Praise

Family Wealth Transition Planning
Advising Families with Small Businesses

by Bonnie Brown Hartley and Gwendolyn Griffith

MW00572424

"If there was no generally accepted definition of success in family wealth transition planning before this book, there certainly is now! This book is both cogent and beautifully written. Anyone looking for a guide to helping families with family wealth continuity, healthy relationships, stewardship, and legacy will find it in this pioneering work. Bonnie Brown Hartley and Gwendolyn Griffith masterfully capture the psychology of individuals transitioning within their family units. This insight makes *Family Wealth Transition Planning* interesting as well as informative."

Valerie Maxwell, PhD
Psychologist
President, Foundation for Learning Development

"*Family Wealth Transition Planning* is an invaluable road map for advisers to families with small businesses. Bonnie Brown Hartley and Gwendolyn Griffith have synthesized and organized the best thinking from many disciplines into a process that will enable advisers to business-owning families. The authors address wealth transfer in all dimensions—both human capital as well as financial capital. Their work brings clarity to the complex, multidiscipline world of family wealth advising. The three case studies effectively illustrate the authors' methodology and holistic approach to advising business-owning families. This book can only help to improve the family and adviser relationship and lead to measurable success for all."

Kathryn M. McCarthy
Independent Adviser to Families and Family Offices
Former Managing Director, Rockefeller & Co., Inc.

"Bonnie Brown Hartley and Gwendolyn Griffith provide a methodology that fully integrates the key factors and variables that professionals from all disciplines who serve family business clients know to be fundamental. It forges them into a coherent and adaptable method customized to the family's unique constellation of family dynamics, sources of wealth and their capacity to grow their financial capital, human capital and social capital. It clearly illustrates how the methodology is applied, guiding the adviser and the client through the planning process when facing change in human lives, business organizations and financial structures.

Family Wealth Transition Planning is a powerful, long-awaited book that should be incorporated into both undergraduate teaching and postgraduate professional development programs for those professionals who engage with family business clients."

Dr. Barbara Murray
Director, Family Business Solutions (UK)
Former Executive Director, Family Business Network

"*Family Wealth Transition Planning* is a must read for everyone advising a family business and for everyone serving on a family business board. More than 80 percent of businesses in America are family owned, yet nearly 95 percent of business schools do not teach family business management. That means that most advisers have had to learn "on the job"—a frightening proposition. By explaining financial capital in the context of social capital and human capital, Bonnie Brown Hartley and Gwendolyn Griffith capture the complexity in family business that is at once the source of competitive power and other times the cause for systemic failure. Weaving the stories of three family businesses throughout the book allows the reader to understand and apply the valuable lessons of family wealth transition planning offered by this book. I recommend it to all the family business advisers with whom I work."

Robin Klemm, PhD
A.E. Coleman Chair in Family Business, Director,
Austin Family Business Program, Oregon State University

FAMILY WEALTH TRANSITION PLANNING

Also available from
Bloomberg Press

Family
by James E. Hughes Jr.

Family Wealth—Keeping It in the Family
by James E. Hughes Jr.

Getting Started as a Financial Planner
by Jeffrey H. Rattiner

How to Value, Buy, or Sell a Financial-Advisory Practice
by Mark C. Tibergien and Owen Dahl

The Investment Think Tank
edited by Harold Evensky and Deena B. Katz

Managing Concentrated Stock Wealth
by Tim Kochis

Money Well Spent
by Paul Brest and Hal Harvey

Practice Made Perfect
by Mark C. Tibergien and Rebecca Pomering

Retirement Income Redesigned
edited by Harold Evensky and Deena B. Katz

A complete list of our titles is available at
www.bloomberg.com/books

FAMILY WEALTH TRANSITION PLANNING

Advising Families with Small Businesses

BONNIE BROWN HARTLEY
and
GWENDOLYN GRIFFITH

With a Foreword by JAMES E. HUGHES JR.

BLOOMBERG PRESS

NEW YORK

BLOOMBERG, BLOOMBERG ANYWHERE, BLOOMBERG.COM, BLOOMBERG MARKET ESSENTIALS, *Bloomberg Markets*, BLOOMBERG NEWS, BLOOMBERG PRESS, BLOOMBERG PROFESSIONAL, BLOOMBERG RADIO, BLOOMBERG TELEVISION, and BLOOMBERG TRADEBOOK are trademarks and service marks of Bloomberg Finance L.P. ("BFLP"), a Delaware limited partnership, or its subsidiaries. The BLOOMBERG PROFESSIONAL service (the "BPS") is owned and distributed locally by BFLP and its subsidiaries in all jurisdictions other than Argentina, Bermuda, China, India, Japan, and Korea (the "BLP Countries"). BFLP is a wholly-owned subsidiary of Bloomberg L.P. ("BLP"). BLP provides BFLP with all global marketing and operational support and service for these products and distributes the BPS either directly or through a non-BFLP subsidiary in the BLP Countries. All rights reserved.

This publication contains the authors' opinions and is designed to provide accurate and authoritative information. It is sold with the understanding that the authors, publisher, and Bloomberg L.P. are not engaged in rendering legal, accounting, investment-planning, or other professional advice. The reader should seek the services of a qualified professional for such advice; the authors, publisher, and Bloomberg L.P. cannot be held responsible for any loss incurred as a result of specific investments or planning decisions made by the reader.

First edition published 2009

1 3 5 7 9 10 8 6 4 2

Library of Congress Cataloging-in-Publication Data

Hartley, Bonnie Brown.

    Family wealth transition planning : advising families with small businesses / Bonnie Brown Hartley and Gwendolyn Griffith ; with a foreword by James E. Hughes Jr. — 1st ed.

        p. cm.

    Includes bibliographical references and index.

    Summary: "In Family Wealth Transition Planning, Hartley and Griffith guide advisers to families with small businesses through the intricate process of preparing and transferring wealth to heirs. The authors take a holistic view of transition planning, focusing on assets that fall under the umbrella of financial capital, as well as other undervalued sources of wealth: human and social capital"—Provided by publisher.

    ISBN 978-1-57660-335-2 (alk. paper)

    1. Family-owned business enterprises. I. Lieuallen, Gwendolyn Griffith. II. Title.

HD62.25.H37 2009

    658.1'6—dc22

2009015807

To my beloved husband and business partner, Mike Hartley

—BONNIE

To my extraordinary mother, mentor, and friend:
Dorothy Taylor Lloyd, MD

—GWEN

CONTENTS

FOREWORD

WHEN BONNIE AND GWEN asked me to consider writing a foreword to their book on planning for families with business enterprises, I asked whether theirs would be a book not about family succession but about family transitions. Would it concern itself with exploring the issues surrounding the various stages of each individual, nuclear family, clan, and tribe that make up the nested systems of a family and how those systems interweave with the life cycles of the family's business enterprises? Happily, as you will find within, the answer to both questions is a resounding "yes"!

Why transitions and not successions? Within a family's long journey, there are not successions as there are between reigns or dynasties; rather, a family's life is a series of lineal transitions over a long period of time, a series of linked lives and systems. These transitions are glued together by the stories of the elder generations and the new stories experienced by the younger members of the family. One of the great wealth planning fallacies is that successions occur in the modern family. This book not only proves that they do not exist, but appropriately replaces the fallacious term "successions" with "transitions." This idea coalesces with the natural flow of family and its enterprises, a flow that is gentle, evolutionary, and, above all, consistent with human development as all individuals and families have experienced it.

Why is distinguishing the issues connected to the life cycles of each individual family member, of each nuclear family, of each clan, of each tribe, and of each business enterprise so important to the success of a family's long-term well-being, including the future success of its business enterprises? Each individual entity represents a singular complex system that is constantly evolving and adapting, at the same time being interwoven into the complex system to which all these entities belong. Essentially, as Bonnie and Gwen teach us, if you plan only for the well-being of the business enterprise and not for the well-being of its owners, of the family, and of each of its members, your plan will likely fail. When you overlook planning, you miss critical current issues integral to each component's life stages. You miss how the resolution of those issues may well turn out positively for one component and negatively for the system as a whole. You will be surprised when the plan devised for the business enterprises doesn't evolve as anticipated, because changes to the individual parts that you did not see or plan for occur simultaneously and blow up the plan. Equally risky, if you plan only for some parts to evolve but not all, the plan may not anticipate and direct how those individual parts and components lead to the fusion of a family as a whole so that the family may exist as something greater than the sum of its parts. Without a plan, it is all too probable, as the shirtsleeves-to-shirtsleeves proverb predestines, that the business family and its enterprises will die out in the entropy of fission or inertia, as nature fates all material things to do. The keys to grasping why the family system performs as it does are understanding the cycles of each component of the whole system, identifying which of the cycles of life each component is in and the issues the cycle presents, and perceiving what transitions are likely to be next. I have long hoped our advisory community and the families it serves would have a road map to these cycles and systems, and now we have it.

Bonnie and Gwen have also given us important insight into the qualities an adviser must cultivate in order to become the most trusted adviser to a family and its enterprises. In my work, I define this role as a *personne de confiance*. As with the qualities that define a great family (a family that reaches its fifth generation in a flourishing condition and dynamically evolves from there), such advisers must be ever patient; must be ever able to adapt their plans to new visions and issues; must be ever resilient, since without this quality no long-distance journey can be successful; must be ever skeptical, asking with complete objectivity why and what if; must be ever loyal, telling only the absolute truth and never mistaking one's position as a serving professional as ever being a member of the family one serves; must be ever prudent so all that is confidential remains so; and, above all, must be forever compassionate and forgiving for the human condition. These are the qualities that Bonnie and Gwen exemplify in their professional work and that are coalesced with their vast experience in the wisdom in this book. A planner must exhibit these qualities if the family he or she serves and its enterprises are to flourish.

Some readers may now be asking a question: "I thought this was about how to manage a family enterprise and the wealth of a family. If it isn't, what is it about?" My answer is that it is about managing a family's wealth and enterprise, but that is only a small part of the book. Bonnie and Gwen teach us that the true wealth of family is not its financial capital, but its human and social capital supported by its financial capital. They, as practitioners, have echoed what Roy Williams and Victor Preisser taught in their book, *Preparing Heirs*: 70 percent of wealth transfer plans for family enterprises fail. And they fail because, as Bonnie and Gwen demonstrate, the family that owns the enterprise has no joint decision-making process at all, no workable governance structure. It is often at a critical moment in the family's and its enterprise's life cycles when the transition between owners, individually or intergenerationally, is taking place, and that is when the family's joint decision systems are at their weakest and least able to meet the challenge. The failure rate isn't, except in very rare cases, because of poor legal or financial advice. The plans fail because the human beings who make up the family are not thriving and growing as they should, and thus the social system they together represent is not thriving or growing. If the owners are in entropy, their business enterprises will soon find themselves there as well.

Bonnie and Gwen make it clear how to identify and assess the state of a family's human and social capital, and then to appreciate how the condition of those two types of capital affects the family's financial capital and its enterprises.

As I hope you now appreciate, this book offers the adviser or family leader the means to learn how to evaluate the deep complexity of a business family system in order to comprehend how that family will best be able to own, grow, and transition an enterprise into a healthy thriving organism. It helps advisers recognize that the true wealth of the family they are serving is the individual members of that family. It guides advisers in helping the whole family system meet its natural life cycle transitions. It helps them discover the core questions they must aks as the family's *personne de confiance*. "Will the transition plan

I devise appreciably help the individual members, the family as whole and the family business enterprises to flourish? Will I help each and all members meet the challenges of the transitions their lives will present so that they can grow and thrive?"

Thanks, Bonnie and Gwen, for giving us a road map on how advisers can guide the families they serve through successful wealth transitions.

JAMES E. HUGHES JR.
Aspen 2009

Acknowledgments

Our heartfelt thanks to Jay Hughes for both his practical suggestions and his profound influence on the field of family wealth advising. Many thanks to our Bloomberg editor, Evan Burton, for his insights, patience and encouragement. Thanks also to Megan Berry for her research assistance. Our gratitude to Doug Murphy, faculty member of the Bowen Center for the Study of the Family, for his mentoring and insights into family systems, and to gerontologist John Gibson for sharing his understanding of life cycles. We also feel deep gratitude to our many client families for trusting us, sharing the ups and downs of their family transition challenges and showing us just how complex their transitions are and how important it is to their well-being that the transition process be handled with sensitivity, respect, and care. Many colleagues over the years have shared their experience and insights with us and for that we are grateful. And finally our deepest thanks to Peyton Lieuallen and Mike Hartley for their infinite patience during the creation of this book and their thoughtful reading of multiple iterations of it.

FAMILY WEALTH TRANSITION PLANNING

Introduction

Business families lead complicated lives. Their major sources of wealth are often illiquid, yet must meet family expectations for support and income. Business families also frequently suffer from an acute lack of diversification, and their wealth is often at the mercy of economic events beyond their control. Family businesses can become all-consuming endeavors for family members, both those intimately involved with the business and those on the periphery. The family business can become the stage on which the family acts out its emotional life, at times recreating the very same patterns of behavior generation after generation. It is challenging enough to manage a family business on a day-to-day basis. When a family seeks to transfer this wealth to the next generation, the complexity of the task can be overwhelming.

If you are or aspire to be an adviser to a business family in transition, this book will help you guide clients toward a successful plan.

As business families begin the process of transferring their wealth, they most often turn first to their trusted advisers, who are the accountants, lawyers, financial advisers, bankers, and business advisers closest to the family. This is not surprising, as these trusted advisers know the family and its history and have often helped family members through difficult situations. A trusted adviser has the opportunity to build an interdisciplinary team that will discover information about the family and its goals, and to guide the family and team through the wealth transition process. This process is called family wealth transition planning (FWTP).

In our work with families and professionals over the years, we became aware of an alarming fact: There is no generally accepted definition of *success* in family wealth transition planning. If we have no definition of success, how will we be able to judge the quality of family wealth transition plans? And how can we guide business families, which are often made up of deeply practical individuals who need to know the purpose of their hard work and their progression toward that purpose? Each profession has its own signposts of progress: Lawyers point to executed estate planning documents, and financial advisers breathe a sigh of relief when families are able to agree on the proper investment strategy for a trust. But these are merely signposts, not destinations. They do not define the desired outcome of FWTP. We offer a definition of success: *family wealth continuity*. Simply put, this is the ability and willingness of a family to make capital available to family members over generations in the right way, at the right time, and in the right amounts. This is easier said than done, of course, for who can predict what *right* means for any particular family over generations? To accomplish family wealth continuity, families and their advisers can focus on three beacons of family wealth continuity: healthy family relationships, responsible stewardship of wealth in all its forms, and the ongoing creation of a family legacy.

In our work with business families and in our own firms, we found ourselves wondering whether there is a clear methodology to family wealth transition planning that can be described and mastered. We concluded that there *is* such a methodology, and much of this book is devoted to illustrating it. Fundamental to this methodology is the premise that every family is part of a complex family wealth system that can and does adapt to changing circumstances. The family wealth system of a business family is particularly complicated, which makes transition planning for business families difficult. The job of an adviser to a business family, then, is to help the family adapt its system to achieve better family wealth continuity. The adviser is an agent of change, charged with creating adaptations that will support healthy relationships, stewardship of wealth, and the family legacy. The methodology for advisers that we suggest in this book is designed to help an adviser by first explaining how to gain a deep understanding of a client's family wealth system, and then describing how to design and implement specific components of a wealth transition plan that will adapt that system toward family wealth continuity.

To illustrate this methodology and the tools that accompany it, this book tells the stories of three business families: the Hernández family of Fresno, California; the Marshall family of Irion County, Texas;

and the Williams family of New York City. These families are fictitious, but to create them we drew from families with whom we have had the privilege of working over the past decades. The three families in this book reflect the dreams, fears, and even obsessions of the real families, and are characteristic of business families everywhere. These families helped us understand why some family wealth transition plans succeed, while others fail. They helped us identify the characteristics that give some families a leg up in planning, and how other families can overcome enormous obstacles in their quest for family wealth continuity.

Because advisers to business families don't have the luxury of an omniscient view into the innermost motivations of family members, we have chosen to present the families' stories through their own voices. In each family, you will hear from family members (as well as a few outsiders) who are working, with various degrees of enthusiasm, on transition plans. Some of these individuals are struggling to keep their family together, while others are wondering if they are a part of a family at all. Some are consumed by stewardship worries. Some can glimpse a possible family legacy, and hope to convince others to share their dream. As in all families, these individuals offer their own perspectives rather than some verifiable truth. We hope that hearing their stories in the first person will help train your ear to listen for information critical to family wealth transition planning, and help you see how what is not said can be just as important as what is said.

Any adviser to a business family in transition can use the methodology described in this book. Less experienced estate planners may want to follow the process in a linear fashion, while those who have worked with various families may want to choose among the methodology's wide range of tools to address specific problems. Families come to their advisers in all stages of planning, and the FWTP methodology is as useful for helping families with fully formed plans survive the rough patches as it is for guiding a family that has no plan in place at all.

CHAPTER 1

FAMILY WEALTH CONTINUITY

WHY DO SOME family wealth transition plans succeed, while others fail? Why are some families more successful than others at creating and implementing a transition plan? Why are business families prone to poor wealth transition outcomes? What are the specific components of a transition plan for business families? How can family advisers help those families transition wealth? Is there a methodology for doing so that an adviser can learn, or must the adviser proceed on instinct alone?

These are the questions business families and their advisers face when they confront the issue of wealth transition planning. The difficulty of composing a successful transition plan can challenge even the most resourceful and experienced advisers and the most tightly knit families. Family wealth transition planning (FWTP) is the methodology set forth in this book for advisers to follow as they guide families through the complex process of transferring wealth in all its forms within multigenerational families.

What is a business family? Business families are those in which one or more family members (1) hold a significant amount of wealth in an operating business in which family members have an ownership stake, and (2) participate in that business in some capacity other than that of holding stock in a publicly traded company as a passive investment. A business family's connection to an operating company creates special challenges in wealth transition planning, not the least of which is defining a successful transition.

The Definition of Success

Traditional estate planning has not provided satisfactory answers to the questions that plague family wealth transition planning. As a field, it has focused largely on the technical aspects of transferring wealth, ignoring the larger issues of defining productivity and success. Tales of family members who fritter away their wealth, waste it in endless litigation, or never speak to each other again illustrate failures, but do not provide the answer to what success in FWTP truly *is*. The emergence of new approaches to estate planning, which focus on family values and family harmony, have helped in the search for a definition of success.[1] But these approaches fail to coordinate the technical side of planning and have left the adviser without a methodology for approaching a challenging family situation that will result in a practical transition plan. This is understandable. FWTP is technical in the extreme and families do not lend themselves to mechanistic approaches.

Fortunately, there is a methodology to the process of creating and implementing a successful plan. It begins with the definition of *success* in wealth transition planning and with the recognition that client families are always in transition. Wills, naming a successor to the CEO of a family business, or creating a new LLC are examples of transactions that may be part of the larger plan. Without a vision of that transition plan, the isolated transactions may have unintended consequences that impact a family for generations.

Family Wealth Continuity

Wealth transition clients usually come to their adviser with specific goals in mind. These goals are usually expressed concretely, in terms such as "I want to make sure my wife is taken care of" or "I've heard you can avoid probate if. . . ." When listening to a client talk about these concrete goals, the adviser is usually categorizing them at a higher level of abstraction as benevolence goals, paternalistic goals, or administrative goals. The FWTP adviser, however, needs to take an even broader perspective than the client does on the definition of success. The overarching goal of family wealth transition planning should be family wealth continuity. *Family wealth continuity* is a family's ongoing ability and willingness to make human, social, and financial capital available to its members at the "right" stage in their lives and in the right way. Of course, it is impossible to define concretely, or even for a particular family, what the right capital is. And even if it were definable, a family's ability to make these transfers will depend on many choices made long before capital is transferred. The way out of this quandary is to look to three pillars of family wealth continuity:

❑ Healthy family relationships
❑ Responsible stewardship of family wealth in all its forms
❑ The ongoing creation of a family legacy

These are guideposts for a successful plan. If a plan generates these outcomes, the family will be much more likely to achieve family wealth continuity. A plan that generates family wealth continuity will create an enduring structure to support a family for generations to come.

Healthy Family Relationships

Based on her interviews with professionals in the fields of education, religion, health care, family counseling, and the nonprofit sector, Dolores Curran defines family as "a group which possesses and implements an irrational commitment to the well-being of its members." In her research, Curran found fifteen characteristics that describe healthy families. These include trust, a sense of play, shared responsibility, good communication and listening skills, respect for one another's privacy, a shared spiritual core, the ability to admit to and seek help with problems, and the teaching of right and wrong.[2]

It is important to differentiate between family health and family culture. Some families are reserved; others are boisterous. Some spend a lot of time together; others are geographically spread out and their members don't see one another very often. Some families share a love of sports or the opera; others seem to define themselves in terms of their shared entrepreneurial spirit. These characteristics do not define the health of the family, but rather, patterns of behavior. Families with these shared experiences may have healthy or unhealthy relationships. Behavior alone does not measure the health of a family.

Families build relationships starting with the core relationship triangle in any family, which is the parents' relationship with each child. Every family has a multitude of such relationship triangles, each alive with emotional activity.[3] The degree to which those triangles function in a healthy way directly affects the overall health and well-being of the family. Healthy families thrive when parents communicate well with one another, help their children learn to become responsible adults, and encourage dialogue about even the most difficult subjects, like the inevitable death of family members.

Creating an enduring family wealth transition plan requires the family and its advisers to focus explicitly upon the creation of processes and structures that will support healthy family relationships. Making choices based in part on whether they will support or undermine healthy family relationships may change the selection of legal transition structures. Leaving assets in trust, for example, may save transfer taxes. Yet if it undermines trust within the family, the family must balance the advantage of saving taxes (an aspect of good stewardship) against the disadvantage of lost trust. Often, with the right plan, it is possible to support both good stewardship and healthy relationships. In FWTP, the impact of choices on the health of family relationships will feature prominently in the family's discussions with advisers.

Stewardship of Wealth

Historically, *stewards* have been administrators or official representatives for homes, ships, or estates who supervise the people, inventory, and activities associated with those assets. In the religious sense, stewards are dispensers of wealth whose purpose is to serve God. Thus, *stewardship of wealth* means the responsible administration, supervision, management, and use of resources such as time, money, people, and talent.[4] It is more than ownership of wealth, as it requires a long-term vision and a sense of responsibility not just to legal owners, but also to all those who have a stake in the administration of wealth and the well-being of the family.

Stewardship of wealth includes, but is not limited to, structures for the transition of wealth between generations. Stewardship must be considered in the context of the client's values, vision or philosophy of wealth, and goals related to the preservation, control, and use of that wealth, and the structures and processes that support the realization of those goals. It involves different processes and actions for each kind of capital (financial, social, and human).[5]

Ongoing Creation of the Family Legacy

In legal terms, any inheritance is a legacy. In this book, however, *family legacy* has a broader context. It is more like the legal concept of an endowment, or even the traditional concept of a birthright. A family legacy may certainly include financial assets, such as property, money, or a family business. But it will always contain a strong symbolic element as well: an expression of the family's values as they have evolved through generations. A legacy speaks to what it means to be a member of a particular family. It also speaks to the responsibilities that are inherent in being a member of a family: responsibilities to self, to family, and to community.

The creation of a family's legacy is an ongoing, collaborative process within the family, and the process is never linear. Legacies evolve over time. Families may leave the family farm, for example, yet the collection of memories the family shares about that farm and its history may continue as an important part of the family legacy, even for members who have never set foot there.

Every family leaves a legacy to its members, consciously or not. One goal of FWTP is to make the legacy explicit, and to ensure that the components of a transition plan support that legacy without entombing it for all time. As part of their planning, some families include their legacy in a family vision statement or as part of their governance systems.

The concept of a legacy is intimately tied to the other two components of family wealth continuity: healthy family relationships and stewardship of wealth. For some families, strong family ties *are* the legacy. Members of these families can rely on each other no matter what. Making sure that value is transmitted and supported over generations requires excellent stewardship of human and social capital within the family. For other families, the legacy will include financial assets, along with a strong commitment to charitable giving. These families will spend more time defining the roles of family members as stewards of financial assets, and finding a common vision for philanthropy.

A Systematic Approach to Family Wealth Transition Planning

Central to the FWTP methodology described in this book is the idea that every client is a member of a family wealth system. Whether a client is an ambitious entrepreneur who has poured every dollar into a start-up company, or is an owner of an established business worth tens of millions of dollars, that client is just one component of a larger family wealth system. The family wealth system is a *complex adaptive system*, with the following characteristics that are critical to FWTP:

❑ The system is made up of myriad *components* and the *connections* between them.
❑ The system is *open*, allowing components to enter and exit the system.
❑ The system has a *memory*, so its current state depends on past events.
❑ The system has subsystems *nested* within it.
❑ The system is marked by *uncertain boundaries*.
❑ The system is *emergent*, i.e., it moves toward greater complexity and is marked by *patterns* created by *feedback loops*.
❑ The system is *adaptive*, in the sense that *agents* inside and outside the system can create changes within the system so that it adapts to new information or circumstances.

In the broadest sense, FWTP is a deliberate adaptation of the family wealth system to achieve family wealth continuity. Selected agents, from inside and outside the family wealth system, come together for the explicit purpose of adapting the family wealth system to help a family achieve its goal of family wealth continuity. There is, of course, no fail-safe recipe for creating family wealth continuity, just as there is no recipe for a happy family. But this book proposes a methodology that any adviser can use to assist any family, particularly business families.

Figure 1.1 illustrates this methodology, which has three basic steps. Each of these steps must be connected to the overall goal of FWTP planning: the creation of family wealth continuity. In Step One, the advisers to a family clarify their roles and responsibilities in the wealth transition process. In Step Two, the family and FWTP team set about understanding the family wealth system of a particular family. Specific aspects of a family wealth system reveal a family's needs, capacities, and constraints in the planning process. In Step Three, the advisers and family develop specific components of a transition plan, each of which is designed to fit the particular family's situation. Figure 1.1 distinguishes Step One from Steps Two and Three because Step One

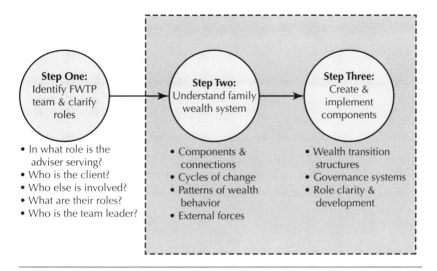

Step One:
Identify FWTP
team & clarify
roles

Step Two:
Understand family
wealth system

Step Three:
Create &
implement
components

- In what role is the
  adviser serving?
- Who is the client?
- Who else is involved?
- What are their roles?
- Who is the team leader?

- Components &
  connections
- Cycles of change
- Patterns of wealth
  behavior
- External forces

- Wealth transition
  structures
- Governance systems
- Role clarity &
  development

FIGURE **1.1**   Methodology for FWTP

is essentially about the adviser(s), not the family. Even prior to engagement by a family, advisers must clarify their role and understand
how that role relates to the obligations of their profession. This clarity
allows Steps Two and Three to proceed with maximum potential for
success.

Despite the linear nature of the methodology depicted in Figure 1.1,
much of this is a nonlinear process. For example, advisers and families
will revisit initial goals from time to time and new needs, capacities,
and constraints will arise throughout the process. If advisers employ
the methodology outlined in Figure 1.1, however, the process will stay
grounded in concrete objectives.

Step One: Selecting Participants and Clarifying their Roles

In the process illustrated in Figure 1.1, a FWTP adviser begins by carefully choosing and articulating his role and the role of others on the planning team, as these individuals will be the agents of change in adapting
the family wealth system. Chapter 2 discusses in depth the issues any
adviser faces in leading or participating in a FWTP team: identifying
a client, managing conflicts, and ensuring an appropriate level of

confidentiality. The often difficult and emotional process of FWTP offers many opportunities for advisers to step out of an appropriate role
and into an ethical quagmire, so selecting the role that is right for the
adviser as well as for the client is a critical first step.

A financially successful family will usually have developed professional relationships to help with its day-to-day legal, accounting, and
management issues. These relationships may involve business and personal advisers, accountants, banking and insurance professionals, and
business consultants, in addition to family systems experts, spiritual advisers, psychologists, doctors, and close family friends. To complicate
matters, in wealthy families some members may have their own teams
of advisers, who may or may not also advise other family members or
the family business. It is important to sort out these relationships early
in the process.

The FWTP process for a business of any significant size will require
team members other than the adviser to develop a deep understanding
of the family and to test the viability of potential wealth transition plan
components. Membership and size of the team will vary, depending on
the family and the size and nature of the business. It is important to
identify those who have a longstanding relationship with the business
and family, and involve them early in the process. If business and family advisers are different, which adviser(s) will be chosen? Is there a
need for an adviser who does not have a long-term relationship with any
participant? It is equally important to identify any gaps in expertise and
find ways of bringing the right people onto the team. The more these
business and family advisers can work as a team, the more successful the
business succession planning process is likely to be.

Finally, coordination of the team of advising professionals is critical
to its success. An adviser representing transferors of wealth in a relatively simple business succession plan may often act informally as coor-
dinator of a team of professionals. In more complex situations, a formal
arrangement may be necessary to ensure the team consistently serves its
function of moving the transition process forward productively.

Step Two: Understanding the Family Wealth System

The FWTP adviser (or team) must understand the internal and external
forces at work within the family wealth system. No analysis will ever

be complete, nor must it be for a plan to be successful. In fact, the complexity and continual evolution of the family wealth system ensure that it can never be fully understood. Yet certain aspects of the family wealth system are particularly important for the adviser to grasp when designing a plan.

When the FWTP adviser analyzes the family wealth system, financial assets remain important, but other kinds of wealth take on new significance. Specifically, the adviser must trace the sources of human and social capital within the family wealth system and discover how a family develops and deploys this capital in its internal and external relationships.

The family wealth system at the outset of the FWTP planning process is a snapshot of the system as it exists at a certain time—and as it will never exist again, because the components and connections of the system are in a constant state of change. The system "remembers" events that shape it, but will never return exactly to a previous form.

Although every family is different, and every family wealth system is different, families share some common pathways of change. Individuals go through more or less predictable cycles of change and growth, although some become stuck along the way. Businesses, as well, often experience specific cycles of growth that can be analyzed and predicted. While these cycles are not universal in the sense that every individual, every family, and every business will experience each in the same way, the patterns are common enough that they form patterns of change that must be considered in the FWTP process. Cycles of change are constant, and change is often invisible to the participants. However, *trigger events* such as death, divorce, childbirth, or midlife crisis create the illusion that change is sudden and bring the impact of change to the forefront. Moreover, especially in business families, overlapping cycles of change can introduce major complexity, so family members often ignore them. The FWTP process must take account of the family's capacity for (and constraints on) meeting change, and build in structures that increase the system's ability to withstand trigger events.

Families bring certain long-standing patterns of wealth behavior to the FWTP process. These patterns will have a fundamental effect on the planning process. Certain patterns of behavior relating to wealth often endure through multiple generations of family members.[6]

These patterns of behavior create feedback loops—both positive and negative—that strongly influence choices about the management of family wealth in all its forms. In turn, these choices inform the family's need for certain kinds of wealth transition structures, governance systems, and role development plans.

The external world brings a variety of forces to bear on the family wealth system.[7] The family wealth system is an open system, meaning that it changes in response to external forces. Income and transfer taxes, as well as economic cycles, business exigencies, and pure luck, affect the family wealth system. The typical family already has certain established structures in place when planning begins, and these must be accommodated and adapted as necessary. The process will generate new structures, including some that a family will grudgingly accept in order to adapt to external forces (such as credit shelter trusts to minimize estate taxes). The internal needs of a family may conflict with external forces, and the adviser must help the family balance these needs. A plan may go through many iterations as a family and its advisers address the conflicts among external forces, established family structures, and the internal needs of family members.

Step Three: Designing and Implementing a Family Wealth Transition Plan

Once the adviser has an understanding of the family wealth system, it is possible to move to the next phase of the process—the creation of the plan. Answering the four fundamental questions of wealth transition in light of the information gleaned in Step Two allows the adviser to develop plan components that meet a family's true needs. By answering the questions in Step Three, the adviser can check assumptions about the future state of components and connections, and ensure that the plan takes into account the family's cycles of change and patterns of wealth behavior.

Four Fundamental Questions

Most clients arrive at their adviser's office with some idea of their desires for wealth transition. They have thought about a provisional plan for addressing some of the four questions discussed in this section, and their estate planning adviser helps them fill in the details.

❏ Question 1: What kinds of wealth are being transferred?
❏ Question 2: From and to whom will wealth be transferred, and will it pass inside or outside the family?
❏ Question 3: When will the transitions occur—now or later, suddenly or gradually?
❏ Question 4: How will each transition occur?
   — Will it be by gift, sale, or both?
   — What conditions will be imposed upon the transition?
   — How will the wealth be shared among recipients, if at all?

Every experienced estate planning adviser is familiar with these questions. The adviser helps the client by listening to what is articulated (and what is left unsaid), offering insight into the viability of different options, and explaining what other families do (and why). While doing this, the estate planning adviser is testing the client's assumptions about wealth transition.

The same is true in this methodology. However, FWTP advisers must take what they have discovered about the family wealth system in Step Two into account in answering these questions. A thorough understanding of the family and its wealth system will often change the answers to these familiar questions, leading to a plan that is more likely to achieve family wealth continuity.

The Three Components of a Plan

Traditional estate planning focuses on the transactions and documents needed to facilitate transition, but often neglects the other key elements of successful wealth continuity. Traditional legal structures are important, but they form only a part of an overall plan. Family wealth transition planning has three different components: wealth transition structures, governance systems, and a plan for role clarity and development. The relative importance of each component will vary from family to family, and some families will need very little in the way of role clarity and development or governance. Business families, however, are likely to need all three components.

The legal transition structures, such as trusts and wills, that traditional estate planning uses are a part of a larger category in FWTP, and are referred to as *wealth transition structures*. This category also includes nonlegal forms of wealth transition, because many of the methods a family uses to transfer wealth do not (and should not) create legal rights and duties. A grandfather teaching his granddaughter how to drive the tractor is as much a part of the process as a qualified personal residence trust (QPRT) for the family farm. Yet the former is invisible as a transition structure, at least to outsiders. The point is that the transfer of human and social capital doesn't happen without planning, and the purpose of FWTP is to anticipate transitions of this nature and put into place specific and appropriate support structures.[8]

Governance systems are crucial to successful transition plans, because wealth transferees are typically more numerous and more diverse than their predecessors. Transferees must often develop their own form of governance. What worked for fathers and mothers may not work for their children, especially when the siblings are far-flung and have diverse interests, capacities, and desires. Their levels of trust may differ significantly from those of their parents or grandparents, and their experiences will certainly differ. This is particularly true in the transition of businesses from one generation to another. As a result, for many families governance systems become an important component of FWTP.[9]

Clarifying current roles and developing a plan for role development is a critical plan component. Particularly when individuals participate in a family business in multiple roles, the transition of wealth changes those roles, requiring family members to be flexible and often to develop new skills and capacities.[10]

The three components of the FWTP process—role clarification and development, governance systems, and wealth transition structures—are intimately connected. At times, a legal transition structure will require a certain governance system as well as help define roles for upcoming wealth transferees. For example, the creation and proper use of a limited liability company (LLC) has the potential to serve all three functions. For most families, these three components, in some combination, will form the foundation of an enduring plan. A family's particular mix of core challenges will determine and prioritize the exact components the family needs.

Putting the Methodology to Work

The Hernández, Williams, and Marshall families are three fictional families struggling through the process of family wealth transition planning. Their stories illustrate how an adviser can approach transition planning as a collaborative experience in which adviser and family have the common goal of family wealth continuity. The final transition plan, whatever it may be, must be rooted in a deep understanding of the family and its needs. It must be the result of the adviser's efforts to help the family learn about itself, and its members' efforts to learn about each other by discovering their shared beliefs, assumptions, and values, as well as their differences and areas of potential conflict. Along the way, advisers may learn a great deal about themselves, which will strengthen their ability to assist future clients. For the less-seasoned family wealth transition adviser, this book provides a road map for this experience and a guide to the intricate and often confusing pathways families take toward their goal. Expert family wealth transition advisers, however, will likely recognize parts of these processes as implicit in the way they already provide advice to clients. For those advisers, placing these parts in the context of a larger methodology may assist them in developing plans that are more effective and in overcoming barriers to family wealth transition planning.

Measuring the Success of Family Wealth Transition Planning

Although family wealth continuity is the overall goal of transition planning, the components of family wealth continuity may be difficult for individual family members to measure in the short term. For that reason, it is helpful to set specific individual and family goals related to the family's wealth transition plan. These goals can involve finding the answers to the four questions above, implementing governance or legal transfer structures, and creating individual role development plans. Goals should be specific and measurable, including both distinct action items and measurement criteria. The family and adviser should identify the resources necessary for achieving the goal, which may include time, training, commitment, and financial resources, among others.

Each goal should have a definite timeline. All goals should be measured against the ultimate objectives of family wealth continuity: If the goal is accomplished, is the family wealth system more likely to create healthy family relationships, responsible stewardship of wealth, and a desirable family legacy?

The Difficulty of Planning for Business Families

The perspectives and methodology described thus far apply to all families of wealth, regardless of their kind or level of wealth. This book, however, focuses on one kind of client: the business family. In some business families, members may work side by side twenty-four hours a day in the business. In others, family members might be board members, beneficiaries of a trust owning stock in a company, or employees of the family company. Whatever their members' level of participation in the operating business, these families face specific challenges in FWTP, including the following, which later chapters will discuss in detail:

❑ Business families tend to hold all their eggs in one basket, making them vulnerable to change both inside and outside the family wealth system.

❑ Cashing out a business is difficult, and this illiquidity often both prevents change and ties family members together.

❑ Business wealth is often most valuable when shared, and families share that wealth in ways that rarely follow the patterns of nonfamily businesses.

❑ Many components of the family wealth system (both people and assets) have an intricate connection to the operating business.

❑ The operating business is vulnerable not only to the cycles of change experienced by all individuals and families, but also to the effects of the business life cycle.

❑ When a business changes hands, the members of the transferee generation are likely to have different kinds of involvement with the business than their predecessors, raising governance questions as well as ambiguity about what is fair in wealth transition.

❑ Transferees are often unprepared for new roles, and transferors often have difficult letting go of old ones.

❏ Compared with liquid investments, businesses are particularly vulnerable to complex external forces, such as a changing tax and economic environment.
❏ Business families tend to mix business and personal relationships
within the business and use the business to attain nonbusiness
objectives.
❏ Business families bring their long-standing patterns of behavior to
bear on the business, which affect both decision making within the
business and wealth transition decisions.
❏ For many business families, the business is much more than a financial asset; it is a significant part, if not all, of their family legacy.

Any of these challenges can cause the FWTP process for a business
family to fail. While experienced advisers are alert for the signs of these
problems, it is difficult to address them piecemeal. The methodology
detailed in this book offers a systematic approach to the problems complexity causes in business families so that the FWTP adviser can create
wealth transition structures, governance systems, and role development
plans that will ensure family wealth continuity for their clients.

The Process for Three Families

As discussed in the introduction, this book will trace the transition planning of three fictional families:

❏ The Hernández family of Fresno, California
❏ The Marshall family of Irion County, Texas
❏ The Williams family of New York City

These families are fictional, yet they are based on real experiences.
They are composites of real families and the challenges they have faced
in real FWTP situations. While these families are quite different in
membership, background, and challenges, they do share some important characteristics. All are business families, and they rely on one or
more family businesses as a source of wealth. In each family, some family
members work in the business, but others do not. Some family members
don't appear to work at all. All three families share wealth among various members of the family, but the ways in which they share it is quite

different. All have taxable estates, but none of the families has established a family wealth transition plan or even family wealth continuity goals. Each family faces different and specific barriers to planning, which they must overcome in order for the transition process to succeed.

The FWTP methodology proposed encourages advisers to seek the perspectives of various family members. Rather than following a traditional approach and giving the reader only a single perspective on the client family, the authors have let members of each family provide pieces of the family's story. These individuals share their stories as if they were participating in an information-gathering process facilitated by a FWTP adviser to help the family and its other advisers develop an understanding of the family and its wealth system. Some family members mine their memories for stories that are important to the family and relevant to the planning process. Others are only interested in what is (or is not) happening in front of their noses. The purpose of these stories is to mimic the real situations advisers must deal with, from the sixteen-year-old who is more concerned with his father's secret drinking than with the family business to the runaway-turned-businesswoman who reflects on her brother's influence on her life. As the characters' stories unfold, the situations they face illustrate the process. Chapters 11, 12, and 13 apply the methodology of this book to each family and reveal the success and failures of each family's plan. Lastly, Chapter 14 discusses how the advisers working with these families helped them. It concludes by presenting how the lessons exemplified by these processes apply to adviser firms seeking to create an effective practice group for business families.

To introduce the families and give readers the first tools for understanding them, the following sections introduce two basic tools: the genogram and trigger events.

The Hernández Family of Fresno

The Hernández family is a multigenerational, multicultural family with roots in Fresno, California. The central figure in the Hernández family is Bartolomé (Bart) Hernández Sr., who is sixty-two years old when he consults an adviser for the first time for FWTP. *Figure 1.2* presents the Hernández genogram, without coding for behavior patterns. The family members' collected stories are interspersed throughout this book.

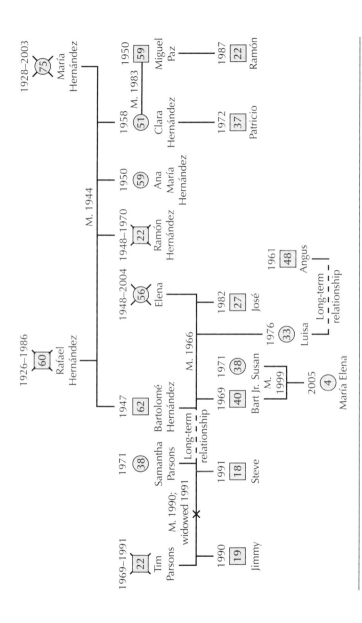

FIGURE 1.2 The Hernández Family Genogram

21

The Hernández family has been quite successful in a variety of businesses. While Bart has always encouraged his other family members to consult with lawyers and advisers, he's never quite gotten around to taking that advice himself. (This is probably a familiar story to most FWTP advisers.) Here is Bart's initial story.

—THE HERNÁNDEZ FAMILY—
Bartolomé (Bart) Hernández Sr., age sixty-two

Ahora bien, my wife Elena died three years ago of cancer. We have—well, I guess now it's just me—three kids: Bart Jr., Luisa, and José. Luisa's a doctor in Los Angeles—I'm as proud as I can be of her. She's just like her mother. Bart Jr. is the most like me—so serious, studying to be an engineer in night school. José is my youngest, 27, and will be the death of me. Wild, but he's a charmer, that one. My Elena babied him, I think because he came along after she had three miscarriages. But it's a blessing my father can't see how he's turned out. My father Rafael and my mother María came to the U.S. from México in 1945 to work in the Bracero Program. They never knew anything but hard work. They were migrant laborers and moved up and down the West Coast following the crops every few months until I was born. Then they settled in Fresno. Then my two sisters were born: Ana and Clara. I had a brother, too, Ramón, but he got into trouble and died in prison. He was twenty-two.

Elena and I bought the hardware business years ago. It's done pretty well, even with all the competition. I had worked there during high school and college and full-time after that, but the son of the family and I didn't agree. So I left and went to work for a big national chain. I got good experience there. It's funny how things come full circle. I ended up buying the store from the family when their son didn't want to run it anymore. We had a couple of good offers to sell it over the years, but Elena and I decided to keep it. It's probably a good thing that we did, because it seems like it's the only place that José can make it. He runs it now. He makes good money there, but spends everything he can get his hands on. I try to stay out of things, it drives me crazy when the inventory isn't right and I don't know what the sales are from week to week. José has a way with the customers, though. We've made a point of making our hardware store a place where women are comfortable shopping and learning how to do home repair. We bought the land where the building is, and over the years, Elena and I bought some duplexes and small apartment buildings. I keep busy managing them. Most people say the [That will be the death of me] "three

Ts" of being a landlord—tenants, trash, and toilets—*serán el colmo*, but I enjoy all the people I get to deal with.

I've done well with residential rentals, and now I'm thinking about buying a little strip center near my house. That's how I met Samantha, the woman I'm seeing. She sells commercial real estate. She has two teenage kids. Her husband was killed in Bosnia. I don't think we are going to get married—I was married for thirty-eight years the perfect woman, and I sure don't need to become a father of teenagers at sixty-two! But you never know. José is still living at home, coming in all hours and mooching money from me whenever he can. I found out he's borrowing money from his sister, too. The one thing he and his brother can agree on—the only thing—is that they don't want Samantha and her kids taking over what they consider their rightful spots. I really blew up at them last weekend. I said I intended to live for a long time, and that I have as much right as anyone to share my life with someone. I told them they were ungrateful and that the two of them had already benefited more than Luisa had from my generosity. So I might just leave it all to her, or to Samantha, or even to the church! But of course, I won't. My sister Clara turned the tables on me last week and gave me some good advice: I just need to get everything straightened out and tell everyone what is going to happen. Then maybe we can all enjoy *El Día de Gracia* for a change.

The Williams Family of New York City

A central figure in the Williams family of New York City is Helen Weinstein Williams, age forty-eight, mother of four, and the wife of John Williams. The Weinstein–Williams clan is smaller than either of the other two families discussed in this book, but is growing. *Figure 1.3* shows the family's genogram, and the family's stories are interspersed throughout the chapters.

Helen Williams is seeking an adviser's help for the first time, but she has plenty of advisers in her future. Here is her story.

—THE WILLIAMS FAMILY—
Helen Weinstein Williams, age forty-eight

I'm not usually the one to push the family about financial things or see advisers. John's always handled all that, and I just haven't had time. I have my hands full with four children and my mother. But earlier this year

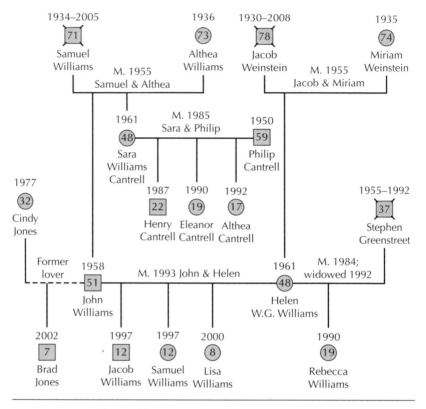

FIGURE **1.3**   The Williams Family Genogram

John had triple-bypass surgery and it made me think: what would happen if I had these four children to raise alone? I used to work. I taught at the Manhattan School of Music and was a concert cellist, but I haven't worked in years. When my father died he left everything with the t's crossed and the i's dotted for my mother—his typical style. Apparently, he provided for a large gift for John and me, and I have to go see his advisers next week to get it finalized or something.

John was supposed to be here with me today, but something came up at work at the very last minute. He owns several jazz bars and a restaurant—the Jazz Jives, do you know them? He works very hard, lots of nights and weekends, but he does his best to make it to the children's school events and the twins' games. We're comfortable now at least, and have plenty of savings from when he was in advertising to send the kids to college and retire on. I've never been a worrier, about money or anything else, but John is different that way.

John and I have been married for sixteen years. I had been widowed and had a daughter who had a three-year-old daughter, Rebecca, whom John adopted. She's in her first year of college, studying music—she's a very talented violinist. We have twin boys named after their grandfathers. We used to call them the Twin Terrors, but not anymore, of course, since 9/11. September 11th had a profound effect on my parents. My mother became more fatalistic than ever. Many of my father's partners at the investment firm died in the attack. He wasn't there—he had retired—but I still think it killed him because he was just never the same.

Our daughter Lisa is eight and has Down syndrome. John's family is from the Midwest and his father died four years ago. He's very close to his mother and we both are (or at least used to be) close to his sister, Sara, and her family—they live in Boston.

I'd like John to sell the business. We could all move out to Long Island and live with my mother. She needs me more and more, and we were happier when we spent summers out there years ago. John doesn't really seem to want to talk about what's going on with the business and just says that this may not be the right time to think about selling. So that's on our agenda. And, in the meantime, I want to make sure that everything is up to date and taken care of if something happens to John, and we both want to make sure that Lisa is taken care of if something happens to both of us. I don't want to leave a mess for anyone else to clean up.

The Marshall Family of Irion County, Texas

The Marshalls are an old Texas family, probably more accurately described as a Texas institution. Johnny Ray and Jenny Lynne Marshall are in their eighties, and are still living on the ranch and involved in the family businesses. One of the central figures in the FWTP story is their son, Robert L. Marshall, known to the family as Bobbie Lee. He moved to Chicago, earned his PhD (the "Piled Higher and Deeper degree," according to his father), and became a professor of economics, but his roots are in Texas with the rest of the Marshall clan. *Figure 1.4* shows the Marshall genogram, and the family's stories are interspersed throughout the chapters.

Robert L. Marshall has been away from the ranch for several years. He's planning a trip to Texas, however, and he has the following talk with one of his family's advisers in Dallas on the telephone beforehand.

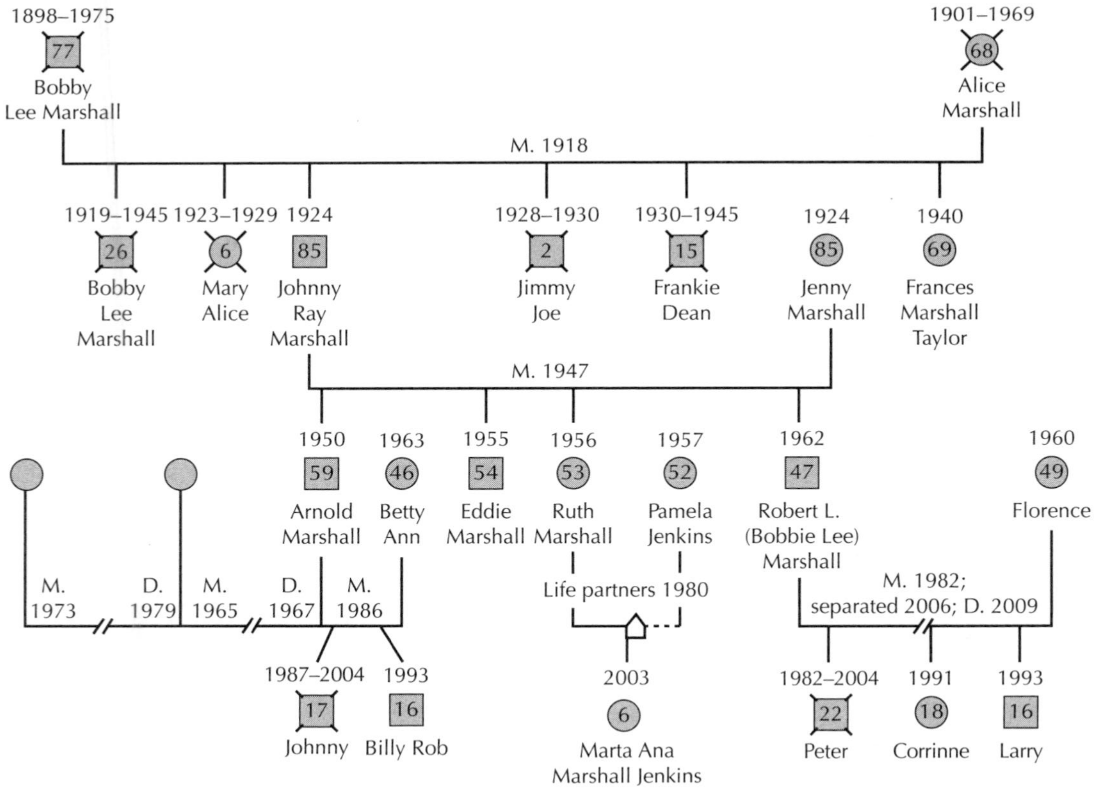

FIGURE **1.4** The Marshall Family Genogram

—THE MARSHALL FAMILY—

Robert L. (Bobbie Lee) Marshall, age forty-seven

Dad hates all the complicated estate planning you have been recommending for years. He finally opened the door a little bit on the phone last week, saying he wanted to do something to keep the government from taking the ranch when he dies. But then what he said shocked me. He told me that he got that local adviser down in Mertzon to write a will cutting my brother Arnie out. He thinks it was Arnie's sinful ways that caused that awful wreck back in 2004. You know, when our boys died and my other son, Larry, got hurt. Somehow, Dad's convinced himself that with Arnie raising Johnny the way he did, Johnny was bound to drive drunk and kill himself and everybody else. Dad's so-called "estate plan" has everything—the ranch and Marshall Enterprises, essentially—going to Eddie, Ruth, and me. All Arnie gets is a case of Jack Daniel's. And, believe it or not, Dad wants me to be the executor. Everybody knows Arnie's lived hard and played harder, but there is no way that I am going to give my brother nothing after all he's been through! And Dad keeps forgetting that all of us kids have homes on the ranch, whether we use them or not. I just don't know how all this is going to work out.

I doubt Arnie knows about the will, but he's threatening to move to Galveston anyway and go to work for the competition unless Dad stops acting up. If Arnie leaves, the drilling business will go downhill in a hurry. Dad thinks he can handle it, of course, but at eighty-five, it's just impossible. And Mom would be lost without Betty Ann to help on the ranch.

CHAPTER NOTES

1. See J. Hughes, *Family Wealth: Keeping It in the Family* (2nd ed.) (Bloomberg, 2004); B. Woodman, and M. Hartley, *Integrating Your Financial Planning, Legal and Estate Planning and Life Planning* (Cambio Press, 2006); S. Fithian, *Values-Based Estate Planning* (John Wiley & Sons, 2000); B. Hartley, *Unexpected Wealth: A Fire Drill for Building Strength and Flexibility in Families* (Cambio Press, 2006); K. Spafford, *Legacy by Design; Succession Planning for Agribusiness Owners* (Marketplace Books, 2006); C. Collier, *Family Wealth* (2nd ed.) (Harvard University Press, 2006); I. Lansberg, *Succeeding Generations; Realizing the Dream of Families in Business* (Harvard University Press, 1999); C. Barnes, and V. Collins, *Best Intentions: Ensuring Your Estate Plan Delivers Both Wealth and Wisdom* (Dearborn, 2002).

2. See Dolores Curran, *Traits of a Healthy Family* (Ballantine, 1983), p. 71.

3. See Daniel V. Papero, *Bowen Family Systems Theory* (Allyn & Bacon, 1990), p. 34.

4. See definitions of *steward* and *stewardship, Shorter Oxford English Dictionary* (5th ed.), vol. II, p. 3026.

5. See Chapter 4 for more detail on the different forms of wealth.

6. See Chapter 6 for more detail on familial patterns of behavior.

7. See Chapter 7 for more detail on the external forces that affect the family wealth system.

8. See Chapter 8 for a discussion of the wide variety of wealth transition structures suited particularly to business families.

9. See Chapter 9 for a discussion of the creation and implementation of governance systems.

10. See Chapter 10 for a discussion of role clarity and development.

CHAPTER 2

THE ADVISER'S ROLE

MOST BUSINESS FAMILIES undertake family wealth transition planning with a team of professionals in place. This team includes accountants, lawyers, financial planners, consultants, and even family friends or spiritual advisers. The expertise of this team will be critical in the family wealth transition planning (FWTP) process, and Chapter 14 discusses how these teams operate. This chapter focuses on one particular role: the adviser, who is the team leader, the facilitator of the process, and the person whose singular focus is always the client's achievement of family wealth continuity.

Clarifying the Adviser's Role

There is no profession known as FWTP adviser. An accountant, lawyer, financial planner, or consultant can serve in this role. Each adviser brings a different skill set, which acts as a lens through which he or she views FWTP. But this kind of engagement is qualitatively different from the usual assistance these professionals give to a family business. The FWTP adviser provides a family with substantive knowledge, process skills, experience, and the confidence that a family can achieve family wealth continuity. The FWTP adviser helps the family take a long-term view, and facilitates the discussion of difficult issues of power, money, trust, fairness, and love. Before taking on this kind of broad engagement, a professional must understand the

FWTP adviser's role and the ethical duties associated with that role. The adviser must ensure that everyone connected to the process understands that role prior to the commencement, and once the process is under way, the adviser must diligently stay within the boundaries of that role.

For any professional involved in the FWTP process, role confusion can bring very real dangers. Embarrassment, malpractice liability, and professional discipline can arise from failing to define a role clearly or straying from the responsibilities of a chosen role. As the process unfolds, the participants will be confiding in and relying upon the adviser for wise counsel. Advisers who have not clearly defined their role will eventually suffer the anxiety of serving multiple interests without clear guidance. Therefore, the adviser must take the lead in selecting the right role and communicating the boundaries of that role.

The adviser and the family members are partners in the FWTP process, and all need clarity about the adviser's role. Family members need to know, early on, how they can (and cannot) call upon their adviser for help in this challenging journey. An adviser who thoroughly understands the advisory role and explains it clearly to the family will be a helpful model for family members, who will likely struggle with defining their own roles as the family business constellation changes. Moreover, such an adviser is less likely to make a serious misstep that brings the process to a halt so the participants can redefine their relationships and resolve conflicts.

Which Ethical Duties Apply to Advisers?

The term *ethical duty* encompasses a wide range of duties that a FWTP adviser owes to clients, nonclients involved in the planning process, and the adviser's profession. In most professions, these duties center around protecting the professional's objectivity and independence, the client's assets and confidential information, obeying the client, and safeguarding the integrity of the profession. A detailed description of the ethical duties applicable to FWTP advisers in their capacity as accountants, lawyers, or other professionals in the wealth transfer process is beyond the scope of this chapter. It is clear that nothing about the planning process exempts professionals from the ethical duties specific to their traditional roles, even though these duties can sometimes create un-wieldy barriers to moving toward a workable transition plan.

Can a professional shed his or her skin and take on a different role as a FWTP adviser? For example, if a lawyer acts as a consultant to a family instead of performing the traditional lawyer's role, which ethical duties apply to the lawyer? This change of role alters the duties the lawyer owes the client as well as the rights the client usually enjoys as part of the traditional client-attorney relationship. A lawyer acting as an FWTP consultant may be able to assist family members whose interests are in conflict with each other, even when such representation would be pro-hibited if the adviser were acting as a lawyer. But this leniency comes at a price: the attorney-client privilege, for example, is not available to the client when the lawyer is acting as a consultant and not as a lawyer.[1] Dif-ferences must be carefully explained to clients. Finally, for many profes-sionals, some ethical duties apply whether or not they are acting in the capacity of their profession. Many state ethical rules impose on lawyers the duty not to engage in conduct that involves "dishonesty, fraud, de-ceit, or misrepresentation," regardless of whether the action involves the representation of a client.[2]

Are FWTP advisers fiduciaries, independent of their professional status? The adviser accepts a position of trust with a client at the outset of an engagement. While there is no authority on whether this, by itself, would create a fiduciary relationship, the expansion of plaintiffs' claims that fiduciary duties attach to various professional relationships seems inexorable.[3] Common sense suggests that advis-ers should protect themselves by carefully setting boundaries, avoid-ing taking control of the client's property, and clearly stating in the contract or letter explaining the engagement[4] that the FWTP adviser is not a fiduciary. When the FWTP adviser belongs to a profession whose members are normally considered fiduciaries, and in particular when that adviser has served in a fiduciary role for a long time, the ad-viser may have a difficult time explaining this change in role to a fam-ily (or convincing a court that the client understood that the FWTP engagement did not create a fiduciary relationship). Therefore, the wise adviser should take care to avoid the usual pitfalls of the fiduciary relationship: self-dealing, departing from the duty of obedience, and accepting conflicting engagements.

The Four C's of FWTP Structure

Whether the FWTP adviser is acting as a professional in a traditional role, or is taking on the broader role of consultant to a business family, the first task is to structure the process to answer four interrelated questions (the Four C's).

- ❏ Who is the *client*?
- ❏ How can *conflicts of interest* be managed?
- ❏ How will *confidentiality* be preserved?
- ❏ What *communication pathways* will be most effective?

The Four C's arise in three different contexts of FWTP: a potential engagement with an unknown client, the extension of an existing engagement with an existing client, and the disengagement of a client.

Who Is the Client?

With whom is the adviser working to define the desired outcome of FWTP: family wealth continuity? Is this a single individual, a couple, or the family as a whole? Who will sign the contract or letter of engagement? Who will pay the bill? In order to be clear about roles, an adviser must be able to identify the client and ensure that all team members understand who their own client is. When functioning in their traditional roles, this is a familiar and solvable problem for most professionals. But in the FWTP process, identification of the client is more difficult because of the complexity of the family wealth system.

How Will the Adviser Manage Conflicts of Interest?

In FWTP engagements, the question is not whether there will be conflicts of interest, because they will always be present. Rather, it is how to manage them. Parents and children, trustees and beneficiaries, and businesses and their owners may all have conflicting interests at some point in the process. The experienced FWTP adviser can predict many of these conflicts and manage them at the outset with the right discussion and waivers. But even the most experienced adviser cannot predict all of the possible conflicts, and so a wise adviser puts in place a system to manage such conflicts as they arise without derailing the planning process.

How Will the Adviser Preserve Confidentiality?

The methodology described in this book assumes that family members will share a great deal of information about themselves and the family wealth system. The FWTP adviser must create a structure that will ensure, to the greatest extent possible, that information disclosed by the participants will not be shared with outsiders without the participants' approval. This can become more difficult as the number of family members and professionals increases.

Even more challenging is the task of clarifying, at the outset and thereafter, the degree of *internal confidentiality* (confidentiality among members of the group) that the group expects. Does the client (or do others) expect the adviser to hold some information in confidence? If so, what information will the adviser hold confidential, and from whom will it be guarded? Will other team members have to preserve confidences under the tenets of their respective professions, and if so, is it appropriate or desirable for them to obtain consents or waivers? It is easy for an adviser to make the mistake of revealing confidential information in the FWTP setting because conversations within a family in a FWTP process can be messy, and keeping track of what information they can and cannot reveal is often difficult. Moreover, often clients view the emotional context of information as more sensitive than the information itself. The adviser must set clear ground rules for confidentiality at the outset of the process if the course of planning is to be smooth. Advisers must also take the time to review the status of existing information periodically and deal with confidentiality issues as they arise. Sometimes, a time-out is necessary to address these issues.

What Communication Pathways Will Be Most Effective?

The FWTP adviser is the facilitator of the process—the person in charge of moving it along productively. Advisers provide the structure for gathering and sharing information, family meetings, assigning and collecting "homework," and responding to family and team member concerns. Together, these processes constitute the communication pathways of the process. The adviser must design communication pathways intended to elicit information while at the same time taking into account the identification of clients (for each team member), the potential conflicts of interest that could arise, and the need to keep certain kinds of information confidential. If not properly managed, any of these issues can create delays and misunderstandings for family members and ethical violations for team members.

The proper structuring of communication pathways is intimately related to the issue of confidentiality. If some information is to be treated as confidential, whether because it relates to prior engagements or is particularly sensitive in the current FWTP process, the adviser must build protections against disclosure into the agreed-upon communication pathways. The adviser should be ready to suggest ways to protect information that is disclosed within the group. For example, it is common for participants in the process to sign a contract not to disclose any proprietary information they receive during the planning process. This contractual obligation could be extended to other kinds of information as well.

The Prospective Client

—THE HERNÁNDEZ FAMILY—

Bartolomé (Bart) Hernández Sr., age sixty-two

My sister Clara suggested that I come see you. You helped her with the sale of the clothing business that she owned with my mother and wife. She liked how you got that done. I have three children: two boys and a girl, Luisa. My two boys, Bart Jr. and José, drive me crazy, and I need to get the family finances straightened out. When Bart Jr. graduated from college, he wanted to start a remodeling and construction company. I had a couple of duplexes that needed remodeling, and so I financed the start-up of the company. But I insisted that Bart include his younger brother; I thought José could use some purpose in life. Bart didn't want to, but he did it anyway. It seemed to be okay for a while, but then the boys started to fight all the time. They're still partners, but in name only. They hardly speak. They still owe me a lot of money from the start-up, but we haven't talked about it in years. I'm thinking I'll call that loan, which might give me some leverage to make these boys get along. I don't want to hurt the business, but something has to be done to make them act like family. I know Bart Jr. is mad about this whole thing, but he keeps his mouth shut. He's done well, and did I tell you he's studying to be an engineer? *Ahora bien*, he wants to take on even more, it seems. Last week he was saying that he'd like to buy the hardware store, to keep it in the family and get it running right. I don't know—he seems to be taking on so much already, and his wife Susan is always after him to spend more time at home. His little girl, María, named after my mother, is only four. And I worry that he wouldn't make a place for José. What I don't tell Bart Jr. is how much I pay José—way too much—but he was Elena's baby and we always took care of him.

To the FWTP adviser, Bart Sr. is a prospective client, i.e., a person who consults the adviser with the idea of potentially engaging the adviser to provide services. This consultation offers the opportunity to consider how two of the Four C's apply to a new FWTP engagement: selection of an appropriate client and confidentiality.

Is There a Client—and If So, Who Is It?

For some professionals, a preliminary interview can inadvertently create a relationship with a client, which in turn triggers specific duties. For example, even if a consultation with a prospective client does not mature into a client-attorney relationship, a lawyer owes some duties of confidentiality and loyalty to the prospective client, which can complicate other client relationships.[5] Moreover, Bart Sr. (like most prospective clients) is wearing multiple (and often invisible) legal "hats": business owner, director, trustee, beneficiary, parent, and prospective spouse, to name just a few. Further complicating matters is the fact that the person seeking advice is likely wearing multiple nonlegal "hats" as well, such as squeaky wheel, rebel, eccentric, conciliator, or dictator. In the initial interview, it is impossible to sort these roles out clearly in anticipation of forming a client relationship. It is too early in the process (if there will be one) to identify who the client will be, and it is important not to cut off productive avenues for structuring the process.

To avoid these problems, the adviser should take two steps. First, prior to the meeting, the adviser's staff should identify the people and entities that are the major players in the family wealth system, and also clarify who will attend the initial meeting and in what capacity. By examining potential conflicts prior to the meeting, the adviser can decline or restructure it as necessary. It is not always possible to explore conflicts ahead of time, of course. In the Hernández family, the adviser would likely need to take some time in the meeting for Bart Sr. to describe the major components of his family wealth system in order to clarify the potential clients in an engagement. The focus of this discussion is merely to gather the facts about the broad outline of the family's financial wealth, the existing business entities, and the legal issues.

Second, the adviser should conduct the initial interview in a way that will avoid creating a premature relationship or creating expectations in the potential client that cannot be met. This is particularly true for lawyers, whose ethical tenets impose limited, but specific, duties to prospective clients. Most importantly, the adviser should explain (ideally in writing at the time the appointment is made) that (1) the purpose of the meeting is exploratory, and (2) both the prospective client and the adviser must decide whether to go forward with the engagement, after having sufficient time to reflect on the "fit" between the needs of the prospective client and the adviser. At the conclusion of the interview, the adviser should propose a process whereby the client can decide whether or not to move forward with the engagement, and if so, how. If Bart Sr. wishes to continue, another meeting may be necessary to determine the best structure for the engagement. If either the adviser or the prospective client decides not to pursue the relationship, the adviser will issue a client nonengagement letter clarifying that no client relationship has been established.

How Will the Adviser Preserve Confidentiality?

At the prospective client stage of a FWTP engagement, it is impossible to identify the range of information that will be disclosed or who will disclose it, much less what information will be confidential. But in many initial interviews, a client unexpectedly offers up secrets, and Bart Sr. does just that. The adviser is now forewarned that some family members know certain information (for example, Bart Sr. and Bart Jr. both know of the idea of purchasing the hardware store, but José apparently does not). Bart Sr. believes he is overpaying José and doesn't feel comfortable telling Bart Jr. Moreover, there appear to be some desires and emotions that Bart Sr. may not want to share with the family. Bart Sr.'s unhappiness with his sons and his desire to protect José are probably in this category, even though these family secrets may be the kind that everyone already knows but won't talk about.

The interrelationship of client selection and confidentiality is immediately apparent in many first interviews. There may be some information that will require the protection of confidentiality, at least at the outset. Inadvertently, in this short interview, the adviser has obtained client confidences that may restrict the adviser's ability to engage any other individual or entity within the family system as a client. If the adviser is a lawyer, this could preclude representation of any other person in the family wealth system, even if that person would be the more appropriate client overall, without the consent of Bart Sr. and a possible waiver to allow disclosure.

Although lawyers are subject to specific ethical tenets, the same issue arises for any FWTP adviser: If Bart Sr. needs his secrets kept, how is the engagement to be structured in terms of client selection and process? It is impossible to explore the need for confidentiality fully in the initial interview, for to do so could easily elicit more confidences and create client expectations that the adviser may not be able to fulfill. To make matters worse, few clients understand the need for appropriate client selection in the FWTP process or the confidentiality problems that may arise from the professions of the adviser and team members and the ultimate structure of the engagement. To prepare for this, the adviser should open the meeting with the gentle warning that this is not the time or place to discuss information that the client might ultimately not want to share with other family members, because it is not yet clear how the engagement will be structured if the client and adviser decide to move forward. It is the adviser's job to strike the right balance between openness and reservation in the initial conversation, and to head off unwarranted disclosures of confidential information.

The Existing Client: Client Identification

—THE MARSHALL FAMILY—

Robert L. (Bobbie Lee) Marshall, age forty-seven

I'm coming down from Chicago in June for a visit. I know I haven't been around for a while and I realize I haven't kept up on Marshall Enterprises, or anything else, like I should have. Things have been rough here, my son Larry's in and out of rehab, and Florence and I are just now back together. We were separated, you know. Thank goodness little Corrine is fine. I guess she's not so little anymore; she's heading to college already. She's a math whiz, wants to be an economist like me. I'm trying to get my life back on track. It seems like the last three years have been a bad dream. Anyway, what I want to do when I'm there is have a meeting with you and just us kids—Arnie, Eddie, Ruthie, and me—to get clear about what would happen if Dad and Mom died tomorrow. I know you've been after Dad to do some estate planning for years. I think this is a good way to start. Also, I realize you haven't spent a lot of time with Eddie, and, well, you'll see he's a piece of work. But I think it's important that he be there along with the rest of us. We know we can't make any changes or anything. I just want to get a sense of what my brothers and sister think will happen or want to have happen. I may or may not tell Arnie what Dad said to me about cutting Arnie out of his will. But I'd appreciate your keeping it under your hat for now, at least until I get a feel for what's going on in the family.

A long-term relationship between an adviser and a business family will often predate any FWTP conversation, but when the conversation turns to this kind of planning, issues of client identification, confidentiality, and client conflicts soon arise. The Marshall family is a prime example. Robert is trying to instigate a conversation that is long overdue by seeking the help of a long-time adviser to the family. They obviously know each other and have worked together before. It is likely that this adviser has also worked closely with the parents and with Arnie, given his role at the ranch and at the farm. But the adviser's relationship with the two other siblings, Eddie and Ruth, is unclear.

An adviser serving long-time clients may not feel that a formal process of client identification is necessary; after all, the adviser has assisted the business and its owners for many years without controversy. Underlying this belief may be the adviser's fear of losing the trust (and the business) of certain family members or entities during this important transition and a desire not to abandon those who have relied on him or her. However, the process of FWTP will raise special ethical questions of conflicts and confidentiality that are usually irrelevant to providing day-to-day assistance to a business and its owners. Identification of client(s) is a necessary first step in analyzing the adviser's duties and structuring the engagement.

The family wealth system for families with businesses may be made up of individuals, business entities, trusts, and other arrangements in which family members play multiple roles. This complicates the process of client identification. To advise the family appropriately, the adviser may have to disengage from some components of the family wealth system and avoid creating a relationship with others. This is of particular concern for lawyers and accountants, both of whom have ethical duties of objectivity and independence. Yet practicality is also important. It is simply too expensive for every individual and entity within the family business constellation to have a separate adviser.

When existing clients wish an adviser to help them in the FWTP process, the adviser's first job is to take inventory of which members (individuals and entities) of the family wealth system the adviser has assisted, and in what capacity. Are these engagements ongoing or in the past? What was the nature of these engagements? What representations were made at the time, if any, about future engagements? Mapping the adviser's existing relationships is critical to structuring the FWTP engagement.

In the Marshall situation, for example, the adviser has long represented Marshall Enterprises in its business affairs (ranching, drilling, and trucking). The adviser has had many opportunities to work with Arnie in the drilling business, and has met with Robert and Ruthie at the annual shareholders' meetings. The adviser has had much less experience dealing with Eddie, because Eddie generally doesn't attend shareholders' or directors' meetings. The adviser's firm has also handled many smaller matters for family members over the years, and is involved in the defense of the lawsuits generated by the car crash. The adviser has helped Johnny Ray make gifts of shares in the company to family members over the years, and was involved in the estate planning that the Marshalls did some years ago.

Selection of the Appropriate Client

If the adviser is a lawyer, the engagement must be predicated upon receiving consents and waivers from other family members and entities within the Marshall wealth system. Even if the adviser is not filling a traditional role, however, it is prudent to include in the engagement letter a disclosure of prior and existing relationships and obtain the client's informed consent to proceed with the engagement with knowledge of these relationships.

The Existing Client: Multiple Client Conflicts and Communication Pathways

—THE MARSHALL FAMILY—

Eddie Marshall, age fifty-four

I don't know why Bobbie called this meeting of us kids, when we all know it's about Dad. Just 'cause he calls himself Robert Lee doesn't make him general of this family. Where's he been these past five years while we've been pickin' up the pieces? And, hey, where's Dad? Look, I'm supposed to be at work. The last thing I've got time for is these damn meetings. I'm not gonna listen to Bobbie lecture us, and Arnie complain about Dad, and Ruthie try to make everyone act all nicey-nice like she does. And you lawyers, I've told Dad for years all you lawyers wants to spend our money to support your Lexus habits. Anyhow, y'all should be ashamed for sneaking around Dad's back. And your wives' backs, too. I'm outta here. Ruthie, you call me later if you want. I'm done with the rest of y'all.

This adviser has a mess to deal with. The adviser probably expected a meeting in which the siblings discussed generalities, made no decisions, and were largely on the same page. Yet even before the meeting could get started, it has been derailed. If the adviser can look beyond Eddie's anger, he or she will see that Eddie is asking all the right questions. Why *isn't* Johnny Ray there? Why did Robert set up a meeting without his father and mother, or the spouses or partners of the siblings? Can the adviser even proceed without these other people? What exactly *is* this meeting about? Eddie is also warning the adviser of patterns of behavior and family roles that could impede progress during the FWTP process if not dealt with early. Eddie's abrupt departure may be a blessing in disguise, giving the adviser time to regroup and address these issues.

This situation illustrates the thorniest ethical problem in the FWTP process: the problem of *multiple client conflicts.* An adviser must be prepared for more than one person to ask for assistance. Having previously analyzed the potential for conflicts of interest, the adviser must be aware of the duties that may be owed to different family members and business entities. Determining whether a conflict exists and figuring out what to do about it are especially difficult in the FWTP arena because of the multiple roles played by family members and the inevitability that these roles will change as the process evolves.

Successful transition planning requires the adviser to conduct two levels of analysis for multiple client conflicts. The first step is to consider potential conflicts from a professional ethics perspective. Lawyers and accountants, in particular, must be alert to situations in which their loyalty to one client precludes them from giving assistance to another. Clients rarely fully understand the details of these ethical concerns, and often brush off a professional's concern that, in the future, conflicting legal interests may develop. The adviser must consider all of the actual and potential conflicts at the outset of the engagement, and obtain the necessary consents and waivers in an engagement letter. In addition, the adviser must have a plan for withdrawal in the event that an irresolvable conflict arises.

While clients often do not understand or care about the niceties of professionals' ethical rules, they do understand the next step in the analysis of the conflict of interest question: when there are hard choices to make, whose desires and needs will be given priority by the adviser? FWTP will bring to the surface conflicts among family members that have remained suppressed in their day-to-day lives. In the Marshall family, Eddie's tantrum is an example. Many of the decisions the adviser will make will raise questions about the identity, worth, and role of family members. Long-standing patterns of family behavior may prevent family members from openly discussing their differences with the lawyer. Changing roles involved in FWTP are intimately tied to family roles, with all their usual opportunities for conflict, as illustrated in this peek into the Marshall family dynamic. What would be an easily negotiated decision in a nonfamily transaction may cause anxiety and conflict in the family business setting and take much more time. Paradoxically, the methodology advocated in this book is more rather than less likely to bring these conflicts to the foreground. However, it is important to discover and deal with family conflicts, because ignoring them can significantly hamper the transition process.

The answer given by a lawyer serving in the traditional role to the question of whose needs will take precedence will likely differ, at least in part, from the answer given by a member of another profession. For a lawyer, the client's interests are paramount. The lawyer may be instructed by the client to propose solutions that are best for everyone, and to challenge the client's own desires and needs. But, at the end of the day, the lawyer's duty of obedience to the client requires that the lawyer look after the interests of the client. By contrast, other professionals (and lawyers acting in a nonlawyer capacity) have greater latitude to disregard one person's interests, or at least not to prefer one person's interests over another's.

Most FWTP advisers using the methodology in this book would agree that the question "Whose interests are most important?" needs reframing. It is the family that must make decisions in charting its own unique course toward family wealth continuity. The FWTP adviser is a facilitator, a tour guide, and a resource for the family on this journey. The adviser's role is to show how different choices affect the family wealth system, and how adaptations either promote or impede family wealth continuity. That discussion is necessarily broad and only rarely comes down to "them or me" kinds of choices. In fact, many advisers would feel that they have failed if decisions come down to such bilateral choices. In most cases, a properly conducted process isn't derailed by the question of whose interests take precedence. That question is the province of families that are ill prepared to make choices, because of trigger events that occurred before the family began the process.

Establishing Communication Pathways

In a long-standing association, a family member like Robert may certainly call a long-time adviser to the family to express an interest in FWTP. But the adviser must be aware that when this occurs, Robert is taking control of a communication pathway. From the moment the adviser moves beyond pleasantries on that call, he or she is sanctioning Robert's selection of this pathway of communication. If the adviser sets up the meeting, the effect is to give Robert's instruction even more credence and to establish a formal pathway of communication (the meeting). Even if Robert previously held the authority to set up such meetings on other matters, there should be no assumption that he has that same authority when it comes to a new engagement on such an important matter.

The skilled FWTP adviser must be prepared to discuss, in that first call, how important it is to establish pathways of communication with which the family members and the adviser will feel comfortable. The adviser can then discuss next steps—what next conversation is appropriate, whom to involve in the next conversation, how to involve them, and most importantly, why all this is necessary. At times, the adviser must explain, the participants may have to call a time-out to clarify communication pathways and confidentiality obligations. Preparation for that call, of course, will require the adviser to analyze potential conflicts and confidentiality issues and create proposed waivers, as necessary.

The Existing Client: Confidentiality and Disengagement

—THE WILLIAMS FAMILY—

Helen Williams, age forty-eight

I thought we made a lot of progress on the estate plan in our last meeting. Frankly, I'm glad John couldn't be here this time, because I wanted to ask you a question. I'm not sure if I'd be able to ask it if he were here. Do you happen to know whether, if my father left money to me, John would have any right to it? Or if the business got in trouble—it isn't, of course—would my Dad's money have to be used to bail it out? My Dad always told me to have at least some money squirreled away for the kids and myself just in case. I always ignored him, in both my marriages. I trust John completely. But sometimes I wonder about things, because John's been under so much stress and he's being even more vague than usual about finances. I found an invoice—$1,500!—from a pediatrician that I didn't recognize, and it was marked "overdue." It's so unlike John not to pay bills on time.

Red flags went up for the FWTP adviser the moment Helen said that she was glad that her husband wasn't there. Now, having heard the rest of her story (which was probably unavoidable), the adviser has acquired two pieces of confidential information: the question Helen might not have been able to ask if her husband had been present, and her discovery of the bill. Both husband and wife are clients, and now both of them are not privy to all information. The FWTP adviser may be able to conclude that these items of information are not relevant to the representation, and therefore need not be disclosed. Or, the adviser may be able to convince Helen of the need to consent to disclosure of this information to John. Nevertheless, the adviser is in an awkward position, not only because of this lack of shared information, but also because the adviser could infer from either of these items that there is much more going on with the Williams family than either Helen or John have revealed so far.

The Williams situation illustrates the problem of confidentiality within a client group. Are all clients to have access to all information given to or received from the FWTP adviser? In the Williams family, this is a reasonable assumption for each client to make, but although it is still early in the engagement, a problem has arisen. At the outset of the engagement, the FWTP adviser should have made it clear that all information received or given by the adviser was subject to disclosure to any member of the client group, and each member of the group should have consented to this. The procedure for withdrawing that consent should be clear, but as Helen's conversation illustrates, the circumstances of withdrawal of consent are often ambiguous.

For lawyers, this is a particularly difficult problem because they owe their clients an almost absolute duty not to reveal confidential information. Without consent, they may not reveal confidential information, and the client can withdraw consent at any time. They may also owe their clients a duty to reveal to clients information that the lawyer has and clients want to know. For example, if the FWTP adviser to the Williams family is a lawyer, John may ask the adviser to give a detailed description of the conversation with Helen when they next meet. In that case, without Helen's consent, the lawyer will not be able to respond fully to John's request, nor will the lawyer be able to tell John of the selective nature of the report. This puts the lawyer in an impossible situation, and the lawyer's only option is to withdraw. The problem is not limited to lawyers, of course. Any other adviser will face the same issue, and other professions' ethical rules may be even less helpful than the lawyer's ethical principles in guiding the professional to the required response.

The confidentiality problem grows exponentially with the addition of more members to the client group and with the addition of team members to assist the client group. In addition, the FWTP methodology may make individual meetings with the adviser desirable.

On the other hand, if they are to speak candidly, family members will likely require some assurance of confidentiality in their discussions with the adviser. The adviser must propose a process that takes into account what kinds of information are to be shared, how it is to be shared, and what the adviser may do with that information. That process must consider each professional's obligation to his or her client, the required consents and waivers, and the consequences if a client changes his or her mind about disclosure.

CHAPTER NOTES

1. See *Olender v. U.S.*, 210 F. 2d 795, 805–806 (9th Cir. 1954) (the attorney-client privilege applies only when the client is seeking legal advice from a professional legal adviser in his or her capacity as such; business advice is not covered under the privilege).

2. American Bar Association, Model Rules of Professional Conduct 8.4 (200g). Model Rule 8.4 applies to all of a lawyer's activities, not just the practice of law. Section 98 of the Restatement (Third) of the Law Governing Lawyers (2000) prohibits a lawyer from knowingly making a false statement of a material fact or law to a nonclient.

3. See, e.g., *Estate of Buonomici, Jr., Alfred Isaacs, Executor, and the Beneficiaries thereof v. Salvatore Morici, CPA & Ostroff Fair & Co., PC Sup. Ct. Del. 2009, CA. No. 08C-10-231 JAP* (claim of breach of fiduciary duty against valuation experts).

4. Most FWTP advisers use an engagement letter at the outset of the planning process that provides a brief description of the anticipated planning process; identifies the scope of activities; sets forth the extent to which information can be shared with professionals and family members; states the financial terms, including how expenses such as travel will be handled; and lists the specific deliverables the client may expect, such as progress reports, project summaries, and assessment tabulations.

5. Although a lawyer has the absolute duty not to use any confidential information to the detriment of a current client, the lawyer for a prospective (or former) client may use this information "to the disadvantage" of that client, but only after the information has become "generally known." Model Rules of Professional Conduct 1.18(b), 1.9 (200g).

CHAPTER 3

THE FAMILY WEALTH SYSTEM

A FAMILY IS NOT just a gathering of people, nor is its wealth just an assortment of assets. Family members and their assets, along with their relationships, dreams, hopes, and habits, participate in a complex system of wealth creation that is more than the sum of its parts. Understanding a family as a *family wealth system* is integral to family wealth transition planning (FWTP).

Every client's family wealth system is unique, yet all family wealth systems share common traits. Understanding these common characteristics allows advisers and planners to describe accurately what they see happening in a family, and allows families to identify the forces at work within and upon the system. Understanding how these forces play out in a particular family ultimately leads to a better selection of plan components, because they will be designed specifically for the characteristics of that family's wealth system.

The family wealth system is made up of numerous tangible and intangible components. The most important are people, including family members and others who are important to the family. Other components include financial assets, skills and talents, ideas, values, and relationships, all of which interconnect in complicated ways. The components of the family wealth system are like the workings of a watch: tinkering with one gear may have a profound impact on how the watch functions. Yet the family wealth system is much more than a mechanical system in which pressing a particular lever produces a predictable result. The family wealth system is an open, adaptive system, with certain characteristics that make FWTP challenging, especially when an operating business plays an important role in the system.

Most experienced FWTP advisers have seen the effects of a family wealth system at work, even if they are not familiar with the theory of family systems. They have experience with the upheavals that can occur in a family when clients makes changes in their estate planning, business planning, or personal life. They have seen clients fail to implement what appear to be "perfect" estate plans for inexplicable reasons. They have seen family members reverse, undermine, or sabotage important decisions. When the adviser properly develops and uses it, a map of a family wealth system can prevent these problems and provide a base for the creation of a FWTP process that serves the ultimate goal of family wealth continuity.

Similarly, clients intuitively understand that their plans are constrained by internal forces within their families and that their actions during the FWTP process will have complicated and long-lasting effects throughout their family. Both of these qualities are characteristic of a family system. From wanting to minimize transition taxes to wondering how to talk with their children about fairness, clients' concerns illustrate the inner workings of their own family wealth system. Although clients would never describe their families as "complex adaptive systems" or their decision-making process as "emergent," they are usually aware of some of the aspects of participating in a family wealth system. This chapter presents an overview of the family wealth system and its nested subsystems.

Systems Theory as Applied to Family Wealth

Systems theory evolved in the 1950s as a model for understanding intricate connections in biology and physics. It was based partly on Ludwig von Bertanlaffy's work on general systems theory.[1] Since then, systems theory has become integral to understanding not only processes in the natural sciences, but also human beings, organizations, and computers. Murray Bowen and others developed family systems theory as a field of study in the 1950s. Applying systems theory to family wealth, however, is a relatively recent phenomenon, pioneered by Peter White in the mid-1980s.[2]

A *system* is a complex grouping of interacting elements that may be dedicated to a common function or goal. In the biological world, *system* may refer to the organs and tissues of a body that are dedicated to a particular function. In computers, a system is a combination of hardware, software, and communication devices dedicated to a particular use, and might also include human users. A system can be populated by people, things, or relationships, and often its most important components are intangible and invisible.

A family wealth system is a *complex adaptive system.* Like any other system, a complex adaptive system is made up of multiple interconnected components. But in an *adaptive* system, agents within the system have the capacity to learn from experience and change their environment. These agents scan their environment, interpret events within it, and translate their interpretations into action. This action in turn causes other components within the system to change, and ultimately causes the entire system to change.

Uncertain Boundaries

In a naturally occurring system, it is difficult to identify the boundary of the system with any certainty. The ecosystem of a lake, for example, is intimately connected to the watershed around it, which in turn is tied to weather patterns. Ultimately, every system is connected to every other system, and boundaries dissolve. However, one must choose a boundary for a system if one is to perform certain functions, such as taking an inventory or assessing the health of the system. Thus, system observers draw boundaries, but these are human constructs and are tied to accomplishing a particular task. When that task changes, so must the boundary.

Similarly, the boundaries of the family wealth system are uncertain. A family's wealth system is connected to other systems, such as another family's wealth system, the tax system, or even the economic system as a whole. The transition process requires a boundary that identifies those components of the family wealth system that are tied to family wealth continuity. The picture of the family wealth system that appears in this section draws a boundary that will facilitate the process, but it doesn't answer all the questions related to a boundary. For example, is the map of the wealth system that of the nuclear family or the extended family? Does "ownership" of an asset determine its inclusion within the system, or does some other claim on it determine its proper place within the system? Addressing these kinds of questions helps create a boundary that facilitates the transition process by focusing on what the client can change or influence. The process can affect what is inside the boundary, but not what remains outside of it. As planning progresses, and the process reveals the full array of wealth subject to transition and the components of the system that the transition will affect, the adviser and the client will redraw the boundaries.

Complex and Nonlinear Relationships

The relationships within the family wealth system are complex and nonlinear. A common example in the family wealth system is the board of directors of a closely held corporation. The actual relationship of the board of a closely held company to the company's shareholders and to other components of the system rarely resembles the legal relationships that statutes prescribe. The interdependency of these connections ensures that change will be communicated throughout the system, often in unpredictable ways. Seemingly small perturbations in one area of the system, or outside it, can generate a disproportionately large effect elsewhere in the system. This is known as the butterfly effect.

Nested Subsystems and Sub-Subsystems

Many naturally occurring systems are made up of a number of *nested subsystems*. The human body, as a system, contains myriad subsystems such as the digestive system, the neurological system, and the circulatory system. In the same way, the family wealth system has a number of subsystems nested within it. The upcoming section on "The Family Wealth System Model" describes the four subsystems of the family wealth system, which are in turn are made up of even smaller subsystems. A family's philanthropic subsystem, for example, may include systems such as coordinated family giving or a family foundation. An operating business subsystem will often be populated by different businesses, such as the Hernándezes' hardware store, construction, and real estate businesses, each of which is a separate subsystem of the operating business subsystem.

The FWTP process generally begins with analysis and mapping of the family wealth system as a whole and, over time, the analysis and mapping of various subsystems. Typically, a family will have special issues surrounding components of a particular subsystem, as business families do when considering the fate of a family business. Increasing the resolution of a part of the picture, however, is obtained at the potential cost of losing sight of the whole image. Examining the detail of an operating business system, for example, could reveal important information about the possibilities of dividing an operating business among siblings. But it cannot so easily reveal the connections between that subsystem and the family's investment office subsystem. The process requires simultaneous attention to nested subsystems and the family wealth system as a whole, and an ongoing awareness of family wealth continuity goals.

Feedback and Feedback Loops

Relationships within the family wealth system create positive and negative *feedback*, as well as *feedback loops*. A feedback loop is the process by which some portion of an output signal cycles back into the input, such as the screech of feedback from an audio system. In fact, a primary function of the family wealth subsystem is to create feedback loops, because they transmit family values across generations. Whether the value is hard work, philanthropy, distrust of strangers, or taking time to smell the roses, feedback to family members, explicit or implicit, communicates those family values.

Feedback can be negative or positive. *Positive* and *negative* in this case do not relate to whether the feedback has positive or negative effects, or to the way feedback is given. Instead, negative feedback dampens or slows an effect, while positive feedback amplifies or accelerates the effect. Repeated feedback between family members can have either effect. Understanding how amplifying and dampening feedback loops work is critical to designing the FWTP process components, particularly the governance system. For example, for families that have a low level of trust but must share wealth, creating governance systems that are a substitute for trust is a critical task. These governance systems will also create an opportunity for positive feedback loops that amplify trust.

Open Systems

The family wealth system is an *open system*. Its boundaries are permeable in both directions, so energy, components, and forces can move into the system or away from it. A family wealth system requires some degree of openness in order for FWTP commence, because the very process involves acceptance of the skills of outside advisers and new ideas.

The openness of the family wealth system to the influx of new people, ideas, information, and opportunities varies from family to family.[3] In some families, a new spouse is immediately welcomed into the family. In others, a spouse may feel that he or she is still on probation decades later. A family may take a different approach in its various subsystems within the family wealth system. A spouse may be welcomed with open arms, yet excluded from investment discussions or participation in the family business.

The openness of the family wealth system is what often propels clients into their adviser's office to talk about FWTP. The family wealth system is always subject to at least some outside forces, such as taxes, regulatory issues, and lawsuits. These forces can dissipate family wealth, draining it away from the family wealth system in unexpected ways. Triggers from outside the family system often propel clients into their adviser's office to talk about their family wealth transition plan. The adviser's ability to work with the client to address the impact of any of those triggers depends to a great extent on the relative openness of the system.

System Memory

When a squeezed sponge is released, it immediately returns to its previous shape and size. Its memory of a presqueeze shape is practically perfect. By contrast, Play-Doh® has no memory: a handful of this flexible stuff can be a tiger today, a snake tomorrow, and all over the carpet the next day. It has no memory of being a tiger, nor any inclination to return to that form.

Like the sponge, the family wealth system has a memory, but it is an imperfect one. The state of the system at any given time is dependent on the past. When change occurs, the system, through the reaction of its components, has a tendency to try to return to its previous state. It is extremely unlikely that the previous state of the system will ever be precisely reincarnated, despite the best efforts of some actors within the system. The components of the system and their relationships to each other will change. Some families, as a way to keep the status quo, deny that change is occurring or has occurred. Others acknowledge the change but try to proceed as if the change has not occurred. The degree of change the system can tolerate at one time is limited, although it varies from family to family depending on each family's adaptability.[4]

The implications of this characteristic for the FWTP process are enormous. The FWTP process anticipates trigger events, those major events of life, such as birth, death, divorce, and disability, which have a great impact on the family system. The process seeks to adapt the family wealth system to weather these kinds of events in ways that promote family wealth continuity, rather than relying on chance to shape the system productively. In this environment, the skill and methods of those introducing change will be of critical importance, and they must counteract the tendency of the system to return to an imperfect imitation of a prior state. Fundamentally, adaptation of the family wealth system to promote family wealth continuity must be an ongoing process, which includes all three components of transition planning: legal documents, governance, and role development.[5]

Emergence

Although the idea is somewhat controversial, many researchers believe that most complex adaptive systems are *emergent* (self-organizing). This means that the system tends to increase in complexity without outside guidance or management. Increasingly organized patterns form within the system, and these patterns evolve in unexpected ways to form new, more complex forms or structures.

The family wealth system is an emergent system. As families and family businesses move through their cycles of development[6] and external forces influence various components of the system,[7] the entire system becomes more complex. The resulting paradox is that families that are successful in promoting individuation among their members and building wealth are rewarded with more complexity, not less. Patterns and structures form within the family wealth system to help a family deal with this increasing complexity. Some of these are patterns of wealth behavior, and others are organic governance systems. For example, a family may implicitly adopt an autocratic governance model when starting a business. This choice could be inspired by family patterns of wealth behavior around issues of control, a need for efficient decision making, or even lack of knowledge of any other way of carrying on business.

Every engagement will encounter these emergent structures, yet at the outset of any engagement, no one really knows for sure what motivates these structures' creation. The role of the FWTP adviser and family members is to reveal these patterns and evaluate their continuing utility in promoting family needs, particularly wealth continuity. During the process, structures may be discarded, adapted, or preserved. Some structures will be artifacts of a previous incarnation of the family wealth system. Still others will easily adapt to the goals of the FWTP process. Entirely new structures may emerge as well, usually explicitly designed as components of the FWTP process.[8] Of course, few clients direct their lawyers to create more complexity in their family wealth system. This is why the process must provide clients with more than documents; it must also help clients navigate the emergent system.

The Family Wealth System Model

The model of a family wealth system is a critical tool for the FWTP adviser team, and a family may find it useful as well as they work with their advisers on the FWTP process. *Figure 3.1* presents a model of the family wealth system and its four major subsystems, which provide a starting place for mapping any family's wealth system.

Four nested subsystems[9] make up the family wealth system:

❏ *The family subsystem*
❏ *The operating business subsystem*
❏ *The investment/office subsystem*
❏ *The philanthropic subsystem*

The dotted circle in Figure 3.1 represents the system's boundary, which defines the components that are inside and outside the system at any given time. In all complex systems, however, the boundary is difficult to identify, and may change as the purpose of the examination changes. The boundary traced in Figure 3.1 could easily go somewhere else in the figure.

Outside the boundary are various entities or systems with which the family wealth system interacts, and the forces that have an impact on the system, such as the wealth system of a related family (e.g., in-laws), certain business relationships, or the Internal Revenue Service (IRS). Inside the boundary are the four nested subsystems: the core family subsystem, the family-operated business subsystem, the family investment/office subsystem, and the family philanthropic subsystem. Note that Figure 3.1 shows subsystems of relatively equal size. In practice, this is never the case. In most families, each subsystem will be of a

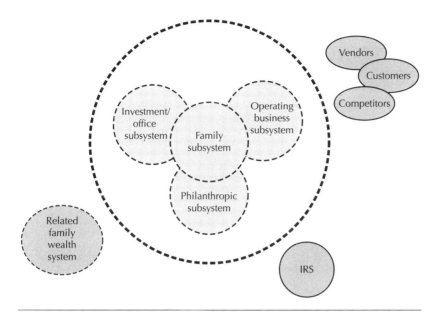

FIGURE 3.1   The Family Wealth System

different size with respect to the number of components within it and its importance in the system.

The heart of the family wealth system, and what distinguishes it from other systems, is the family subsystem: the family members, their roles, and their relationships. It includes the family's history and their dreams, hopes, and fears for the future. Thus, the most important components of the family wealth system are the family members.

Not every family wealth system incorporates every other subsystem. Some families may only have a family business. Others may have sold the business and now manage the proceeds as investments. Some families have generated wealth through stocks and bonds, or retirement accounts, and have created a family office to manage their investment, tax, and legal activities. In some cases, families have created foundations as the vehicle for their philanthropic activities; other families may rely on tithing. In some business families, the operating business subsystems may dwarf philanthropy or investment subsystems.

In order to illustrate the subsystems more clearly, Figure 3.1 shows relatively little overlap among the systems. In practice, it is unrealistic for the family subsystem not to overlap with the other subsystems. In many families of wealth, all or most of the subsystems will overlap, in the sense that a given component will be a critical component of more than one subsystem.

The family wealth system is engaged in a continual cycle of change and equilibrium. Many families start with one or perhaps two of these systems and add others as the needs of the family change. Subsystems die off as businesses are sold or retirement accounts drained. New subsystems emerge when a family member starts a business or a charitable project. A picture of the family wealth system is valuable, just as a balance sheet is valuable: it is a snapshot of the system as it exists at a moment in time. This snapshot offers valuable information about a family and its wealth. But it does not capture the details of the family wealth system in the past, nor does it necessarily predict the future.

Functions and Components

Each subsystem of the family wealth system fills a different role in building family wealth. The function of the core family subsystem, for example, is the creation of individual identity, mutual love and support of family members, and the transmission of family values. The investment/office subsystem is the place for family savings for retirement, education, health, and personal development. The philanthropic subsystem guides resources to recipients outside the system. The operating business subsystem builds family wealth through the creation, expansion, and ultimate disposition of businesses.

Various components contribute to the unique function of a subsystem, and any component may have an important role to play in more than one subsystem. These components include:

❏ **Financial capital:** Assets and liabilities, such as cash, equity interests in companies, real estate, retirement or education savings accounts, loans and other obligations, life insurance policies, and intangible assets such as proprietary knowledge

❏ **Human capital:** People and their competencies, including family members (living or in memory), close non–family members, advisers, key employees, decision-making protocols, and governance structures

❏ **Social capital:** Processes and methods, including formal and informal governance systems, understandings of "the way we do things around here," statements of values or vision, contractual agreements, family traditions, connections within family and community, and philanthropic efforts

Chapter 4 discusses these different kinds of capital in detail and the complex interconnections among them. For now, the important point is to understand that each subsystem is made up of many different components, all of which interconnect within a subsystem and potentially with other parts of the family wealth system.

The Family Subsystem

—THE MARSHALL FAMILY—

Jenny Lynne (Mrs. Johnny Ray) Marshall, age eighty-five

I used to start every day the same way. I'd put on the coffee, let the cat in. I'd look out over the hills and ask God to help each member of my family find their path. And to give me enough sense to know how to help them best or to get out of their way. You know, it always worked, always. By the time Johnny Ray was slurping his coffee, I just knew we were all going to be fine.

Now I can't pray anymore. I figure nobody's home up there. He moved out three years ago, no forwarding address. But I try to pray anyhow, I truly do. I try to pray that my husband won't run Arnie off for good so I don't lose my grandson. And that Eddie will find some peace inside all that anger. And that my dear Florence will forgive us for her son's death.

But it's not working. We're on our own. And we're not doing so good.

Jenny Lynne Marshall, the matriarch of the Marshall clan, is worried about her family's core system: *the family subsystem*. This subsystem has served the Marshalls well over the years, providing priceless intangibles to family members, such as love, trust, approval, and acceptance, and providing a forum for the development and transmittal of family values. Most family subsystems are intensely focused on the raising of children, and the Marshalls' is no exception. These personal and family values are reinterpreted and passed on from generation to generation. The family subsystem is the starting place for analysis of the first component of family wealth continuity: healthy family relationships. It also is the home of feedback loops that continually amplify or dampen family connections and values.

The family subsystem is an open system, although the degree of openness varies from family to family.[10] People enter the family subsystem through birth, adoption, marriage, and long-standing partnership. During their tenure in the family subsystem, they are connected by roles and relationships with both legal and cultural dimensions. Although people leave the family subsystem through divorce, death, and repudiation, in a sense, no one ever leaves the family system, because departed members have an ongoing influence within the family.

The relationships among people within the system have both legal and nonlegal characteristics. Husbands and wives, or parents and children, have legally defined relationships, with legally imposed rights and responsibilities. The legal rights and duties of unmarried partners are continually being redefined. However, in day-to-day life—the primary concern of most clients—the roles of family members are defined by emergent patterns of relationships, cultural expectations, family dynamics, and family history.

Of the four subsystems shown in Figure 3.1, the family subsystem is in some ways the least transparent. Families come in all shapes and sizes, ranging from couples with no children, to single- and two-parent families, to blended families and multigenerational clans like the Marshalls. Because of this great diversity, a family subsystem can be defined in a variety of ways. It can include only one branch of a family or multiple branches, and one generation or multiple generations. Deciding which family members are included in the analysis of a family subsystem and its boundary depends on the purpose of the analysis and the attitudes of the family.

Like the family wealth system as a whole, the family subsystem has a "memory." People need not physically be present to be and remain important. Patterns repeat themselves through generations. For example, a pattern of cutting off is not unusual. In some families, individuals or segments of the family may sever ties with the rest of the family, which may or may not be eventually rebuilt. Even if death, divorce, or abandonment has removed a person physically from the system, that person is present whenever a current participant takes an action informed by a memory of the departed or displaced family member. The Marshalls, for example, are still reeling from the events of 2004, when two grandsons were killed and another wounded. If Jenny Lynne is in despair, the family subsystem is probably in jeopardy.

It is not only people in the physical sense that constitute the core family subsystem. Any system populated by people will include multiple sets of beliefs, ideas, and values, which inform how participants interact with others within the system. For example, most families have some topics of discussion that are traditionally taboo, ranging from family scandals or the sexual orientation of family members to the family's level of wealth and its plan for self-preservation and distribution.

As Ruthie will reveal later in this chapter, the Marshall family refused to acknowledge Johnny's drinking as a teenager, with tragic results. Any pattern can repeat itself through feedback loops that amplify a particular pattern. Long-standing family patterns of behavior (discussed in detail in Chapter 6) have an important bearing on how people in a family interact, as well as how they create, manage, and expend wealth within the family wealth system. In the Marshall family, whatever their ways might have been, they reflect important family patterns that have potentially enormous implications for FWTP.

The Operating Business Subsystem

—THE HERNÁNDEZ FAMILY—
Bart Hernández Jr., age forty

Luisa teases me that I'm a throwback to my grandfather, Rafael Hernández. Everybody says I look just like him. I hope I'm like him, too. He came to this country in 1949 and worked hard. Just like me. He died falling off a roof while rescuing a neighbor's cat. *Bueno pues.* I'm studying to be an engineer at night school, and I work at the construction company during the day. We started out remodeling homes, and when that went well we branched out into new construction. We're doing okay, even in a recession. I make good money to support my wife and daughter. It's a lot of work, and we run things lean and mean because it takes money to acquire new land and put in the improvements, and all that has to be done before you can sell a single lot or build a single house. That worries my father—and me too sometimes. Papá financed this whole thing in the beginning, and even now will cosign on loans if I need it. When there's a piece of property I want to develop, Papá will help me negotiate for it and he'll be a partner in it too. I've been trying to tell Papá that I'd like to buy the hardware store, to keep it in the family. But I know that will

bring up the whole business of José. Everybody but him knows we have
to get him out of the construction businesss . . . but I don't want to start
that fight up again with Papá, who just tells me to have a more generous
spirit. That goes nowhere.

The *business subsystem* is alive and well in the Hernández family
wealth system. Bart Jr. is operating the construction business. Luisa has
opened a medical practice. Bart Sr. owns, and his other son, José, is running, the hardware business. Bart Sr.'s late wife and his sister created
a successful business, which they sold. And the real estate appears to
be increasingly important to Bart Sr. Even though Bart Sr. is an owner
only of the hardware and real estate businesses, all of the Hernández
businesses will become important in the FWTP process, because his influence permeates all of the businesses in which his family participates.
Responsible stewardship of wealth in all its forms, including all the different kinds of wealth deployed in and created by these businesses, will
require careful attention to wealth transition structures, governance
systems, and a plan for untangling Bart Sr. from at least some of his
roles and realigning the roles of other family members.

The common denominator of businesses within a family wealth system is the presence of a significant connection between family members
and the business. Family members may own all of the company, they
may be minority owners, or they may even be shareholders in a publicly traded company. The family's level of involvement in the day-to-day
management and its board-level strategic direction varies depending on
how many generations the family has owned the business, its size, and
the family's interests and skills. Nevertheless, family members always
have some identifiable connection with the operating business beyond
that of the typical individual investor in a publicly traded company.

The business subsystem serves both tangible and intangible functions within the family wealth system. As with any other business, the
function of a family business is to create wealth in the form of cash flow
and increase the value of the company. In the family-operated business,
this begs an important question: for whom is the wealth created? Traditional corporate law suggests that the goal of a business is to generate
wealth for the owners of the company. Bart Jr. relies on the construction
business to support his family, and a portion of the profit is directed to
his brother, José. But modern corporate law refutes the singular focus

on owners,[11] and certainly in a family business this focus is too narrow. A business, particularly a family-owned business, exists to create wealth not only for owners, but for nonowner family members as well, in the form of employment opportunities, perks, and roles (such as lessor of property) that allow cash flow to be directed to family members. It can be a training ground for some family members and a social security system for others. Financially, it can be a cash cow or a black hole of expense. The Hernández operating businesses reflect all of these potential functions.

A family-operated business serves a multitude of intangible and symbolic functions. The business is a place to practice the values and beliefs of the family. The family business can be a creative outlet, a place of acceptance, or a symbol of legacy, for good or bad. For some family members, it is nothing more than a stone around the family's neck. Understanding the true functions of each operating business for each of the various family members connected to the planning process is critical to mapping this subsystem.

Analysis of the business subsystem should include not only the businesses and the assets of each business, but also the multiple roles of family and nonfamily members involved in the business and the complex connections among this subsystem and the others. The butterfly effect is particularly prevalent in the family-operated business subsystem. Small changes in this subsystem are usually communicated throughout the system quickly, and changes elsewhere in the system can have disproportionate effects within the operating business subsystem. The greater the overlap between the business and family subsystems, the greater the potential for disruption is, and the more important planning for this disruption becomes.

Finally, an operating business subsystem usually has at least one explicit, formal governance structure in place. The business will likely be organized as a limited liability entity, such as a corporation (S or C), a limited partnership (LP), or a limited liability company (LLC), to protect nonbusiness family assets from the risks of the business. In many cases, there will be more than one business entity, because owners seek to protect the assets of each business venture from the risks of other ventures. As every lawyer knows, however, most families ignore the formalities of an externally imposed governance structure, much to the dismay of their advisers. Instead, governance patterns emerge to meet the needs of the family business and the family at any given time. Most families report that this is successful as long as the founding generation is at the helm. When a business is changing hands within a family, however, long established decision-making structures often fail. As founders become less involved in the business, other family members may have less confidence in the new managers' decision-making ability. When some family members run the business and others are passive owners, fissures of distrust can form. Often, the informal governance structure that worked so well in the founding generation must give way to some other decision-making process in order to achieve the goals of continuity. Methods for structuring new ways of making decisions are discussed in Chapter 8.

The Family Investment/Office Subsystem

—THE WILLIAMS FAMILY—
Miriam Weinstein, age seventy-four

Jacob always made sure that all the i's were dotted and the t's were crossed in absolutely everything he did, and so of course his estate plan was right up to date before he died. The advisers are handling everything, and they are taking forever to get it done. I thought, at least until this year, that I would have plenty of money; it's all in stocks and bonds and Jacob and I planned ahead for how all this would work, just in case. Or at least I thought he was planning with me. Helen and John are going to get some money, too, but Helen has to go in and sign some papers and she's been putting it off. Jacob and I agreed that John—that's our son-in-law—was who I could turn to if I needed anything. Anyway, John was going to be a trustee of my trust—with me, of course—and also he was supposed to be on the power of attorney so he could handle things if I lost my marbles. Just before he died, Jacob changed all of that without telling me. Now I have some junior banker I hardly know as trustee, not John. Now, this banker person and Helen are on the power of attorney together. I never even met the man before Jacob died, and now he's always talking nonsense to me on the telephone. Helen has never been interested in money decisions, although it's past time for her to learn. Sometimes I do think I'm losing my marbles, like when I walk into a room and can't remember why I'm there. I'm not going to tell that to Mr. Junior-banker and Helen. They'd put me in a home.

Both Miriam and Helen are now forced to address a large part of their family's *investment/office subsystem*: the system devoted to the goal of saving, investing, and preserving wealth for family members' future needs. Savings can take any number of forms, including savings for specific needs, such as education, health or retirement, or simply for the freedom to do as one pleases. It includes savings designed to replace earning power, including life and disability insurance. Typical components include retirement plans, 529 plans and other educational savings vehicles, brokerage accounts, insurance policies, and various kinds of deferred compensation. This system also includes real estate held for investment, as well as the major asset of most families: the family home. Vacation properties may be either part of this system or part of the family system, depending on the point of view of the family. Some savings, of course, are held outright, but interests in trusts, custodianships, and other management vehicles are often important components of this subsystem.

In some families, this subsystem also includes the *family office*, which serves the coordination function for families. Miriam and Helen may find that coordinating their investment and tax preparation services, for example, may save them time and better help them preserve wealth. Some family offices provide personal services to family members, such as scheduling for family vacation homes. Others even provide concierge services such as buying concert tickets or walking dogs. In large multi-generational families, the functions of a family office may expand to include managing the family's wealth, coordinating its philanthropic activity, overseeing its operating businesses, and handling real estate sales and acquisitions. The office can become the center of the family's lifelong learning programs for family members.[12]

Some families view themselves as too small financially to justify a family office. They have the option of joining multifamily offices (MFOs) that are managed by private banks, investment firms, or other families who have created economies of scale, enhanced expertise, and invest-ment advantages by operating together.[13] Family offices are sometimes attractive to families that have recently sold their operating company or who do not want to dedicate resources to staff and run an in-house family office. An adviser who considers recommending an MFO as one of the vehicles for a family's ongoing wealth management must research the various options carefully to find an appropriate fit for the family.[14]

The life cycles of individuals, families, and businesses greatly affect the investment/office subsystem. For example, during the founding stage of a business, its insatiable appetite for cash may preclude any significant savings. Young families often struggle with the choice between funding retirement plans and college savings plans. Older adults try to balance their support needs with their desire to make gifts to members of the younger generation. The cycles of change and equilibrium within this subsystem can be traced over time and mapped to the life cycles of those involved in this system. These tracings reveal not only the family's savings stability, but also its beliefs and values about savings, investments, and spending.

A family with significant assets in this subsystem will be subject to multiple governance structures. When a family uses a vehicle such as a qualified retirement plan, an education savings account, or a marital deduction trust to obtain the desired benefits of these arrangements, state and federal law requires specific governance structures to be adopted and implemented. This structure will identify which assets are available for which benefits, define who has decision-making authority over the assets, and set forth the "rules of the road" for managing the assets. Typically, state or federal law also imposes specific obligations on the vehicle's owners and other participants, who are the "quid pro quo" for the benefit conferred by that vehicle, whether it is limited liability, tax benefits, or something else.

There is often a great deal of crossover between the investment/office subsystem and the other systems. Most commonly, when there is an operating company, the family office is staffed through that company. The office manager or bookkeeper of the operating business wears dual hats, working for the business and handling myriad personal matters for family members. (Whether such a structure is desirable is a separate question.) Similarly, the philanthropic activities of a family may be carried out in part through a family office, even if there is a separate family charitable enterprise.

Mapping the investment/office subsystem is the most familiar process for many advisers. Taking stock of the family's savings in its myriad forms, such as stocks, bonds, real estate, retirement plans, educational savings vehicles, and the like, is a relatively straightforward process for which most advisers already have effective tools. If a family has a family office, however, mapping the roles and relationships of this subsystem becomes more complex. As in the operating business subsystem, organizational charts assist the family and its advisers in pinpointing roles, relationships, and decision-making authority. If the office serves multiple generations and family branches, the family office may also require diagrams showing beneficiaries, trustees, and trust protectors or advisers. This is especially helpful if family members serve in those capacities for multiple trusts. Family offices may have written investment protocols, adviser and asset manager profiles, and criteria for hiring, evaluating, and changing asset managers or advisers. Some families have protocols for identifying the responsibilities of trust beneficiaries, trustees, and others related to a trust. These tools are helpful, both for staff and for family members who must learn to be responsible investors. They also help family members and outside asset managers understand roles, boundaries, and expectations.

The Family Philanthropic Subsystem

—THE MARSHALL FAMILY—
Ruthie Ann Marshall, age fifty-three

That car crash in 2004 just tore my family apart. My nephew, Johnny, was driving his truck and had a head-on collision with another car. There were six people in Johnny's truck and everyone had been drinking. Three of them were riding in the truck bed, which everybody does out there, even though it's just plain stupid. Johnny died, and so did my other nephew, Peter, who's Bobbie Lee's boy. Bobbie's other son, Larry, was thrown from the truck and had really serious injuries—a crushed pelvis, for one. He didn't die, thank God. Johnny's girlfriend broke her neck and was left a paraplegic. Another of the girls was in a coma for six months. Even though the couple in the other car was wearing their seat belts, the steering wheel crushed the husband's chest and he died too. Thank God their little two-year-old daughter was in a car seat. Amazingly, only her arm was broken. But her mother's disabled and she's growing up without a daddy.

Bobbie Lee has been AWOL from the family ever since. Larry spent months on pain pills, and when his doctor wouldn't give him any more, he started buying drugs on the street. He quit college and is in and out of rehab. Florence and Bobbie Lee split up. They're back together, but that's touch and go, she says. I talk to her more than to my own brother. Florence is right when she says anyone could've seen this coming, the way the Marshalls always protected all the kids from consequences. When Johnny was sixteen, he was caught driving drunk more than a couple of times and nothing happened; my father pulled strings with the DA, of course. It happened a few more times, and nobody—not Arnie, not Daddy, not Bobbie Lee—did a thing. "Boys will be boys," was what they all said. Even my mother kept quiet.

My parents have already shelled out, on their own, almost a million dollars to the victims of that crash. That didn't stop the lawsuits, though, and there's no end in sight. My mother and the other church ladies visit with Johnny's former girlfriend all the time. But nobody in our family is talking about the crash or Johnny or Peter or Larry or us as a family. And last week my sister-in-law told me that she and Arnie are probably going to move off the ranch, which will just kill my mother. Right then Pam and I decided: That's enough! We don't care anymore if Daddy accepts Pam and me or not. Pam and I can both take a leave of absence from our jobs, so what we're going to do is move back to the ranch with our little girl and stay right there until my family is a family again. They need to stop viewing our family as the center of the universe and find some way so this never, ever happens to any other family. Pam and I have made a lot of good things happen with young people here in Dallas over the years and we can make it happen out in West Texas, too. One thing everybody knows about us Marshalls is that we are stubborn, and I'm as stubborn as they come.

The Marshall family's focus has always been directed toward building family relationships on which family members can rely. Ruthie's confidence that there is a place at the ranch for her, whether or not her father approves of her sexual orientation, is proof of that. The family's philanthropy appears to be directed toward their church, and individual family members such as Ruth have made inroads on their own. As the fabric of the family starts to unravel, however, Ruth has other plans. Although she would never refer to it as such, she wants to develop a *family philanthropic subsystem* as a means of healing the family.

The family philanthropic subsystem is devoted to directing resources *away* from the family, outside the boundary of the family wealth system, through charity, other kinds of gifts, and even taxes. It may serve secondary goals as well, as a training ground for family members or a way to save income or estate taxes. Many families are surprised to find that their family wealth system includes a philanthropic system, but it is rare for a family of wealth *not* to devote at least some of its resources to philanthropy, and practically all families are concerned with taxes. From dropping a check into the weekly collection plate, to spearheading a major charitable campaign, to establishing a private foundation, family charitable efforts are a major part of funding for charities and will probably continue to be so in the future. Families whose charitable giving is individually directed or ad hoc may not see this as a system, but simply as a part of their family's values.

As more and more charities solicit gifts from family members, and as the size of potential gifts becomes more significant, a family may desire to coordinate its individual, ad hoc efforts and to incorporate other goals (such as reduction of taxes) into a family-wide charitable giving plan. This plan can be as simple as trying to coordinate the amount and timing of various family members' gifts to charity, or as complex as establishing a charitable remainder trust or private foundation. The more formal the gifting structure, the more likely the family will be subject to a governance structure. Charitable trusts, for example, must follow specific guidelines in order to preserve their tax-exempt status and qualify donors for a tax deduction. Private foundations are subject to arcane and complex rules regarding the relationships between family members and foundations.

A map of the family philanthropic subsystem emphasizes the pathways by which various kinds of family wealth are directed from the family wealth system to those outside the boundaries of family wealth. To whom are charitable requests directed? Who makes the decisions about charitable gifts, and how? There may also be protocols for how family members may become involved as donors, board members, or project managers for charitable activities. How are the changing needs and interests of family members taken into account in structuring philanthropic activities? Determining how much to give, and when, will depend on the needs of participants in the other subsystems. There must be an internal process for making these decisions with the assent of other family members. For the most formal philanthropic structures, such as private foundations, the map of the philanthropic system will be similar to the map of an operating business, including organizational charts, roles and responsibilities, and lines of authority.

Implications of Family Wealth Systems for Business Families

—THE HERNÁNDEZ FAMILY—

Bart Hernández Sr., age sixty-two

Elena and I had thirty-eight wonderful years together. Before she got too sick, we were able to do some of the things she'd always wanted to do, and I'd always said I was too busy to do, like ballroom dancing. I had time to say goodbye. Luisa was wild to move back home when her mother got sick again, but I said she shouldn't, because I knew she really needed to stay down in LA. After all, she's only two years into her practice; it's just now starting to take off. She's no quitter. Bart Jr. didn't spend a lot of time with his mother at the end. He wouldn't even talk about her being sick. Now he's just working harder in his business and going to night school. José's the same as ever. I've had to keep after him at the hardware store all the time. I'm working on my real estate and Samantha is helping me do a rent review for all the properties. She told me I should think about doing the opposite of what we did all those years with the hardware store rent. We kept it low to help the business, but she says it's better tax-wise to take money out as rent than as wages to me.

Taking a systems view of a business family changes what the FWTP adviser looks at and looks for. Instead of focusing almost exclusively on financial wealth and its transition, the adviser will look for multiple kinds of capital within the nested subsystems of the family wealth system. The adviser will pay careful attention to the connections among people and assets inside and outside the system, and at how the system's boundary is defined. The adviser will look for emergent patterns, feedback loops, and vulnerabilities to external forces that are likely to affect the viability of transition structures.

In the Hernández family, Elena's death had a huge direct impact. But it also affected the family in subtle ways: Bart Jr. started working even harder, and Luisa wanted to (or felt she should) move back to Fresno despite the demands of her new medical practice. This is evidence of the tendency of the family wealth system to seek a return to a prior state. By telling his daughter clearly that she should "stay put," Bart Sr recognizes that there is no going back, but his new relationship with

Samantha is creating unexpected reverberations in the system. While Bart Sr. seems to welcome Samantha's advice, how open the family wealth system will ultimately be to her influence remains to be seen. Along the way, has anything changed for José? No one knows.

The activities within each subsystem have an enormous impact on the other subsystems. In the family subsystem, sibling rivalry between José and Bart Jr. affects family gatherings; in the business subsystem, that rivalry influences transactions between the construction company and the hardware store and the internal governance of the construction company. The relatively illiquid nature of the businesses ties the sons together even though they cannot seem to work through their differences. The untested and possibly erroneous assumptions about José's needs, abilities, and roles in the family and business subsystems put the hardware store at risk, affect José's relationship with his father and brother, and seriously affect José's self-confidence and well-being. They may also place undue burdens on Luisa if she tries to mediate the family's business and personal relationships from afar. The two sons' inability to communicate directly with one another creates a feedback loop that amplifies their mistrust, increases risk, and reinforces poor decision making in all the family's subsystems.

As later chapters will illustrate, taking a systems view also changes what the adviser seeks to accomplish. The FWTP adviser seeks to create components that fit each particular subsystem and the needs and constraints of the family, in order to satisfy the most important goal: family wealth continuity. The patterns of transition within each subsystem are likely to be different, but they must align so the system will promote the three key elements of family wealth continuity: healthy family relationships, responsible stewardship of wealth, and the ongoing creation of the family legacy.

CHAPTER NOTES

1. This graphic shows not only the subsystems but also how the different sources of capital flow into and out of those subsystems.

2. Also influential were John Levy, Jay Hughes, Joanie Bronfman, and Lee Hausner; John L. Levy, *Inherited Wealth: Opportunities and Dilemmas* (BookSurge Publishing, 2008); James E. Hughes Jr., *Family: The Compact Among Generations* (Bloomberg, 2007); Lee Hausner, *Children of Paradise* (JP Tarcher, 1990); Joanie

Bronfman, PhD, *The Experience of Inherited Wealth: A Social-Psychological Perspective* (Brandeis University, 1987).

3. This is discussed in Chapter 6.

4. See Chapter 6.

5. These are discussed in Chapters 8 and 9.

6. These cycles are discussed in Chapter 5.

7. These forces, particularly taxes, are discussed in Chapter 7.

8. See Chapters 8, 9, and 10 for discussion of the components of FWTP.

9. The original two-circle model for a family business was created by Davis and Tagiuri. It showed two overlapping circles, one representing the family and one representing the business; Davis, J. A., and R. Tagiuri, "Bivalent Attributes of the Family Firm," *Family Business Review*, Vol. 9, No. 2 (June 1996).

10. This pattern of wealth behavior is discussed in Chapter 6.

11. The nexus theory of the firm suggests that shareholders are just one of many participants that provide input for the firm, along with employees, vendors, customers, and others. The firm is a method of amassing these inputs and allocating the fruits of their efforts. A complete discussion of the Cosean impact on corporate law is beyond the scope of this book, but see generally F. Easterbrook and D. R. Fischel, *The Economic Structure of Corporate Law* (Harvard University Press, 1996).

12. See "Family office or family wealth management?," "How the family office can educate the family," and "US and European family offices: sea change" in the January 2003 issue of *Families in Business*.

13. Within the wealth management field, there is a wide range of opinion about whether such organizations are really MFOs or merely an extension of the larger institution's financial management services.

14. In the late 1990s another evolution of the MFO took place. The advent of the virtual family office (VFO) represented the formation of professional teams as the result of strategic alliances among several firms. Attorneys, accountants, investment consultants, insurance professionals, and others formed collegial teams designed to provide the services required to achieve a particular family's goals. The adoption of standardized communication protocols assured accountability and continuity. The adoption of standardized roles, such as relationship manager and engagement manager, avoided many of the problems of ad hoc teams. These VFOs are highly scalable and able to continually refine their scope of services to accommodate the ever changing needs of a family.

See Woodman and Hartley, *Master Plan: Integrating Your Financial Planning, Legal and Estate Planning and Life Planning* (Cambio Press, 2006).

COMPONENTS AND CONNECTIONS

ADVISERS OFTEN MEET families who are astonished by their own financial wealth. From family members' perspective, they started with nothing and ended up with more money than they could ever have imagined. Closer examination reveals that these families rarely began with nothing, even though their balance sheets from twenty years ago were flimsy by any standard. Although they may have lacked financial capital, these families often enjoyed strong ties to others, both within and outside the family. They often insisted that family members get an education, investing in the human capital of the family even when it seemed unaffordable and unattainable. They supported each other in reaching out for experiences that led to financial opportunities. These families may have been bereft of financial capital at one time, but they had deep stores of human and social capital.

Clients often focus on financial capital as an impetus for family wealth transition planning (FWTP), but a wealth transition adviser listening closely to family members will also hear about the less tangible assets that make a family wealthy. These include the resources of *human capital:* the perspectives, values, beliefs, expectations, interests, education, competencies, and experiences that comprise a family's heritage. These intangibles may also include *social capital,* which is the web of rights and responsibilities of having wealth, such as the rewards and duties of being an accountable beneficiary, the obligation to give back to the community, steady employment, and the skills required to manage ongoing relationships with family, friends, strangers, and even the Internal Revenue Service (IRS). Together, the trio of financial, human, and social capital makes up the total of family wealth.

As families evolve, their peculiar blend of capital always changes, both qualitatively and quantitatively. One family may start with only strong family bonds and end up two generations later with significant financial assets, a shared philanthropic mission, and the same strong family bonds. The family next door may start with a strong financial base, but little social capital. They may end up two generations later as paupers, astounded at the dissipation of their financial capital.

The difference between these two families is how their family wealth system adapted, or failed to do so, in ways that promoted family wealth continuity. FWTP is a means of positively adapting the family toward that goal. To adapt the system successfully, however, an adviser must first understand the current makeup of the family. This chapter turns to the process of charting the components and connections of that wealth system so as to prepare the adviser for adapting that system to achieve family wealth continuity. Mapping will not only reveal what kinds of wealth must be transferred, but it will also begin to reveal the areas in which the system as a whole must adapt if the ultimate goal of family wealth continuity is to be achieved.

Mapping the Family Wealth System

Each subsystem of the family wealth system is populated with components: people, financial assets, ideas and beliefs, governance systems, and legal structures. Of these, the most important component is people: the family and non-family members who generate and consume wealth within the family wealth system. Family members are what make the family wealth system unique. Therefore, family members are the best place to start when mapping the system as a whole.

Mapping components of the family wealth system is not the end of the story, however. All the subsystems of the family wealth system, and the components of each of these subsystems, interconnect in explicit and implicit ways. When change occurs in one subsystem, these linkages convey the change to other systems, where the reverberations of the initial change are perceptible. *Explicit* linkages are usually easy for advisers to spot. There may be legal or economic relationships that link components in two or more subsystems, or family members may readily acknowledge an existing link. *Implicit* linkages are more difficult to identify and address in FWTP. These do not arise from legal duties or economic necessity, but instead arise from long-standing patterns of behavior, the exigencies of overlapping life cycles, or external forces at work on the system. The adviser must identify these linkages in order to adapt the system to serve the goals of family wealth continuity more effectively.

One caveat: it is simply impossible to understand fully any system, or to map it completely. Fortunately, one does not need that degree of detail in order to commence the FWTP process. As planning progresses, and as it becomes important to focus on one or more components of the system, more detail will emerge.

The Genogram

A *genogram* is a tool used to understand family relationships within the family wealth system. Just as genealogists create family trees to illustrate the relationships among members of a family, family systems professionals use genograms both to show these relationships and to offer a way of mapping roles, interactions, and patterns of behavior in the family system.[1] Genograms almost always include multiple generations: great-grandparents, grandparents, parents, and children. They also include stepparents, stepchildren, stepsiblings, and their spouses or life partners. Typically, a genogram also shows ex-spouses and deceased family members. Coding on a genogram can track family relationships and highlight behavior patterns that influence decision making and relationship management. For example, a genogram might show a pattern of divorce or alcoholism within multiple generations of a family.

Figure 4.1 illustrates a simple genogram for three generations of the Smith family. This simple genogram shows only basic information about dates of birth and death, marriage and divorce, and sibling birth order and gender.[2]

Incorporating a basic genogram as part of an initial family client assessment helps an adviser understand a family more effectively. It identifies family events and development, as well as patterns of behavior that pass from generation to generation. In its more detailed format, it provides the adviser and the client family with insights into patterns of behavior that span generations, such as entrepreneurial or philanthropic mindsets, patterns of marriage and divorce, substance abuse, or

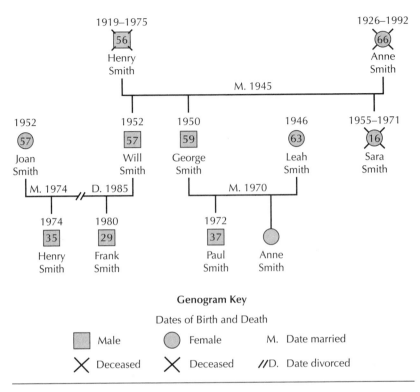

FIGURE 4.1   Sample Genogram

dysfunctional behavior. It can incorporate patterns of cutoff and triangulation in family relationships. The adviser may also draw genograms to differentiate between owners and nonowners of a family business.

The Three Forms of Capital

Once the adviser maps the core family relationships in a family system, the next step is determining which kinds of wealth the family enjoys. Family members generate and consume wealth within the family wealth system and export wealth out of the system. This wealth, which may include investments, savings vehicles, family homes, vacation properties, and interests in closely held businesses, is generally referred to as *financial capital*.

Two other kinds of wealth within the family wealth system are at least as important to the health of the family wealth system as financial capital. The development of individuals within the system generates human capital, and the connections among these individuals with each other and with others outside the system generate social capital. A blend of these three kinds of capital constitutes the family wealth system.

While one kind of capital might be more important in a particular subsystem than another (financial capital may be relatively less important than human capital in the family subsystem, for example), the adviser should be careful to look for wealth of each kind within each subsystem. *Figure 4.2* provides a summary of the important forms of capital within each subsystem, although myriad other kinds will figure prominently in many families.

FIGURE **4.2**   Important Forms of Capital Within Each Subsystem of the Family Wealth System

	Family Subsystem	Business Subsystem	Investment/ Office Subsystem	Philanthropic Subsystem
Important Forms of Human Capital	*Relational competencies:* • Emotional intelligence • Conflict management • Ideas about importance of family	*Business competencies:* • Management skills • Understanding of oversight roles • Ideas about entrepreneurship	*Investment competencies:* • Evaluating and monitoring investments • Understanding taxes • Ideas about saving versus spending	*Charitable competencies:* • Generosity • Knowing how much is enough • Ideas about giving back to community and sharing wealth
Important Forms of Social Capital	• Connections among family members • Openness to new members • Ideas about participation in family	• Good relations with those outside family wealth system • Ideas about collaboration	• Understanding how to choose and work with advisers • Ideas about needs and wants	• Close connections with those outside family wealth system • Ideas about sharing wealth
Important Forms of Financial Capital	• Family home • Vacation property • Health Insurance • Emergency savings	• Equity interests in entities • Real estate • Employment relationships	• Savings: education, retirement, "rainy day" • Insurance	• Gifts of financial assets • Split-interest trusts • Charities and private foundations

Human Capital

—THE WILLIAMS FAMILY—

Sara Williams Cantrell, age forty-eight

My mom always said, "No matter what, your education will always be yours. No one can take it from you." Sure, I was a little wild in high school (probably reacting to John's big-man-on-campus routine), but it never occurred to John or me to even get a bad grade, much less drop out of high school or not go to college. So we both ended up getting our MBAs. John owns his own business and I am a marketing consultant. We've always known Mom and Dad are proud of us. Last Christmas Mom told me they had set up an educational trust for each grandchild. While Phil and I have been able to save some for college, I greatly appreciate their help. By the time our kids go to college, it will probably cost $200,000 a year!

I love Helen like a sister. She is a total sweetie, and you'd never know her dad was super-rich. She had to pull herself out of a deep depression after Lisa was born, and she did. Yeah, they had a nanny and all, but Helen does everything for Lisa. Helen's daughter, Rebecca, is a marvel, a music prodigy like her mom. I admire Helen's decision to give up her career to devote all her time to her family. I know it was hard for her. Me, I could never do it. I'd go crazy.

I used to see John, Helen, and the kids all the time when I was in New York on business. Now, not so much. A couple of months ago John told me something awful: a few years ago, he had a brief affair with one of his managers, and she got pregnant and had a child. He's seven years old now and his name is Brad. Of course, John's never told anyone about this, but as Brad gets older John's realizing he needs to be part of his life in some way. And the woman still works for him, imagine! Now that I know John's big secret, I just can't sit in their living room and act like everything is normal. So I tell Helen, "Sorry, I'm just too busy." My husband says I'm a bad liar, and Helen is going to be really, really angry with me when she finds out that I knew and didn't tell her. I keep worrying about how Mom will react to all of this. She relies so much on John now that Dad is gone.

People are the critical element of the family wealth system, and those people and their competencies make up the family's storehouse of human capital. When a family acquires a new member, whether by birth, marriage, or partnership, its human capital account usually increases, unless the new member introduces serious problems. When a family loses a member, whether through death, divorce, or schism, its human capital account decreases. This is not only because family members are valued for who they are, but because each member brings one or more competencies or skills to the family wealth system. A major challenge of retaining human capital is preserving and utilizing the best competencies of each member, and developing competencies to replace those that disappear with departing members.

The map of human capital in every family will be different, reflecting both the history and the values of the family. Sara Williams Cantrell makes it clear that her family values education: Sara and her brother John were destined for college, and probably graduate school, from an early age. Their parents continued this commitment to developing the family's human capital by creating educational trusts for their grandchildren. The Weinsteins, the family John married into, similarly nurtured their only daughter's dreams of a career as a cellist.

Human capital doesn't just reside in advanced degrees. Helen Williams's choice to give up teaching to devote time to her family represents an investment in human capital for the family as a whole. It represents a decision that at that particular time, the family needed a full-time mother more than a cellist or a wage earner. When Helen got help for her depression, the therapy, too, was an investment.

Helen Williams isn't the only one making an investment in her family. John's care of his mother after his father's death is certainly an addition to the family's human capital account. His newfound attention to his health after the bypass surgery scare represents an investment, particularly if he finds ways to enjoy yoga, meditation, or playing music with Helen. But John's decision to stray from the marriage, and to keep his big secret, represents a huge withdrawal from the family's human capital account. His mistakes are causing a loss of trust within the family and making him unable to nurture any of his children properly. The secret is beginning to sever family relationships, too. Even if Helen doesn't discover John's secret, as he dwells on self-recrimination and worries about discovery, he is distracted from the task at hand: developing his family's human capital. When Helen discovers John's misdeeds, the bonds of trust within the family may be broken forever.

A family as a whole is likely to have a broader range of competencies than any one of its members, who potentially provide resources to family members and others within the family system. Families can develop competencies that complement one another to maximize family efficacy, if they explicitly set out to do so. A relatively small family like the Williams family will likely have to reach outside the family to increase the members' storehouse of skills and experiences.

Human capital is not usually represented as an asset because it cannot be transferred readily in the marketplace. Therefore, the focus in wealth transition planning is not usually on the owner of the wealth, but instead on the person whose experience or education gives rise to the wealth. In divorce situations, professional degrees inhabit that in-between land of quasi property, and in family businesses, where salary may substitute for dividends, a similar situation can arise. In family businesses, the flow of cash to a particular person will not necessarily reflect the human capital of that person. Rather, it may be a form of support, a tax strategy, or both.

In some families, human capital within the family may be under-developed or overly focused on a few key family members who hold positions of leadership. There is, of course, no formulaic mix of human capital. The need for different kinds of human capital can change dramatically from generation to generation and in response to changes in both the external environment and the family wealth system. For example, a grandfather may have relied on practical experience to build financial wealth in the form of a family business. His daughter may obtain a professional degree to continue that business, but her son may reject formal training. This attitude is likely to alienate his mother, but is one that his grandfather may more readily understand.

Mapping Human Capital

Mapping a family's storehouse of human capital is not as easy as putting together a balance sheet or inspecting an income statement. During transition planning, there are a number of competencies that are particularly relevant to the planning process. These competencies center on the skills, talents, and experiences likely to support a family in its search for wealth continuity. Of course, every family will have some unusual talents to take into account. For example, Sara Williams Cantrell's wide-ranging travels may give her an edge in adapting to new environments. Perhaps Rebecca needs to learn some skills from her Aunt Sara before she leaves for college. Similarly, some competencies are peculiar to families in business together, or families with a family foundation; other families will not need them. All tools and processes for mapping human capital must be tailored to the specific situation of each family.

Human capital is a critical component of wealth in every subsystem of the family wealth system. In the family subsystem, relational competencies will be most important. Family members with high emotional intelligence, good conflict management tools, and ideas and beliefs about the need for participation in family bring important competencies to the table. While these relational skills are important in any endeavor, in business a different set of competencies is required, such as the ability to understand and implement management tools and oversight functions.[3] In the investment/office subsystem, human capital is expressed through knowing how to evaluate and monitor investments, having and teaching the ability to defer consumption (save), and understanding how the family approaches taxes. In the philanthropic subsystem, a mindset of generosity, knowing "how much is enough," and an interest in finding creative ways to direct family resources to others are critical competencies.

Competencies can also be mapped to the three kinds of capital. An added benefit of focusing on capacities early in the process is that it is generally a positive experience for families to see how rich in human capital they really are. While they are tempted to focus on the "holes" they see and create a plan for filling them, that is premature. A plan for developing capacities within the family will come in due course. For now, the focus is on taking an inventory of values, experiences, skills, and talents to generate a deeper understanding of the family and its members.

Social Capital

—THE MARSHALL FAMILY—
Billy Rob Marshall, age sixteen

If you could see it, you'd think the Marshall ranch was kind of a crazy place. There's the old house, where everybody used to live all together. Now only Grandma and Granddaddy live there. My parents and all my aunts and uncles have built houses on the ranch, really nice houses. There's even a little airstrip and hangar, where my Grandma used to fly her plane. Grandma says that once you have the Marshall name, there's always a place here at the ranch for you, whether you're a person, a pig, or a petunia. And she's right. My great-grandparents took in my great-aunts when their husbands died, and all the children too and everybody still hangs around, more or less.

I worry all the time that Dad and Granddaddy are finally going to have the biggest fight we've ever seen around here. All the time I was growing up all they ever did was act like best friends. But ever since my brother, Johnny, died they keep going after each other for no reason. Dad's saying he's going to move us down to Galveston and never look back. Mom tells him, "Settle down, honey, you know Johnny Ray will get over it," but she's mad all the time. Me, I swear, I'll run away if they try to make me go to Galveston. Grandma would take me in. She'd have to after everything she's said about petunias.

Social capital is the connection among individuals within a community and the connection of an individual to his or her community.[4] In families, a critical component of social capital is the resources the family develops through activities that support and give back to the community, including involvement with religious, philanthropic, and political groups. Although charitable activity often directs financial capital away from members of the family group, this activity builds social capital by strengthening the relationships and shared values of the family. Some families of wealth cultivate social capital from a very young age by encouraging young children to save part of their allowance to give to charities or community-based projects or by encouraging all family members to contribute time and money to others in need. Others create family foundations or actively serve on not-for-profit boards. The ways in which a family creates and distributes social capital relate directly to the family's values, experience, and desire to be of service to others.

Compared to inheritors who have already lived with inherited wealth opportunities and threats, first-generation entrepreneurs may be more concerned with generating wealth than with the impact of that wealth on their children. There are notable exceptions, including John D. Rockefeller. In his autobiography, David Rockefeller describes the source and object of his grandfather's commitment to philanthropy as a combination of the entrepreneurial freedom to create wealth through achievement and the obligation to give back to the community that had nurtured him.[5] He was aware of an obligation to teach his children that same value of giving back.

Younger wealth generators and executives may be more inclined toward "venture philanthropy" as a way of maximizing the value of gifts and improving the performance of grant recipients. They may set specific outcome requirements for the projects they fund, create matching gifts, or find ways to be directly involved in the recipient organization.

The Marshall family demonstrates that social capital isn't just about philanthropy. It is the sum of a family's relationships: the complex web in which the family interacts internally, and with others, in the personal, business, and community spheres. Whereas human capital arises from the personal and collective cache of competencies within a family, social capital is created when those people, with their competencies, interact with others to build value. Social capital can be expressed in any number of ways, from smoothing ruffled feathers at a family meeting to effectively supervising money managers, from running a business to rallying donors for a fund-raising campaign for a local charity. The relationships that make up social capital can be formal or informal, short or long term, officially sanctioned or off the record.

The Marshall family focuses its social capital inwardly. The family is religious, but so far it doesn't seem involved in philanthropy. Yet there are strong family bonds of responsibility reaching back at least to Billy Rob's great-grandparents. That Billy Rob knows the story of his great-aunts—a story that played out long before he was born—shows that the Marshall family is intensely interested in creating a family culture of care and support. In the Marshall family, you can *always* go home again.

Social capital can be destroyed when relationships fail, even if personal or collective competencies remain. That's what appears to be happening in the Marshall family. The effects of the terrible car crash that killed Billy Rob's older brother and cousin, and left another cousin severely injured, have torn the family apart. Robert Marshall's story suggests that Johnny Ray blames his son, Arnie, for bad parenting. Yet it appears, at least to Billy Rob, that there is no purpose in their fighting, which means that nothing is being resolved. Arnie is threatening to leave the ranch and the family business. That would be the second son to jump ship, because Robert and his family haven't been around much.

They have their reasons: Robert and Florence have been separated, and they have been struggling with their son's addiction. And Robert's return may be rocky, if his brother Eddie's attitude is any indication. As for Billy Rob himself, there is both good news and bad. He appears to feel intimately connected to the family, particularly his grandmother. Yet what he *doesn't* say is troubling. For a sixteen-year-old not to mention once his friends or activities outside the home is anomalous. Billy Rob may be experiencing isolation as yet another result of the crash, or may even be another Uncle Eddie in the making. While further inquiry may ruffle family feathers, it may help the family make progress. It is unlikely that a transition plan can proceed without the family coming to grips with the crash and its effects, and recognizing its impact on Billy Rob may be the lever that the family needs to break through their pain.

The Marshalls' strong family ties illustrate the value of social capital in the family subsystem. In the operating business subsystem, good relations with outsiders, including employees, vendors, customers, and even rivals, form a web of support for the business. In the investment/office subsystem, having a team of advisers in place is important, but perhaps not as important as knowing how to choose and work with old and new advisers.

Mapping Social Capital

Mapping social capital is even more challenging than mapping human capital. By its nature, social capital is built through relationships within and outside the family, and mapping requires taking stock of these relationships. But this potentially leads the family into an emotional quagmire: the quality of those relationships. *Who's the better aunt: Kat or Anne? Who likes our financial adviser? John says he's a snake and Sabrina says he's a teddy bear.* It is better, at least at the outset, to identify existing relationships in terms of competencies, i.e., those skills, experiences, and talents that allow a family to build a good storehouse of social capital. *Figure 4.3* (p. 92) provides a sample tool that advisers can use to take stock of those competencies.

Exploring how the relationships among family members and the relationships of family members to others sustain and bring value to the family usually helps a family begin to understand its storehouse of social capital. They begin to see how stewardship of financial and human capital will depend in large part on a successful transition of the social capital: the web of relationships that support these other kinds of capital.

Financial Capital

—The Hernández Family—
Clara Hernández Paz, age fifty-one

Things turned out fine for me, but only after I made a lot of mistakes. It would have been easier if I had just listened to Mamá and Papá, but I guess I had to learn the hard way. I got pregnant at sixteen and ran away with my boyfriend rather than telling my parents. He went to prison, and I was on my own with a little baby. Those were hard years and I did some things I'm not proud of. Finally I couldn't handle it any more and I begged Papá to let me come home. I learned years later that my father and my brother, Bart, had a terrible fight over this, the only one they ever had. Papá gave in and I was able to come home.

Papá never let me forget what I'd done and watched me like a hawk. Mamá said her usual *a lo hecho, pecho*—look forward, not back—and that it was my job to make something of myself and provide for Patricio. I studied at night to get my GED. Mamá let me work in her sewing business. Mamá had worked as a seamstress while I was growing up. The most fashionable ladies in Fresno always wanted her to sew their clothing. I started out sweeping, graduated to cutting, and was finally allowed to sew alongside Mamá. That's when I discovered I could design clothes. Lots of people wanted the clothes that I designed and Mamá sewed. Bart said we could turn this into a valuable business if we did things right.

We had to get a lot of money together to build inventory. Bart loaned us some, and Mamá and Papá took out a second mortgage on their house, which made Papá really nervous. We got an SBA loan for $25,000. I earned my degree in fashion design and designed a line of infant and toddler clothes—I had lots of cute *sobrinitas* as models! There were some scary times, because fashion is a fickle industry and you can end up with a warehouse full of clothes nobody wants. We knew the big retailers were *sinverguenas*, so we sold to lesser-known stores who loved our clothing and stayed loyal to us through the years. We were blessed. Elena helped us with the books. From a start in my mother's garage, we ended up with a company with millions of dollars in sales. We sold it a couple of years ago for more money than any of us had ever dreamed of. I stayed on for about six months to help with the transition, but now I'm done with that. With my share, I tried to pay off my eldest son's student loans, but he laughed and turned me down flat. So, even after taxes, I have a good little nest egg.

I don't think we could have built the clothing business without Bart's help, and I don't mean just from the loan. He has an MBA, and he always says that there is no problem that doesn't have a solution. He married his high school sweetheart and started a family young. He owns the hardware store he worked at part-time in high school and full-time after college. That wasn't as easy as it sounds. As I understand it, he got crosswise with the son of the former owners. He left and went to work in sales for a national hardware chain. He could have gone far in that company, but he wanted to stay in Fresno because the entire family is here. Luckily, when the former owners figured out that their own son couldn't run the place, they sold it to Bart. There was lots of back-and-forth about price and terms, and he had to put on the table everything he and Elena owned to buy it, including their retirement savings. He got an SBA loan and repaid it early, just like us. They've had some nibbles from people wanting to buy the store over the years, but Bart has refused to consider selling. Now my nephew José works full-time in the hardware store, which is a little surprising because José is one wild kid, at least according to my Ramón. Bart and my nephews also buy houses and fix them up to sell.

Mamá died in 2003. I never really felt Papá forgave me. He always loved Patricio, though, and even accepted my son's father—Miguel—into the family when we made a new start of it. Papá died right after we had Ramón. I guess that's all you could ask for. Elena died of cancer in 2004 and we all just went to pieces. Now it's just me and my sisters to carry on the family traditions. We don't think of ourselves as old, or at least we didn't until Bart brought around his new girlfriend, Samantha, who is only thirty-eight years old! I tease him, but he knows I really do like her, and if anyone deserves to have love in his life, it's Bart.

Financial capital includes the assets traditionally associated with family wealth transition planning: cash, real estate, portfolios of stocks and bonds, collectibles such as coins or art, and other investments that provide a family with a financial return. It also includes individual participation in a family business in any role that generates a financial return, whether as an owner, an employee, a creditor, or a lessor.

A family's financial wealth changes as a family moves through generations. A first-generation entrepreneurial family may put all of its disposable income back into its business and only diversify its holdings after that business matures. A second- or third-generation family may live partly on earned income and partly on distributions from the family business, which is run by others. Some families are asset rich and cash poor because they have invested in illiquid assets like land. Some third- or fourth-generation family members may have grown up in relative affluence but find that the growth of the family in size or its rate of spending has outstripped the growth of its financial assets, so they will have fewer financial assets than their parents did. In some families with multigenerational trusts, younger family members may grow up without any ability to influence investment policies or the distribution of the trust's resources. All these variables influence how family members view their wealth transition options.

The Hernández family built its financial capital over several decades. Clara says she and her mother were "lucky" in the clothing business, but their success was likely not a result of luck, but rather born of hard work and willingness to take big risks. The industry they chose was intensely competitive and subject to unforeseeable changes in consumer tastes. Furthermore, the business's ability to increase the prices charged for goods would likely have been limited, while their cost of production could have increased at any time. This could have potentially reduced profit margins to unacceptable levels. Fortunately for everyone involved, the business's expansion permitted the timely repayment of funds advanced by María and Rafael as well as the SBA loan. Failure could have resulted in María and Rafael losing their home and having no retirement savings. Given Bart's loyalty to his family, one wonders if he would have allowed that to happen.

When Clara looks at Bart's situation, she attributes his success to his hard work and business sense. His starting a family at a relatively young age created a tremendous incentive to produce enough steady income to support a wife and eventually children. Bart's full-time job in the hardware store was attributable to more than just being in the right place at the right time. Staying in the industry he knew well allowed Bart to build on his prior experience and to begin to save. His new position gave him added security in terms of an advantageous retirement program and health insurance benefits that were important to his growing family.

Bart and Elena's decision to purchase the hardware business further illustrated this family's high tolerance for risk. Bart liquidated a diversified equity investment account and invested the proceeds into a single, leveraged investment: the new business. He accepted significant new liabilities along with the new assets and left the secure income from a good-paying job with benefits for the insecure income of an entrepreneur, with fewer benefits. Clara says Bart put everything on the line, including his retirement fund, to make the deal happen. For example, if his 401(k) account had been earning an average of 8 percent per year, and he was in the 25 percent federal marginal income tax bracket, the equivalent rate of return in a taxable account would exceed 10 percent per year. He would have to expect to earn more than this on the capital in his new venture to begin to justify such a strategy. Certainly, Bart had the skills to undertake this analysis, as he had earned his MBA. For entrepreneurs, however, financial analysis takes a back seat to the noneconomic rewards that come from building a business.

The Hernández family's financial wealth seems to be developing an investment side in addition to the operating businesses. Clara now has her nest egg, and her son appears to have inherited the family penchant for independence. Bart and his sons' real estate empire is growing. In the meantime, it is clear from Bart Sr.'s stories in Chapters 1 and 2 that trouble has been brewing for some time between the two sons and between them and their father. Is it a human capital problem of José's not having the necessary skill set to participate in the hardware or construction business? Or is it a social capital problem arising from the deaths of María and Elena so close together, plus the boys' strained relationship, plus the introduction of the new girlfriend into the picture, all of which are putting a huge strain on family relationships? Or is it a financial capital problem, because the hardware store is not contributing to the bottom line? The family's situation makes it clear that the three kinds of capital are so closely intertwined that almost any family wealth problem must be viewed from the perspective of each kind of capital if one is to grasp the whole picture.

Financial capital doesn't just reside in the operating business in the form of equity interests, employment arrangements, or real estate. It figures prominently in the investment/office subsystem in the form of savings for education and retirement. In the family subsystem the family home, vacation property, and health insurance figure prominently, as do emergency "stashes" to help family members through rough patches. In the philanthropic subsystem, split-interest trusts provide charitable gifts as well as income for family members.

Tracing Complex Connections in the Family Wealth System

—THE HERNÁNDEZ FAMILY—

Bart Hernández Jr., age forty

When I say we do this or we do that in my construction business, who I mean is Chuy and me and sometimes Papá. Chuy's my main project manager and we think the same way on everything. I sure don't mean my little brother. José is part owner—well, half owner—of the business. Papá made me set it up that way years ago when we started out. José was young and wild. Papá thought the business would settle him down, teach him the value of real work. Didn't happen. Won't happen. José and I can get into it over anything, really fast. At first, José helped with the remodeling part of the business—he does have a good sense of what people want—but now he doesn't do a thing. I used to give him 50 percent of the profits, but not any more. After all, I do all the work and also I have a family to support— a wife and a little girl—and he doesn't. José still lives at home with Papá, even though he's twenty-seven years old. I need to reinvest more in the business, anyhow. José was getting me good prices on materials, but lately he seems to be screwing around with the pricing all the time. Papá should know what's really going on.

Even this brief piece of the story from Bart Jr. reveals the tangled connections among the components of the Hernández family wealth system. In this family, as in many others, people and sources of wealth interact in complicated ways, so even a provisional "sorting through" of these relationships seems daunting. Yet understanding the complex connections among components of the family wealth system is critical to creating a transition plan, particularly when a family business is at stake. There are three reasons for this.

First, understanding the components and how they connect helps the FWTP team create appropriate wealth transition structures for financial, human, and social capital. To take a simple example, circumstances surrounding the Hernández hardware store require a deep understanding of how the store is tied to the construction business and the development of José's human capital.

Second, understanding the roles that each person plays within the family wealth system is critical to creating a role clarity and development plan. In the Hernández family system, Bart plays an important role within each subsystem. He and the rest of the family may not understand his central role or how it creates feedback loops within the system. Almost any change in the financial or social capital within the family will implicate him in some way. For example, if Bart Jr. or José want to make a change in the way they share wealth, Bart Sr. will be a critical element of that change, because he plays the roles of lender to the construction business, father, and owner of the hardware store. If Bart Sr.'s roles are to change, the family needs a plan for clarifying these roles and developing new ones.

Third, if wealth is to be shared in succeeding generations, a governance system must be devised to ensure that the right people participate in the right way in decisions about that wealth. This requires an understanding of who has a stake in the outcome of decisions. For example, if Bart Jr. and José are to continue to share wealth in the form of the construction business, some method must be devised to help them share responsibility for this wealth. This begs an important question, however: who has a legitimate stake in the outcome of this venture? Are these two siblings the right people, or the only people, who have a legitimate claim to the outcome of this venture? Answering these questions requires an understanding of how people and assets are connected within the family wealth system.

A number of methodologies can assist the adviser to understand complex familial connections. Perhaps the simplest is to chart the active subsystems of a family wealth system by people and sources of wealth and have the family identify the connections. Beginning with the family system, a genogram will identify family members and their relationships. Tracing connections within a subsystem before looking at connections among subsystems is useful. For example, all is not well within the core family system. José and Bart Jr. "can get into it over anything" and

Bart Jr. is keeping at least one secret from his father. Has Bart Sr. fully grieved over Elena's death? For that matter, has anyone else in the family grieved? How is this affecting the family's ability to function? Despite this loss, the family system appears rich in social capital with close and supportive family relationships and seems to have successfully transmitted the value of hard work to most family members.

The Hernández operating business subsystem is populated by a number of businesses—real estate, hardware, construction, a medical practice—all of which potentially form a large base of financial capital. The members of the family also bring a large storehouse of human capital to the family wealth system. Within the Hernández family, there is significant overlap between the family and business subsystems. Family members work in the businesses, own businesses together, and structure their business lives to encompass the transmission of family values.

At this point, we know little about the Hernández investment subsystem, or about how the family manages its finances. We know even less about its philanthropic subsystem. What is clear, however, is that Bart Sr. has intricate connections to every subsystem within the Hernández family wealth system: he is father to three children, an owner of the hardware store, lender to Luisa's practice and the construction business, partner in land development with Bart Jr. and José, real estate mogul, and potential new partner with Samantha. His financial assets, too, play multiple roles, including supporting himself and his family members and their various business activities.

Stakeholder Analysis

Of particular use in mapping the complex connections within the family wealth system is *stakeholder analysis*. This is because people are the most important component of the family wealth system. They include those family (and nonfamily) members who play roles and have complex relationships within some or all of the subsystems of the family wealth system. Each person within the family wealth system is a potential stakeholder, i.e., a person who has a stake in the activities of the family and its wealth.[6]

A number of stakeholders with common roles or interests within the system constitute a *stakeholder group*. Family members make up one stakeholder group. Other stakeholder groups might be owners of the family business, trust beneficiaries, employees, or family members with an overriding interest in charitable activities. The perspective of each stakeholder group arises out of its particular needs, experiences, and assumptions, which are rarely (if ever) fully articulated or discussed within that group or between groups. The membership of a stakeholder group will change as the individuals, family, and businesses move through their life cycles and as the structure of family wealth changes.

A peculiar mix of legal rights and family culture determines whether a person is a member of a particular stakeholder group. Legal rights create potential stakeholders. A spouse's right to take action against a will and a shareholder's right to inspect books and records make them stakeholders in an estate plan or the operation of a company. But family culture is more important than legal status in establishing membership. Not every shareholder, for example, is a real stakeholder in a company. In some families, particularly when gifts of ownership interests have been made for tax planning purposes, it is clear that some shareholders hold only nominal positions. Nevertheless, the existence of legal rights means that at some point in the future, when family culture changes, these rights could be enforced. Family wealth transition planning advisers are usually sensitive to this issue, but they are more likely to trip up when family culture creates stakeholders who have no enforceable legal rights. A husband, for example, may own 100 percent of the stock of an operating company, but his wife may, by family culture, be an equal stakeholder with her husband. A new daughter-in-law may, by family culture, be entitled to the "right" to a job in the family business because her husband already works there. An in-law who has received shares in the family business as part of a performance bonus system may have to sell those shares as part of a divorce settlement, depending on the structure of the company's buy/sell agreement. How people become real stakeholders will vary from family to family, and will also vary within a family over time.

In each family subsystem, multiple stakeholder groups operate according to implicit roles, and in each subsystem, most individuals participate in more than one stakeholder group at the same time. In a multigenerational business family, an individual may simultaneously have roles as an adult child, a grandchild, a spouse, a parent, a sibling, and an in-law. These various roles are generally accepted as the fabric of family, rather than consciously delineated or separated. The blurring of stakeholder roles is a major source of potential conflict within families of wealth. The principles and processes that govern one group may not be suitable for another. This can occur within a subsystem or between subsystems. A family may subscribe to a principle of unconditional love and acceptance for family stakeholders, but how well does this translate to acceptance of new in-laws? Are they treated as family members? As between systems, does entitlement to unconditional acceptance mean that those who are family stakeholders are also unconditionally entitled to a place in the family business? Because roles, rights, and responsibilities are not likely to be well articulated within the family wealth system, conflict between stakeholder groups and within groups can easily occur. Methods for dealing with conflict are discussed in detail in Chapter 9. But to address stakeholder conflicts properly, the adviser must first map stakeholder groups to understand which stakeholder groups exist and how they interconnect.

The number of stakeholder groups in any family varies with time, the number of family members, the degree of wealth, the number of operating business entities and philanthropic organizations, and the complexity of the family investment management system. For many families engaged in FWTP, the only relevant stakeholder groups will be those that include family members. Other families rely heavily on nonfamily members to serve on boards, carry out investment functions, and serve other roles. For these families, the stakeholder groups will be more complex. *Figure 4.3* is a map of a family wealth system that shows fourteen possible groups with fully developed subsystems.

❏ **Stakeholder Group One:** The members of Group One are actively involved in all four of the family's subsystems: they are members of the family, managers or owners of one or more operating companies, asset managers, family office executives or investors in family funds, and members of the foundation board or the family's more informal philanthropic efforts. In many families, only one or two people are in this spot: a founder and his or her spouse, or a founder and one or more adult children. This can be an enormously stressful position, but it is also the place of greatest influence and control. This is also the place where clear boundaries between subsystems and roles are required. A founder who is also the supervisor of his or her adult children who work in the company may find it challenging to evaluate their performance. The adult children who are managers may find it daunting to give criticism or oppose parents, siblings. or cousins who

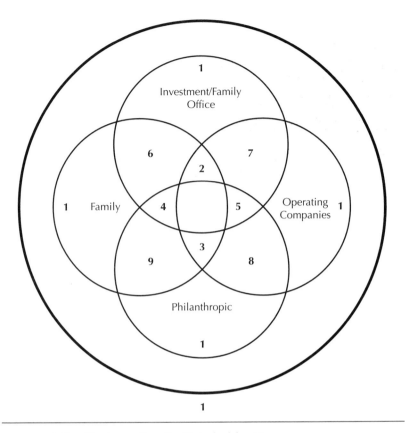

FIGURE 4.3   Business Family Stakeholder Groups
Source: © 2004 Transition Dynamics Inc.

are theoretically their peers as owners or managers. However, this is also the spot where people potentially have the deepest understanding of the needs, strengths, and weaknesses of each of subsystem. This is frequently where the adviser's client is before FWTP. After succession or the sale or gift of shares of the operating company, that individual will move to another stakeholder group.

❏ **Stakeholder Group Two:** Members of Group Two are in the family and are involved in the investment group either as investors, recipients of family office services, or executives in the family office. They may be principals in a family operating company, either as members of the board, shareholders, or executives.

❏ **Stakeholder Group Three:** Group Three includes only family members. They either sit on the board of a family foundation or are actively involved in the family's philanthropic efforts. They also have some involvement with the operating company, either as employees or owners. They are not involved in the investment/family office aspect of the family.

❑ **Stakeholder Group Four:** People in Group Four have a stake in the family, the family investments/office, and the family philanthropic activities. They are not involved in any operating companies. In some cases, they are members of a family that has sold the operating company and focuses its business activities through an investment group or family office.

❑ **Stakeholder Group Five:** In Group Five, there are no family members. It includes nonfamily board members, executives, account managers, or program directors who are actively involved in the family office or investment group, the operating companies, and the family foundation.

❑ **Stakeholder Group Six:** Family members who benefit from family investments, receive services from the family office, or work there fall into Group Six. They are not owners or employees of any family operating companies and do not have any direct involvement in the family's philanthropic endeavors.

❑ **Stakeholder Group Seven:** Members of Group Seven have no active involvement with philanthropy and are not family members. They are employees, directors, or advisers to the family office and one or more of the family operating companies.

❑ **Stakeholder Group Eight:** Group Eight comprises people who are actively engaged in both the operating companies and the philanthropic efforts of the family. They are not family members. They may be people who have responsibility for corporate giving programs or they may be executives or board members of both groups (a family operating company and the family foundation). They may be employees who volunteer for programs underwritten by a family foundation.

❑ **Stakeholder Group Nine:** Group Nine includes members of the family who are actively involved in its philanthropic efforts. It could include children who participate in philanthropic activities or shadow the board as part of their learning process. They are not owners or managers of the family's operating companies and don't actively participate in the investment activities or family office.

❑ **Stakeholder Group Ten:** Group Ten comprises family members who are not actively involved in the family's operating companies, investment or family office activities, or philanthropic endeavors. It may include children and extended family members. In some cases, it may tangentially include family support staff such as nannies, housekeepers, drivers, advisers, or even family therapists who provide services to the family, but don't work in the operating companies, investment or family offices.

❏ **Stakeholder Group Eleven:** Group Eleven comprises nonfamily executives, staff, financial analysts, investment account managers, and tax and legal advisers who work with the family under the umbrella of its family office or its investment group.

❏ **Stakeholder Group Twelve:** Employees, managers, board members, vendors, customers, clients, and corporate tax and legal advisers belong in this group. They are not family members and have no direct involvement with the other realms of the family. However, what happens in the family affects them either directly and indirectly.

❏ **Stakeholder Group Thirteen:** In Group Thirteen are nonfamily staff, board members, program volunteers, and beneficiaries of the family's philanthropic activities, whether those activities occur through a family foundation or other philanthropic vehicles.

❏ **Stakeholder Group Fourteen:** Group Fourteen consists of people and entities, including the community at large, that are "outside" the family wealth system but have some connection with it. These might include vendors, customers, the IRS or other regulatory agencies, or related family wealth systems.

Implications of Components and Connections for Business Families

—THE MARSHALL FAMILY—

Betty Ann Marshall (Mrs. Arnold Marshall), age forty-six

My husband works really hard, and usually he doesn't think much about the future. He was pretty wild before he moved back to the ranch when Johnny Ray had that heart attack. I guess a lot of veterans came back from Vietnam with habits; well, at least his was mostly alcohol. Anyway, he got on the wagon, and we met and married. Before the wreck, he used to be happy if he could just hunt, fish, coach our sons' teams, and have his nights out with the boys. Now, with only our Billy Rob left, everything is different. Billy Rob doesn't play sports anymore, he doesn't even want to get his driver's license, and he and Arnie don't talk much. Arnie told me last week that he is going to move us off this ranch and down to Galveston. He says he and his dad just can't make things work anymore. I didn't say much then, but I've been thinking on this really hard. Arnie and I almost always see eye to eye on things, but not on this. Last night I put on what Arnie calls my determined look and asked him about all those years he's put in, is that all down the drain? "What about all those promises your dad made?" I asked him. "You're supposed to get a big chunk of the business. You're the only one who knows how to run it, and your brothers and sister have just stood around for years and watched while you've worked your fanny off. All of us have about lost our minds the past three years. I am not letting Billy Rob lose the only home he knows. And we are not running off like a pack of scalded dogs," I told him. "You get yourself right over there and work whatever this is out with your father, Mr. Marshall!" He knows when I call him Mr. Marshall that I am really serious.

Understanding the components of the family wealth system— financial, human, and social capital—is fundamental to understanding what kinds of wealth the transition plan must take into account. Cataloging components is not enough. Understanding the connections between the components is critical, particularly for the business family. The connections between people and wealth within the FWTS are complex and nonlinear, and the system as a whole is peppered with feedback loops. Creating a plan for just one component, such as a type of financial wealth, is likely to create unexpected reverberations throughout the system and lead to a less than optimal plan.

The Marshalls, like any business family, will face particular challenges in mapping the components and connections of their family wealth system. Their wealth, like that of most business families, is focused in the business operating subsystem, and this wealth is probably illiquid, which binds the family together for better or worse. Moreover, in the Marshall family, there is usually a great deal of overlap between this subsystem and the others. The same people and components play important roles within multiple subsystems and the functions of each subsystem are blurred, with family, business, investment, and philanthropic goals often overlapping as well. This overlap magnifies the impact of change throughout the system, making it particularly vulnerable. Minor changes in the business can have enormous impacts elsewhere, and vice versa. In the Marshall situation, for example, it is unlikely that this family is fully aware of the multiple ways Arnie, Betty Ann, and even Billy Rob are connected with the other components of the family wealth system. If Arnie and his family do leave the ranch, reverberations will be felt throughout the system, which is still reeling from the multiple losses of the past three years.

The vulnerability generated by this component overlap is exacerbated by three forces at work within and without the family wealth system. These forces are discussed in the next three chapters. First, business families experience multiple overlapping cycles of change. In addition to the individual and family cycles of change experienced by every family, business families must take into consideration the business life cycle. Second, family patterns of wealth behavior take on particular importance when played out in a family business. Whether these are issues of control, rebellion, or trust, doing business together will bring them to the forefront. Lastly, external forces, from taxes to interest rates, play a particularly important role in shaping components of the system for business families.

CHAPTER NOTES

1. See generally Monica McGoldrick, Randy Gerson, and Sylvia Shellenberger, *Genograms: Assessment and Intervention* (Norton, 1995).

2. See Roberta M. Gilbert, MD, *Extraordinary Relationships: A New Way of Thinking About Human Interactions* (John Wiley & Sons, 1992) and Fredda Herz Brown, *Reweaving the Family Tapestry: A Multigenerational Approach to Families* (Booksurge LLC, 2006) for more detailed information about family systems and genograms.

3. See discussion in Chapter 9 on governance systems that achieve the right blend of management and oversight for families sharing business wealth.

4. See, e.g., David Halpern, *Social Capital* (Polity Press, 2005); Nan Lin, *Social Capital: A Theory of Social Structure and Action* (Cambridge University Press, 2001); and Robert D. Putnam, *Bowling Alone: The Collapse and Revival of American Community* (Simon & Schuster, 2000).

5. See David Rockefeller, *Memoirs* (Random House, 2002).

6. See Randel S. Carlock and John L. Ward, *Strategic Planning for the Family Business: Parallel Planning to Unify the Family and Business* (Palgrave, 2001).

CHAPTER 5

CYCLES OF CHANGE AND EQUILIBRIUM

IN THE SAME WAY that an individual cell has a cycle of birth, development, maturation, and death, so do people. An individual's life cycle from birth to death comprises many stages of personal development. Families and businesses experience life cycles as well. In each of these life cycles, periods of change are followed by periods of relative equilibrium until a new phase begins. Thus, the components of each nested subsystem of a family wealth system are continually experiencing cycles of change. New connections form; others wither away.

In each cycle, an individual, a family, or a business is fully engaged in certain developmental tasks. Consider an adolescent whose prime directive is clear: autonomy. This developmental task doesn't leave much room for the tasks of other stages of life, such as finding meaning or establishing intimate relationships. In each stage, a participant in the cycle has specific capacities and needs, and operates under predictable constraints. Of course, individuals, families, and businesses may depart from these predictable life cycles, or their development may become arrested for some reason. Cultural differences may also play a role in changing the usual patterns. But most people, families, and businesses follow predictable developmental pathways.

The cycles of individual, family, and business change layer overlap, so that any particular client is likely to be enmeshed in multiple cycles of personal, family, and business development. These overlapping cycles have a major impact on family wealth transition planning (FWTP). This is particularly true for business families, because their businesses become the focal point for multiple sources of wealth as well as multiple cycles of change. As the life cycle of a family business plays out, individual family members connected with the business bring their own developmental tasks to the business environment. Because their families are intimately tied to the business, the challenges and needs of those families affect business operations.

An understanding of life cycles helps family members see their development: where they've been, where they are now, and where they are likely heading. A planner who can help individuals, families, and businesses see how these multiple cycles affect them is more likely to help families create enduring transition plans.

Trigger Events

Even though the family wealth system is in a constant state of change, family members are prone to ignore these changes until a trigger event occurs. *Trigger events* are familiar to FWTP advisers. These are the events that propel clients into their adviser's office to discuss the planning process. Trigger events can be births, marriages, deaths, serious illness, sales of businesses, changes in jobs, and even midlife crises. These trigger events, and their reverberations within the family wealth system, present the illusion of sudden change within a family. The truth is, however, that change is constant in a family and its wealth systems. While trigger events are familiar to most FWTP advisers, organizing them within each of the family wealth systems helps the adviser to develop a deeper understanding of the family wealth system (*Figure 5.1*).

Trigger events take on a special importance in the FWTP process. Family wealth transition planning advisers are familiar with the syndrome, common to many clients, of denying that these kinds of trigger events will occur in their families and in their lives. Because change is the only constant in life, an adviser may have to find ways to educate family members as to the inevitability of these trigger events in the life of the family.

At the other end of the spectrum, family members who are acutely aware of the inevitability of these events use them to entice the more reluctant members of the family to the adviser's office. These agents of change within a family usually recognize the potential for trigger events

FIGURE **5.1**   Trigger Events in Business Families

Family Subsystem Triggers	Operating Business Subsystem Triggers	Investment/ Family Office Subsystem Triggers	Philanthropic Subsystem Triggers
• Birth • Adoption • Death • Serious illness • Marriage • Divorce • Commencement (graduation) • Empty nest • Revelation of a secret • Midlife crisis • Change in career • Retirement	• Formation • Significant change in business operations • Sale • Reorganization • Admission of new owners • Change in key employees • Liquidation • Transfer to family members • Changes in external environment, e.g., tax laws • Lawsuits	• Liquidity event • Need for funds, e.g., extended illness • Sale of assets • Change in type of assets • Change in investment advisers • Need for new services • Change in external environment, e.g., tax laws • Lawsuits	• Change of family members' interest in charity • Change in charitable needs • Tax law changes • Regulatory inquiries or penalties

to drain family capital of all kinds. A marriage, for example, may require a wedding, setting up a new household, a prenuptial agreement, and a will. A serious illness requires significant financial resources and an even more significant commitment of time and energy by family members. A lawsuit may require a new way of making decisions within the family. The FWTP adviser helps family members understand that planning for cycles of change, not just for trigger events, is a more effective means of deploying capital.

Most important, trigger events offer the opportunity to test the effectiveness of a transition plan. In the face of a major life event, will family relationships be strengthened, or will they crumble? Is there a plan for the stewardship of wealth when there is change in management? Will the family legacy be strong enough to survive difficult transitions? A family with an effective plan will be ready for these trigger events and will see them as an opportunity to review the larger issue of healthy transition within the family wealth system.

Individual Life Cycles

—THE HERNÁNDEZ FAMILY—

Susan Hernández (Mrs. Bart Hernández Jr.), age thirty-eight

When the family gets together, someone will invariably tell the family leg-
end about my father-in-law, Bart Sr., and his paper route, even though it
embarrasses him. He had a paper route at age ten. That was too young,
even then, but he got one of the neighbor boys who was three years older
to sign up for it, and then Bart actually did all the work and paid that boy
something, I don't know what. Bart didn't tell his father, of course, that he
was too young under the paper's rules, or that he had involved the other
boy. With Bart at the helm, it wasn't going to be any old paper route. He
went around and introduced himself to all the people on the route, and
asked where they would really like their paper delivered—driveway, front
porch, side porch, wherever. On holidays, he would tie the paper up with
a ribbon, red and green for Christmas, black and orange for Halloween. He
earned lots of tips on top of the regular payment for the route. He acquired
other boys' routes and pretty soon, he was the paper route king. All this
came crashing down one Saturday afternoon when Bart came home from
baseball practice to find the other boy's father visiting with his own dad.
The newspaper had called the other boy's house to tell him he had won
an award for increasing sales on his routes, and the other boy's father had
just happened to take the call. I'm sure Rafael—that was Bart's dad—was
secretly proud of Bart, but he couldn't let the lying go by. He let Bart sweat
it out for a few days, and then made him go see the owner of the paper and
tell him what he had done. They all worked it out so that Bart could keep
the route for a few more years, with his father's help, but his father made
him give a quarter of his earnings to the church. Everyone laughs when they
tell this story, and always gets to talking about how hard the Hernández
family works, but then my Bart makes a point of looking right at José and
sometimes he even says, "So, what happened to you?" I feel bad for José and
tell Bart not to do that. It can only make things worse between them.

In his book *Identity and the Life Cycle,* Dr. Erik Erikson identifies
eight individual life cycle stages associated with identity and a healthy
personality.[1] In the first year, healthy children develop a sense of basic
trust. By year two, a sense of autonomy develops, and by year six, they
acquire a grasp of the meaning of industry. Healthy preadolescents

develop initiative and confidence in their abilities to accomplish their goals. Adolescence is a time for children to develop their own special identity, and by early adulthood, they have learned to form intimate relations with those outside the family. Middle adulthood can bring crises of *generativity* in connection with one's capacity or opportunity for productive and meaningful work and one's need to nurture and care for children and aging parents. Finally, in late life, a developmentally healthy individual integrates all these life experiences in a sense of completion.

Figure 5.2 illustrates the life cycles experienced by individuals, based on Erikson's divisions. Advisers benefit from understanding client issues in the context of the life cycle stages of their immediate client as well as the client's extended family.

In the Hernández family, for example, Bart Sr. was clearly developing a sense of industry and competence by age ten. He showed initiative in creating the opportunity for the paper route and creativity in making it work. These qualities have been passed through generations, probably starting with Bart Sr.'s father, Rafael, and passing in turn to Bart Jr. This begins to emerge as a kind of family pattern of industry, particularly when Elena and Clara's business, Luisa's medical degree, and Clara's son's refusal of her offer to pay off his student loans are included in the picture. The one holdout in the industry department appears to be José. This raises questions. Why is he not industrious? Did he somehow miss out on a way to develop these traits? If so, how did this happen? Is there a remedy? Or is he really a holdout at all?

Life cycles are *epigenetic*. If an individual doesn't accomplish the work of one stage, that gap interferes with the work of the next stage and with future activities unless the individual goes back to address

FIGURE **5.2**   Individual Life Cycle Stages

Life Cycle Stage	Challenges or Opportunities
Stage One: Infancy (Ages 0 to 1)	Trust Versus Mistrust
Stage Two: Toddler (Ages 1 to 2)	Autonomy Versus Doubt
Stage Three: Early Childhood (Ages 2 to 6)	Initiative Versus Guilt
Stage Four: Early School (Ages 6 to 12)	Industry/Competence Versus Inferiority
Stage Five: Adolescence (Ages 12 to 18)	Identity Versus Role Confusion
Stage Six: Young Adulthood (Ages 18 to 40)	Intimacy Versus Isolation
Stage Seven: Middle Adulthood (Ages 40 to 65)	Generativity/Caring Versus Stagnation
Stage Eight: Late Adulthood (Ages 65 to Death)	Integrity/Fulfillment Versus Despair

Source: Adapted from Erik Erikson, *Identity and the Life Cycle* (Norton, 1994).

the needs of the earlier stage. For example, if siblings grow up in a family where they learn to mistrust those outside the nuclear family, cousins who work together in a family enterprise, office, or foundation have to build trust with one another consciously and directly if they are to be effective as partners. In José's case, has he left important adolescent work undone, making his resolution of his sense of his role in the world somehow incomplete? While the life cycle stages above indicate the ages when children typically resolve these issues, it is not unusual to see an individual working on trust or autonomy well into his or her midlife. To do so will require more than the help of a FWTP adviser, and referrals to other professionals may be advisable. The adviser, however, must be able to recognize in general terms the stages completed or left unfinished in order to help the family select the appropriate components of a plan.

Mapping Individual Life Cycles: Capacities and Constraints

When an individual successfully negotiates a life stage, that individual acquires identifiable capacities that can be used in the FWTP process. Likewise, an individual's inability to complete a stage, whether due to age, upbringing, or other reasons, imposes certain constraints. For example, psychologist and family business consultant Dr. Ken Kaye notes that when children grow up in an entrepreneurial or family business environment without an opportunity to individuate, they may become parents with low self-esteem and poor ego development. As parents, they resist their own children's need to differentiate from their families.[2] These capacities and constraints also help point the adviser in the right direction for selecting the components of a plan and setting planning priorities.

The most fundamental example is trust. *Trust* is the willingness to be vulnerable to another person because of a good expectation of that person's abilities, integrity, or benevolence.[3] In some families, all or most members have successfully negotiated Stage One of the individual life cycle, and have a basic willingness to be vulnerable to each other. These families typically need less help with the creation of complex governance systems than do families whose lack of trust requires a continual check on the veracity and activities of other family members. Trust may vary greatly within families as well. Members of the founding generation may trust each other implicitly, while their children, who are cousins, may have a much lower level of trust. The adviser must explore whether this is because of actual negative experiences, or because they lack experiences that test trust.

Figure 5.3 provides a summary of the capacities and constraints that result from a client's successful or unsuccessful travels through these stages of development. While these stages are typical, not every family or its individual members will follow them.

The only way for the FWTP adviser to find out about these issues is to listen to the family story. Susan Hernández, Bart Jr.'s wife, offers a compelling insight into the development of initiative and competence by both Barts, and perhaps José as well. By contrast, in the Williams family, a FWTP adviser might listen for questions of intimacy and isolation in the Williams household, both in their families of origin and in

FIGURE 5.3   Individual Life Cycle Stages: FWTP Implications

Life Cycle Stage	Capacities if Successfully Completed	Constraints if Not Successfully Completed
Stage One: Trust Versus Mistrust	Ability to trust others' abilities, benevolence, and predictability	Need for structures of accountability and a willingness to use them
Stage Two: Autonomy Versus Doubt	Ability to be independent	Undue caution, inability to make a decision
Stage Three: Initiative Versus Guilt	Ability to create own reality	Lack of boundaries, enabling behaviors
Stage Four: Industry/ Competence Versus Inferiority	Ability to believe in one's work and positive results from work	Dependency issues; fear of loss when asked to take risks
Stage Five: Identity Versus Role Confusion	Ability to articulate true goals and dreams	Lack of ambition and inability to "stick to it"
Stage Six: Intimacy Versus Isolation	Ability to be honest and open with others	Fear of connection and unwillingness to share ideas
Stage Seven: Generativity/Caring Versus Stagnation	New energy for new ideas and patterns	Need to cling to the familiar
Stage Eight: Integrity/ Fulfillment Versus Despair	Ability to imagine different futures; belief in change	Fear of letting go; depression

Helen and John's nuclear family. While it is not the role of the adviser to be the family's therapist, sometimes the adviser may need to help clients address these issues during the wealth transition planning and implementation process. Red flags may surface as it becomes clear that trust, autonomy, or industry are problem areas between members of different generations. In some cases, referral to other professionals is appropriate. In other cases, the adviser may only need to help the client family identify the appropriate challenges and explore options for meeting them.

Family Life Cycles

—THE WILLIAMS FAMILY—

Miriam Weinstein, age seventy-four

I hardly remember those two years after my Jacob died. I don't know what I would have done without Helen and John. Before Jacob died, he and I went round and round trying to figure out what to do about our Long Island home. Our Manhattan apartment was much more practical for us as we got older. But Helen wouldn't hear of us selling it. She grew up here, and she and John used to bring their children out here for the summers. Those were such wonderful times! It would break her heart for me to sell the house now. But it's money down the drain all the time, and I'm always worrying about it when I'm staying in the apartment. Helen says she'd like to move her family to Long Island, but that's just her living in that dream world of hers again. John has his business in the city, and the kids are involved in their schools and activities there. Is she going to uproot everybody and make them relive her childhood? I've been telling my daughter, "I know you don't want to hear this from me, but I'm telling you anyway: This house, it really is too much for me." She doesn't want me to sell it, she says I have too many memories there, but memories are something I can take with me. I'd rather just live in the apartment and enjoy life!

In the same way that individuals move through life cycle stages, families also evolve from one developmental stage to another. Each of these stages brings its own challenges for FWTP. Family business organizational development experts Jane Hilburt-Davis and Gibb Dyer define six family developmental stages in terms of critical tasks, risks, and participation in the family business:[4]

- ❏ **Stage One:** Young, single adults who leave home to find work and form personal and business relationships
- ❏ **Stage Two:** New couples who redefine boundaries and relationships with extended family because of this primary relationship
- ❏ **Stage Three:** Families with young children
- ❏ **Stage Four:** Families with adolescents
- ❏ **Stage Five:** Families launching children into adulthood and facing the loss of older family members (parents, siblings, cousins)
- ❏ **Stage Six:** Families in later life

Stage One: Singles

Stage One of a family's developmental cycle comprises young single adults, often exploring a variety of jobs and personal relationships. Both John Williams and his sister Sara probably explored a number of careers before settling on their chosen pathways. Both may also have tested a number of potential relationships before marrying. Certainly we see that exploratory trait in John's midlife change of career, which is likely different from his own father's history. In trying out alternative futures, John and Sara's experiences are probably very different from those of their parents, who most likely chose a path early and stayed with it. The younger generation may value adaptability, while the older generation may value commitment. These values, as well as other generational differences, become important in creating a FWTP process.

Stage Two: New Couples

Stage Two comprises new couples. In today's world, that may include young couples as well as mature couples who marry or create long-standing partnerships for a second (or third or fourth) time. These relationships are often scrutinized carefully by other family members and their advisers in the context of the larger family and business needs and expectations. The greater the difference in background, status, and lifestyles between members of the couple, the greater the potential scrutiny, and the greater the potential for family discord. In the era of serial marriages, this stage will also test a family's openness to newcomers. Are they welcomed warmly, or do they have to prove themselves? How much time will it take for the family to adjust?

When John Williams married Helen Weinstein in 1993, he was thirty-seven and she was thirty-four. They were in the second stage of family development: seeking to redefine boundaries and relationships with extended family because of this primary relationship. Stress probably arose from their different religious backgrounds (Jewish and Episcopalian) because of differing family expectations and traditions. Their respective parents may have taken a fully supportive role or a "wait and see" approach, or simply encouraged sensible protective measures. For example, as we will see in Chapter 6, Jacob Weinstein insisted that John Williams sign a prenuptial agreement before marrying Helen, a move that caused some conflict within the family.

Stage Three: Families with Young Children (Including Blended Families)

In Stage Three families, the focus is on young children. These families often have little free time, even when they have nannies. If both parents work outside the home, this further exacerbates that lack of time. An added burden can arise from the blending of stepchildren from previous marriages and children born to this couple, as the family must seek to merge different values, experiences, and lifestyles. A custody issue from previous marriages, a separation or divorce, or a family illness places even greater demands on parents and children. The flurry of activity makes it difficult for Stage Three families to plan, given their immediate focus. It is often hard for them to imagine any other stage of life or understand others' perspectives.

When John and Helen Williams married, not only were they in the second stage of family development, but they also immediately entered the third stage as a couple with a dependent child: Helen's daughter Rebecca (age three in 1993), whom John legally adopted and considered his daughter. How Rebecca's paternal grandparents felt about John's adopting Rebecca isn't known, but it may have been a source of either discord or support, depending on how they perceived this move as affecting their continuing relationship with their granddaughter.

John and Rebecca had seven years to bond before the twins, Jacob and Samuel, were born. Although Rebecca's birth father was deceased, the family still experienced some characteristics of a blended family. Rebecca had three sets of grandparents, aunts, uncles, and cousins; the twins only had Helen's parents, John's parents, and his sister Sara's family. Their extended family was more complex than many, given the religious mix. Did Rebecca view her brothers as brothers or as stepbrothers? And did she introduce John to others as her father or her stepfather?

Helen and John were both professionals who worked outside the home. For them, this third stage of family development was characterized by hectic schedules and a high cost of living. The focus was on managing time and relationships in the moment, with little thought given to longer-term individual or family goals. Their lifestyle in New York ate up most of their income, especially when Helen took a leave of absence after Lisa's birth. Although they were putting away some money in John's 401(k), they also counted on an inheritance from Helen's parents to secure their own retirement and to fund their children's education. John probably assumed that he would work until at least his mid-sixties.

Stage Four: Families with Adolescents

Adolescents bring their own set of challenges to any family as their search for identity and role clarity intensifies, abetted by surging hormones, the prevalence of drugs in schools and communities, the threat of AIDS and other sexually transmitted diseases, and the attitude that anyone else's parents are preferable to one's own. Teenagers bring lots of activity and unpredictability to the home, and often forge new bonds with outsiders, with or without parental approval. Parental concerns about financing education and their teens' futures mark this as an important stage of family wealth development. John and Helen have one teenager, Rebecca, who appears to have embarked on the same pathway that her mother followed. When the twins become teenagers, the couple will doubtless have its hands full.

Stage Five: Families Launching Young Adults and Losing Seniors

In this developmental cycle, one branch starts to grow away from another. The children enter Stage One of the family developmental cycle as young adults. Their parents and grandparents are most likely in Stages Five and Six. To picture the family's development, visualize the family genogram as a tree. In every family, there are multiple stages, and at times new branches start to move out in a different direction as others die off or break away.

Some families experience divorce in this developmental stage, with one spouse marrying a younger woman (or man) and starting a second family. Obviously, this is not predictable. Blended families may also appear in Stages Three and Four. In whatever developmental stage they occur, blended families increase the complexity of family dynamics, boundary definition in relationships (especially when there is a family business involved), and the wealth transition process.

In Stage Five families, the parents are in the middle of the family sandwich. They are still caring for their children, even as the children launch their young adult lives, and are beginning to provide more care to their parents, who, if they are still living, will in all likelihood require more emotional, physical, mental, and sometimes financial support as they age. It is most likely that individuals will be in Stage Five when they visit the FWTP adviser to begin a family wealth transition plan. Their elders may or may not have created a wealth transition plan. They may or may not have shared that plan with their adult children. So the planning process is often filled with unanswered questions about the level of wealth the parents will inherit and the timing of that increase in their own net worth. Likewise, they are facing their own retirement and mortality, and probably beginning to lose friends to cancer, strokes, and heart attacks.

Stage Six: Families in Later Life

In Stage Six, families face more inevitable and predictable losses than in other stages. People celebrate marriage and birth. They rarely celebrate death and divorce. Letting go is a central theme of families in this stage. As Miriam Weinstein is learning, family members may have to let go of a family home where they've lived for decades. One spouse may die, leaving the other alone. Some widowed or divorced spouses may remarry during this stage, causing a flurry of speculation about whatever existing wealth transition plan has already been created. If there is no plan to date, such a late marriage may cause even more concern among the heirs. Families in this stage are also letting go of their physical, and sometimes their mental, health.

Miriam Weinstein finds herself in Stage Six after the premature death of her husband. She appears to be coming out of a long period of mourning, in which she relied heavily on her daughter and son-in-law. Now she is struggling with the issues of letting go of her family home and living a different kind of lifestyle. Yet talking to her daughter about these issues is proving difficult, as Helen is not only in a different stage of family life but also appears to have trouble accepting her mother's evolving status.

Family Life Cycles: Needs, Capacities, and Constraints

The individual life cycles bring certain identifiable needs, capacities, and constraints to the FWTP process. So, too, does the family life cycle. Each family, at its own particular stage of development, has special needs in FWTP. For example, a family with young children is typically intensely interested in plans that address the specter of the parents' premature death. Despite the statistical unlikelihood of both parents dying while their children are young, they may spend what little extra money they have for life insurance, and will debate for months about which individuals the family they should ask to be guardians for their children. These needs can create conflict between generations. Parents of Stage One families are generally in the middle of their adulthood and starting to think about retirement. Aging specialist Dr. John Gibson notes that these two generations within the same family often have different key experiences, memories, ambitions, values, heroes, and beliefs,[5] all of which can lead to very different perceptions of what is important during the FWTP process.

Similarly, just by being in a particular stage, a family brings certain capacities to the table. The Stage Three family with small children is motivated. Stage Five families are typically in their highest-earning years, and can accommodate changes to savings and spending habits to achieve their goals. Young adults, even teenagers, bring a special capacity for flexibility to the planning table that can help everyone imagine a different future.

Finally, each stage of family development is accompanied by a special constraint or challenge in the FWTP process. The young family typically feels it has neither time nor money to spend on planning. The family of an adolescent may be in doubt as to whether their teen-ager is destined for college or life as a couch potato, so they defer planning. Stage Six families may be coming to terms with whether they truly trust the next generation to manage wealth. For all families, regardless of stage, time is a major constraint: time to devote to the planning process, time together for discussion and reflection, and the time necessary to create and implement the plan. The methodology suggested in this book requires more time, not less, than the typical estate planning engagement. A family embarking upon the FWTP process needs a realistic assessment of the required time from their advisers.

Mapping a family's stage of development is the easiest of the mapping processes for cycles of change. However, every family is different, and a family may suddenly depart from the usual cycle. In the Hernández family, for example, Bart Sr. was comfortably in Stage Five, but he may return to Stage Four if he marries Samantha. *Figure 5.4* summarizes the

FIGURE 5.4   Family Life Cycle Stages: FWTP Implications

Stage of Family Development	Needs in FWTP Process	Capacities in FWTP Process	Constraints in FWTP Process
Stage One: Young, single adults	Begin to understand wealth and management of it	Flexible	Inability to imagine "old," attention, or focus
Stage Two: New couples	Develop shared values, goals, plan	Energetic	Time, experiences with each other
Stage Three: Families with young children	Provide for untimely death	Motivated	Time, money
Stage Four: Families with adolescents	Plan for college and retirement	Practical	Time, changing roles and needs not yet clear
Stage Five: "Sandwich families"	Plan for retirement, health care costs, death	High earning ability	Time, confusion as to desires for future, uncertainty about inheritances
Stage Six: Families in later life	Retirement needs, taxes, death	Age brings a reality check and a new practicality	Trust in next generation, willingness to "let go"

needs, capacities, and constraints that families typically bring to the table, based on their stage in the family life cycle.

Business Life Cycles

—THE WILLIAMS FAMILY—
Cindy Jones, age thirty-two

Okay, so I was a walking cliché: I was sleeping with my boss. But it was only for two months. Who would have thought I would get pregnant? I had been around this business for years, but had just started working at Jazz Jive as a bartender when John bought it from Stan. John didn't know the first thing about running a bar, that's for sure. But, you know, he's not a typical guy. He's not afraid to ask for directions. So he learned fast, from me and anyone else who could help him. He also knew jazz and knew how to make the bar a special place—not snooty like with Stan, but friendly and fun instead. He still has a lot of friends from his old job. They're great customers, and they really help us out when something comes up. Like when we found out that our waitstaff was skimming—well, more like scooping it up with both hands. John's buddies got us set up with a real accounting system—on the cheap, too—so we could keep a better eye on expenses. Now I can tell you on Tuesday morning if a steak walked out the back door on Monday night, and probably who it walked out with, too!

When I got pregnant, John was horrified. He had four kids, one of them a new baby with Down syndrome, and his wife was in a major depression, completely out of it. I knew I had messed up big time. So we broke it off right away, but I decided to have the baby. Thank God, my parents helped. I went back to work—as a manager for John, believe it or not. Anyway, it was hard at first, but my Brad is seven and the love of my life. Things worked out at Jazz Jive, and I'm happy with my life. No, John and I haven't been lovers since. We're good friends and we work together. Period.

I know John poured a lot of money into the bar. He spent all of his time at the business. His work finally started to pay off though, and now there are three Jazz Jive bars and a restaurant too. They're all doing great. I'm John's general manager. He can trust me to make sure everything is running smoothly so he can do what he does best—get customers in the door. I make good money—we worked out a deal so that the business basically pays my child support through salary. I can set my own hours, which is important because of Brad. He always comes first with me.

Okay, so, last year a guy from one of the hotel chains was asking
John about buying the business, and for a good price, too, but he wanted
John to stay on for a year or so to transition it, and John said no. I was
only half kidding the other day when I said to John, "Hey, let's buy a
few more bars and we'll apply our secret formula to 'em." John actually
snapped at me, "No more!" He seems so distracted and edgy these days,
after his surgery.

In addition to understanding individual life cycles and family developmental cycles, the adviser should understand the basic business cycles
that may affect transition plans. Businesses have predictable cycles of
development, just as individuals and families do. The stage of the business that is generating family wealth, as well as the stage of any business
in which family members are engaged, may influence the family wealth
transition plan a client needs or expects.

The Start-Up Phase

In the start-up phase of the cycle, the business family needs capital,
a business plan, a marketing plan, basic legal and financial structures
through which to conduct business, and sufficient staff. It also must
offer products or services that meet a market need, and have a way of
providing those products or services to customers that keeps those customers coming back and telling others about the new company. There is
usually a high degree of passion and enthusiasm for the venture among
the founders. They often eschew written agreements because they don't
have time to write them, or their business situation seems to change too
quickly to make planning worthwhile. They wait to consult their lawyer
until there is a crisis or an immediate need, sometimes to their detriment and often because they are concerned about the expense.

Whether starting from scratch or buying a business from someone
else, start-ups are time and labor intensive, as John Williams and his
family discovered. Frequently the founders take on multiple roles in
the company until the volume of business allows them to hire other
staff. Sometimes those businesses are run out of a garage or a basement.
They demand attention twenty-four hours a day, seven days a week. An
entrepreneur's family members often see little of the founder unless
they, too, are involved in the business. They sometimes think that the

founder loves the business more than he or she loves them, based on the amount and the quality of time spent with each.

Cash flow is sometimes precarious and usually closely monitored. Entrepreneurs often invest their own savings, borrow money from family, friends, or banks, and occasionally take on partners or investors or use credit cards as their financing vehicle of choice. This is what John Williams did to cover payroll from time to time. Most successful entrepreneurs have failed at least once and have learned from their failures. Because many entrepreneurs are independent thinkers who want to be in charge of their own destiny, if a company has a board of directors, it usually comprises the founder and a few family members or close friends. This board, if there is one, may be a rubber stamp, supporting and validating what the founder wants to do. The entrepreneur's strength is product or service development and marketing. This type of client is more likely to focus on maintaining control, and less likely to focus on creating formal governance structures and processes.

The Growth Phase

In the growth phase of the business cycle, the business owners' need for systems, structures, processes, and protocols becomes more urgent, but their willingness to devote resources to those tasks is low to moderate. They balance their opportunities to grow against how they'll pay for that growth. They often reinvest profits and build equity to keep debt/equity ratios healthy. If they borrow money from family or friends to finance the company's growth, those loans may lack proper documentation or collateral. In the best of circumstances, their business planning becomes more strategic; in the worst, they grow too soon in the wrong markets. They may start related companies to become more vertically integrated, e.g., property management companies that own the property where they locate their businesses. However, they may not have arms-length lease agreements with these related companies (or any lease agreements at all).

The management team and board of a growing business may become more knowledgeable about governance, although control usually continues to rest exclusively with the founder. Owners may also receive frequent offers to sell their business in this phase because it is successful.

During the growth phase, founders may also start to bring in family members whom they trust to fill management or board roles, rather than looking for qualified outsiders whom they don't trust. Family members may work without job descriptions, performance evaluations, or performance- or market-driven compensation. This can lead to long-term issues about entitlement that affect the morale of the nonfamily employees, the self-esteem of those family members employed in the business, and the relationships between those family members and other ones who are not employed there. It is during this phase that the business begins to evolve from an entrepreneurial enterprise into a family business. For that reason, it is during this cycle that it becomes critical to address ambiguity of roles and boundaries among the family, management, and ownership subsystems of the business.

John Williams may be in this predicament. Cindy Wallace is his general manager, but also the mother of his child and his former lover. He has merged the family relationship and the business relationship by paying Cindy a higher salary to cover child support. Although Cindy seems competent, whether Cindy is or is not qualified is impossible to tell. Her use of the words "we" and "us" when talking about the business suggests that she views herself as a member of the team. Is it more than that? Is this language a cue that she views herself in the role Helen would normally fill? Testing this will begin to reveal how tightly interwoven John's second family and his business really are.

The Cash Cow Phase

In the cash cow phase of the cycle, there are many opportunities for formalizing business governance structures and processes, both at the management and the board levels. If the board operates more professionally in this phase, it will probably have active committees for functions such as audit, compensation, nominating, and strategic planning. There may be a need to create more internal controls in accounting, inventory, production, and sales and marketing functions.

This is also a cycle in which increased profits make the business owner begin to think about acquisitions. The business owner has more disposable income and the company has more profits than during the earlier years of building the business, so the owner may start to diversify personal investments and may increase gifting to family members.

The business owner may look at outside investments in real estate or consider purchasing a second home. This cycle may also coincide with the time at which members of the next generation start to work in the business. The business owner may look for ways to invest in the careers of adult children or the education of younger children or grandchildren, even if they don't choose to come into the business.

The Expansion Phase

During the business expansion phase, entrepreneurs need to hone their strategic management and forecasting skills. It is also important to make sure that the internal controls to manage expansion are in place. In some cases, expansion takes the business owner into different industries. Owners must clearly understand the opportunities and threats in the new industry, as well as differences in demand on staff and other corporate resources. Some businesses may grow horizontally, as John Williams's did when he bought two more bars and a restaurant. Others grow vertically, going from retail to distribution to production or vice versa. The owners may find this expansion more challenging than they anticipated. Instead of creating economies of scale, expansion may overly tax their resources. This appears to be John Williams's view, although it may be that the confusion of family and business roles is also causing him to refuse to expand further.

The Maturity Phase

During this phase of the cycle, business families address how the business will revitalize itself in its changing marketplace, how they will manage increased or changing competition, and how they can adjust aging facilities, governance structures, and processes to ensure that they are meeting the present needs of the business and the family. It may be a period of divestitures in the operating company system. It may also be the cycle in which the family investment office is formed in response to changes in the sources of financial capital and the means to grow that capital.

In many business families, the business maturity phase parallels the senior generation's need to consider retirement, estate planning, and leadership development in the next generation. This may also be the period in which the family decides to formalize its philanthropic activities under the umbrella of a family foundation. Some families formalize governance structures and processes in the family by creating a family council to address planning, communication, and relationship management challenges within its multigenerational, multibranch family.

Mapping the Business Life Cycle

Many business families have multiple businesses, each in a different cycle of development. From a planning standpoint, what matters is that the pertinent FWTP structures and processes be aligned with the business entities' needs and their governance structures and processes. Inspecting the usual financial tools, including balance sheets, income statements, cash flow statements, and dividend or distribution history, helps the adviser obtain a basic understanding of the financial wealth the business has created, and may help reveal its stage in the business life cycle. It is the family members' perspectives on the history and future of the business, however, that are most critical to understanding the business cycle. The following questions will help the adviser map the family's perspectives:

- ❏ How did your family business get started?
- ❏ What were its turning points, and why were they important?
- ❏ Who is involved in your family business and how? Family members? Key employees?
- ❏ What are your expectations about how much time these people should spend working in the business? What is the reality?
- ❏ Who relies on the business for financial wealth? What kinds and amounts?
- ❏ Who decides what's going to happen in the business, and how?
- ❏ What demands, financial, emotional, or otherwise, does the business make on you and your family?
- ❏ What oversight exists for these people?
- ❏ What is it about your business that has given you the greatest satisfaction?
- ❏ Have you ever considered selling the business? Closing it?
- ❏ What was the biggest failure of the business? What did you and your family learn from it?

❑ What would be your greatest concern for the business today if you were to die tomorrow?

❑ How much does your spouse know about the day-to-day operations of the business? Would the business survive if your spouse had to run it temporarily because you died suddenly or developed a catastrophic illness that made it impossible for you to work?

❑ Do you have vendors or customers who might go to your competitors if you died or suddenly became incapacitated?

❑ Do you know whether anyone else in your family has any interest in running the business when you are ready to pass the torch? If so, what are you doing to prepare that person to take charge? What are you doing to help yourself learn to let go?

Overlapping Cycles of Change and Equilibrium

—THE HERNÁNDEZ FAMILY—

Luisa Hernández, age thirty-three

I'm the only one who doesn't live right there in Fresno. I live in Los Angeles, but to hear the rest of the family talk about it you'd think it was another planet, not just a few hours away. Papá always told me to "get out there and be somebody." He always told me I could do anything I wanted to. So when I wanted to go to college, I set everything up secretly—the plan, the scholarships, everything—and just presented it to Papá as a done deal. Later, I went to Stanford School of Medicine on scholarship and did my residency in dermatology. At first, I joined a big group in Los Angeles. But about two years ago, I opened my own practice.

When I was deciding whether or not to open my practice, Papá came down from Fresno and we spent an entire week together. He helped me make up my mind. I was scared to make the move, but I really wasn't happy in such a big group, with all its focus on profits instead of patients. So we went over my options and figured out what it would cost to open up a practice, and how I could get financing and all that. He loaned me some money so I could pay those first few months' salaries before the fees started coming in. I really couldn't have done it without him. He brought my mother's old desk with him when he came to help me. When I was a little girl, I always played underneath it while she worked on the books for the businesses. Now I have it in my office.

I need to get up to Fresno soon, although I haven't got time to even breathe, much less take a trip home. My brother José's been calling a lot lately and I figure there's something on his mind, though who knows how I'll get it out of him. I also need to do some refereeing between José and my brother Bart. They just don't get each other, and it drives Papá crazy. Bart was born serious, grew up serious, and will die serious. He works all the time. I don't know how he has any time to see his beautiful wife and little girl. José is just the opposite. He can charm the birds from the trees, and is an artist at heart. Dad keeps him employed at the hardware store, but I think he's just marking time.

My mother died five years ago, and my grandmother the year before that. That left Papá and José alone in the house, but now I hear that Papá's new girlfriend is moving in. At least that's what José says. He says she's twenty-five years younger than Papá—practically my age—and has two teenagers. That will send my brother Bart over the edge, for sure. Like I have room to talk. I haven't yet introduced Angus to my family. I'm not sure why, except he's not Catholic and he is a lot older than me. I promised my mother on her deathbed that I would get married and have children, but I just don't know how that's going to happen. I work all the time and so does he. Maybe after my practice settles down I can think about that.

At any given time, a business family is experiencing multiple cycles of individual development, family development, and business development. Really understanding a family requires understanding these cycles, not just individually, but as an interwoven whole. An adviser to the Hernández family would begin the life cycle analysis using the most tightly focused lens: an individual's overlapping stages of individual, family, and business development. This process reveals the answers to three critical questions:

❏ What does this individual need, and what is he or she likely to need in the future?
❏ What special capacities does this individual bring to FWTP that can help the family wealth system adapt productively?
❏ What constraints must the adviser recognize as a result of the life cycles of this individual?

The natural individual on which to focus in the Hernández family is Bart Sr., and *Figure 5.5* summarizes his life cycles. However, the same

FIGURE **5.5** Bart Hernández Sr.: An Example of Overlapping Cycles

Bart's Individual Life Cycles	Bart's Family Developmental Cycles	Bart's Business Developmental Cycles
Stages One–Five: 0–18 Years Trust, autonomy, initiative, competence	Family of origin: His parents with Stage Three and Four young children and teenagers	Start-up (the "paper route king")
Stage Six: 18–40 Years Passage to adulthood: career and intimacy	Bart's first, second, and third family cycles: Young adult; new couple; parent of three children	Entrepreneurial start-up cycle: Bart and Elena buy hardware store.
Stage Seven: 40–65 Years Nurturing career and family; midlife crisis	Bart's third, fourth, and fifth family cycles: Raising young children and adolescents; launching young adults; losing loved ones (Bart's parents and wife die). Bart contemplates second marriage.	Business growth, cash cow, and expansion cycles: Bart and Elena expand store; acquire rental houses; underwrite sons' construction business; reject offer to sell store.
Stage Eight: 65–Death Reflection, fulfillment, letting go Does not yet apply to Bart	Bart's sixth family cycle: Families in later life Does not yet apply to Bart	Does not yet apply to Bart

analysis can be applied to any family member. Applying this process to individuals other than a central client figure can often generate important insights into family members who may appear to be obstructionist or uninvolved.

Bart Sr. successfully navigated the early and middle stages of individual development, and every member of his family has at one time or another depended on the storehouse of human capital he developed. The years 2003–2004 were significant transition years for Bart Sr. He was in his fifties. Life cycle stage experts identify the fifties as the birth of one's second adulthood.[6] This is the time when both men and women start to pay attention to changes in their bodies due to the aging process. Some men become more nurturing during this stage of life, and this may very well be true for Bart. He probably expected to enjoy this time of his life with Elena, without working quite as hard as they both had throughout their lives, and he may feel robbed of that opportunity. In those years, both his mother, María, and his wife, Elena, died. Bart had always been a strong, confident decision maker. Yet he had to face life-and-death situations over which he had no control. He lost two of the three most important women in his life—his mother and his wife—and even his daughter seems far away. Bart could not help but face his own mortality as a result. Yet he appears to be moving on with his life, remaining engaged with this family as well as forming new relationships. His new willingness to embark upon FWTP may be the result of the natural tendency at midlife to measure the remaining years as well as his recognition of his failure to plan ahead for Elena's death.

From a family developmental perspective, Bart was fully engaged in a Stage Five family, but suddenly found himself at a loss. Bart may feel some guilt about courting Samantha, and may feel disloyal to Elena, but he also wants to enjoy this stage of his life. If Bart remarries, he will also have stepchildren, and his home will suddenly become a Stage Four household. He will need to address the issues surrounding the first blended family in the Hernández clan.

Although Bart began as an entrepreneur by acquiring an existing business, his business life has become much more complex. He and Elena had expanded the hardware store, and in the past, it produced significant income for them. When Elena sold her part of the clothing business, it produced liquid capital, so they began to invest in real estate. At this stage, Bart and Elena's wealth was growing, but they may not have felt very wealthy as they directed capital toward developing opportunities for their own children. Bart financed the boys' construction and remodeling business and helped Luisa establish her medical practice. He is now involved in businesses in four different stages of development, from a start-up (the medical practice) to a cash cow or mature business (the hardware business), with the construction and real estate businesses somewhere in between. Each of these businesses has made significant demands on him over the years, with no change in those demands in sight. A wise adviser will focus on how well these demands fit with the needs and constraints of his individual and family life cycles.

Each of Bart's stages in the individual, family, and business life cycles brings with it certain needs, capacities, and constraints, as we discussed in previous sections of this chapter. An adviser to the Hernández family would carefully analyze these, as preparation for comparing and connecting them to others' life cycles.

A Wider Focus

Family wealth transition planning requires widening the lens beyond the individual to include the multiple, overlapping life cycles of other members of the family. This focus is on the present state of affairs, and brings into the picture other family members, comparing and connecting their stages of individual, family, and business development to the stages of development of a particular individual.

Figure 5.6 is a map of the overlapping life cycle stages of Bart and his children that an adviser to the Hernández family would create in the early stages of FWTP. This kind of map will help the Hernández family see that in every family, individual life cycles in a senior and junior generation are often at odds with each other. The issues each person considers important, trivial, or even tedious will differ depending on that person's individual stage of development. A wise planner helps a family see that these differences are a natural part of growth and development. In fact, these differences show that the family is on track developmentally, and this is certainly true for the Hernández family. However, this map also demonstrates the gulf between José's and the other family members' individual stages of development. By framing

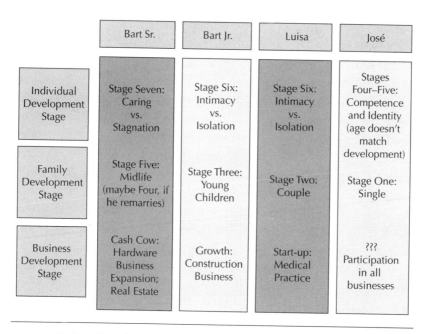

	Bart Sr.	Bart Jr.	Luisa	José
Individual Development Stage	Stage Seven: Caring vs. Stagnation	Stage Six: Intimacy vs. Isolation	Stage Six: Intimacy vs. Isolation	Stages Four–Five: Competence and Identity (age doesn't match development)
Family Development Stage	Stage Five: Midlife (maybe Four, if he remarries)	Stage Three: Young Children	Stage Two: Couple	Stage One: Single
Business Development Stage	Cash Cow: Hardware Business Expansion; Real Estate	Growth: Construction Business	Start-up: Medical Practice	??? Participation in all businesses

FIGURE 5.6 Overlapping Cycles for Bart Sr. and His Children

the conflict as structural rather than about character or motivation, the adviser helps the family move away from value judgments about José that are counterproductive and may further entrench family members. Instead, a focus on life cycles can lead to a discussion of how José can acquire the necessary experiences to get unstuck and move through his life cycles. This will ultimately raise important issues of FWTP, including why Bart Sr. has held on to the hardware store long after his interests have shifted to real estate, and will necessarily involve José in a discussion of his involvement in that store.

The stages of family development in the children's lives illustrate how their needs, capacities, and constraints in FWTP will differ. For example, Bart Jr. may expect a quick fix, because the demands of a growing business and young family mean he has little or no time to devote to a planning process. His father (looking through the lens of Stage Six in his individual life cycle) would likely view Bart Jr.'s perspective as shortsighted and yet another example of how he doesn't want to treat his brother well. Moreover, some or all of the children may be constrained by the ambivalence they feel (but cannot express) about their father's relationship with Samantha. They likely expected their father to follow the usual course of family development, and now have mixed feelings, wanting him to be happy but not wanting the upheaval of a return to a Stage Four family. The adviser to the Hernández family will use the map to find out how differences in family development stages may create fault lines within the family.

Finally, the Hernández family has four businesses in which various family members participate. These businesses are at different stages of development, which place a variety of demands on family members, particularly Bart Sr. The map of overlapping life cycles illustrates the degree to which the developmental needs of an individual or a family complement (or collide with) the developmental needs of a business. For example, the hardware store may be in the cash cow stage. Bart and Elena could have sold it in the early 1990s, but they kept it to create a place for José. The question for FWTP is whether, today and tomorrow, José will be willing and able to mange that cash flow and take the business to the next stage. Particularly for families who are mired in stories and value judgments about members, life cycle analysis provides an objective way to discuss these issues. The needs, capacities, and constraints typical of each stage of development become beacons to guide the discussion. Are José's developmental needs and capacities consistent with the skills he needs to accomplish the business tasks at hand? What about Bart Jr.'s expressed interest in taking on the store? In either son's case, if the desire is present but the capacity is not, the question becomes what needs to change in order for this to happen? Finally, does Bart Sr. have the capacity to manage the store if his sons cannot? The same analysis can and should be used, of course, for any of the Hernándezes' endeavors, and must ultimately be applied to the construction business and the real estate business as well.

Implications of Cycles of Change for Business Families

Understanding a client family's overlapping cycles of change offers enormous potential for successful planning. At a practical level, these cycles establish the priorities for planning. Locating family members, families, and their businesses within their respective cycles of change focuses the family and its advisers on likely future trigger events. Preparing for immediate events takes precedence over longer-term concerns, yet it also grants family members a peek at the coming long-term challenges.

Each phase of each cycle brings its own special needs, capacities, and constraints to the FWTP process. Cataloging these issues can help the FWTP adviser predict where special challenges will arise and where conflict may erupt. The lesson of these ever changing life cycles is that many challenges are structural, not personal. Conflicting needs, goals, and constraints arise naturally from differences among generations, different stages of family life, and various incarnations of a business. Yet these can also be healthy for a family, because complementary needs, capacities, and constraints can strengthen the family wealth system. Without an understanding of the cycles of change, families often identify differences as personal ones relating to the character of an individual, the quality of a family, or the importance of a business. This misidentification can slow or stop the process.

Moreover, a deep understanding of how the family deploys capital within the system requires a map of the overlapping stages of individual, family, and business development. A family deploys its financial capital differently during various phases of the cycles, but human and social types of capital also have different roles at different stages. Mapping a family's storehouse of capital requires understanding not only how capital is deployed at a given point in time, but also how changing stages within the life cycles will affect that deployment.

The multiple cycles of change have broader implications as well. Like most complex adaptive systems, the family wealth system has a memory: its current state depends on past events, including the overlapping cycles that existed at a particular point. The constellation of life cycles that existed for a family at one moment can be the genesis of particular structures or processes that the family now considers permanent features of the family wealth system. A family will be more willing to let go of structures and processes that no longer serve their true interests when its members understand their origins. Moreover, the entire family wealth system is sensitive to change anywhere within itself, and the changes inherent in these cycles will have reverberations throughout the system. Predicting and managing those effects is an important part of FWTP. Finally, the needs, capacities, and constraints of each phase in a cycle can be complementary to those in other cycles, but also can easily create conflict. As cycles collide, new connections arise and others are destroyed. Understanding these cycles will help the FWTP adviser predict the likely impact of implementing certain components of a wealth transition plan.

CHAPTER NOTES

1. See Section 2, "Growth and Crises of the Healthy Personality," in Erik Erikson, *Identity and the Life Cycle* (Norton, 1994).

2. See Ken Kaye, "When the Family Business Is a Sickness," *Family Business Review*, Vol. 9, No. 4 (Winter 1996), pp. 347–368. Kaye defines individuation as a lifelong developmental process beginning in the first year that is characterized by the questions "Who am I and how am I distinct from my parents, siblings and other caregivers, relationships, and their expectations of me?" (p. 355) and ego as the "internalized capacity for self-regulation as well as the experience of oneself as a whole person (p. 360).

3. See Kacie La Chapelle and Louis B. Barnes, "The Trust Catalyst in Family Owned Businesses," *Family Business Review*, Vol. 11 (March 1998), p. 1.

4. See Jane Hilburt-Davis and Gibb Dyer, *Consulting to Family Businesses* (Pfeiffer, 2003), pp. 134–136.

5. See Hartley and Gibson, *The Dynamics of Aging Families* (Cambio Press, 2006).

6. For more detailed explanations of the various life cycle stages, see Gail Sheehy, *New Passages* (Ballantine, 1996); Frederic Hudson, *The Adult Years* (Jossey-Bass, 1999); and Erik Erikson, *Identity and the Life Cycle* (Norton, 1994) and *The Life Cycle Completed* (Norton, 1998).

CHAPTER 6

PATTERNS OF WEALTH BEHAVIOR

EVERY COMPLEX SYSTEM produces repeating patterns created through feedback loops. The individual components of a system create these patterns, but the patterns transcend them. Like eddies in a stream, the individual components that make up the patterns change, but the pattern remains.

The family wealth system is no exception. Each family has unique feedback loops that encourage certain behaviors and discourage others with respect to human, social, and financial capital. Over time, these feedback loops create ingrained patterns of behavior that have a profound impact on the family wealth transition planning (FWTP) process. These patterns influence the selection of individual components of a plan as well as a family's readiness to engage productively in planning and, ultimately, to achieve family wealth continuity.

Family systems theorists have developed useful models to analyze family behavior patterns. Therapists use these models to treat families and change their patterns. While treatment is not the function of FWTP, these models can help the FWTP adviser understand how families behave with respect to their wealth. Although a family may gain valuable insights about its patterns through the process, the adviser cannot change them. Instead, the FWTP adviser must use these models to bring into focus a family's unique needs, capacities, and constraints during the planning process, and ultimately to design the appropriate wealth transition plan.

Feedback Loops: How
Patterns Develop and Change

Patterns of wealth behavior are created when individual components of the system, particularly family members, have multiple interactions with other components in which one component's behavior affects another's, which in turn affects the original actor. These countereffects are *feedback loops*.

The feedback cycle can go on indefinitely, establishing patterns of action that produce positive, negative, or bipolar feedback loops. Positive feedback amplifies or accelerates an effect, while negative feedback dampens or reduces it like a regulatory effect. Bipolar feedback can have either effect.

In the family wealth system, each pattern of behavior is supported by multiple actions of family members and others, who are likely unaware of how their actions support the pattern. In times of equilibrium, these patterns are practically invisible as family members manage their accustomed relationships. In many families, a trigger event will suddenly reveal these patterns. That revelation, while sometimes painful, offers an opportunity to examine the extent to which existing patterns of behavior support the true goals of the family.

Understanding how family behavior patterns are created by feedback loops is critical to the design of a wealth transition plan. For example, a controlling business founder probably generates a tendency in his children to abdicate their responsibilities in managing wealth. The more they abdicate, the more his control manifests itself. The planning process for this family will either involve creating an interruption in this positive feedback loop, or accepting it as unchangeable and working around it. Ignoring it, however, is not an option. In other cases, a feedback loop produces desirable behaviors, and the components of FWTP should support that loop.

Family Typology

The *Circumplex Model* of assessment and treatment of families, developed by Murray Bowen and David Olson,[1] is a typology of families that focuses on three fundamental characteristics, described here and illustrated in *Figure 6.1:*

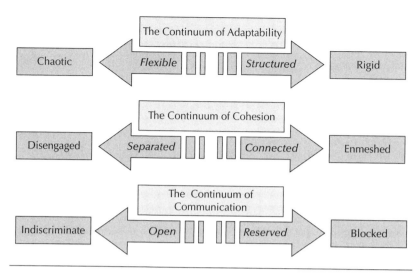

FIGURE 6.1 Family Typologies

❏ **Cohesion:** The degree of togetherness (*we-ness*) versus individuality (*I-ness*) within the family
❏ **Adaptability:** The degree of flexibility in handling change
❏ **Communication:** The degree of productive communication within a family

Because each family enjoys these characteristics to a different degree, one may envision each characteristic as a continuum. Each continuum manifests the degree of a characteristic that leads to healthy and productive patterns of behavior. The extreme ends of the continuum are reserved for the characters of Southern fiction. Real families and their individual members reside somewhere along the continuum.

Cohesion

Cohesion reflects the degree of emotional bonding within a family. Some families are extremely close (*enmeshed*), and these families expect both a high degree of involvement and a high degree of family loyalty. The Hernández family is a classic example of an enmeshed family. At the other end of the spectrum, some families are extremely distant (*disengaged*). In these families, there is limited contact and involvement among family members. In between these two extremes are those families with low to moderate cohesion (*separated*) or moderate to high cohesion (*connected*). Measures of cohesion include boundaries, coalition, space, time together and apart, how decisions are made (collectively or individually), and shared interests and recreational time together.

Adaptability

The *adaptability* continuum ranges from rigid to chaotic. In a *rigid* family, there is authoritarian leadership, roles seldom change, and there are strict consequences for deviation from the rules. Change is extremely difficult in these families. At the other end of the spectrum, *chaotic* families lack leadership altogether. There are few rules and even fewer consequences for breaking those rules. People take on and shed roles constantly, and there is little predictability in family members' lives. Between the extremes of rigid and chaotic families are flexible and structured families. In a *flexible* family, members share leadership, and roles can change, but in a more rational way than in a chaotic family. Decisions are democratic and members can make changes when they are necessary. In a *structured* family, members sometimes share leadership. Roles are relatively stable, but the family can change when it is necessary.

Communication

Communication in FWTP encompasses two separate dimensions. First, each family and its members have a style of communication that is considered normal for that family. Some families talk over each other, while others are quiet and reflective. Some families understand that throwing the dishes means "listen up!" while in others a raised eyebrow serves the same purpose. How the family communicates, whether by telephone, e-mail, or the annual Christmas letter, also reveals its style. The frequency, inclusiveness, and methods of communication help create a family's unique communication style, and create expectations for family members about behavior. A visitor from the Williams family would marvel at the decibel level at the Marshall family dinner table, for example, while a Marshall might be astonished that the busy Luisa Hernández telephones her father five times a week for a lengthy conversation. Moreover, family members often differ in their style of communication.

A middle child may be the only quiet member of a family of talkers, for example. More broadly, experience and learning styles greatly affect a person's preferred means of communication.

No matter what style of communication a family or its members adopt, there is a second dimension to communication: the family culture of what is and is not acceptable to talk about within the family. Even a gregarious family may treat some topics as taboo, including those that are most critical to FWTP: money, love, and power.

By assessing family communication styles and culture, an adviser can classify families along a continuum, the extremes of which are "blocked" and "indiscriminate." In a family where communication is *blocked*, family members cannot be frank about their needs, or there are many taboo topics. At the other end of the spectrum, there is no such as thing as too much information. Some families, or some family members, have trouble distinguishing the important from the trivial. The resulting background noise makes planning challenging. Moreover, some family members are unable to moderate how much information they share, with whom they share it, and how they share it. Openness is good, but such indiscriminate communication can create the feedback loop of increased guardedness by other family members. If an adviser leaves this problem unattended, some family members may ultimately begin to mistrust the FWTP process.

Use of Typology

Typology is helpful in FWTP because it alerts the planner to certain familial characteristics that will affect a family's ability to achieve wealth continuity. Therapists and advisers share an interest in healthy family relationships as a core goal. Moreover, a family's place on the continuums of cohesion and adaptability affects its ability to achieve the other key components of family wealth continuity. Families on each end of the adaptability, cohesion, and communication continuums typically interact in ways that create positive feedback loops, reinforcing and extending the characteristics of a given extreme. Families in the middle ranges of the continuums typically interact in ways that produce negative feedback loops, regulating the forces that might move them toward an extreme.

The cohesion continuum is critical in assessing the particular challenges a family will face in sharing wealth. A disengaged family is unlikely to want to share wealth, but if wealth must shared, such a family will face difficulty in developing stewardship models involving the entire family. Their lack of ongoing experiences with each other may lead to a lack of trust, and the family may need to use special governance systems as a substitute for trust. At the other end of the continuum, the enmeshed family will typically opt to share all kinds of wealth, whether or not doing so is the best model for stewardship. In addition, these two kinds of families face special challenges in developing a legacy. A disengaged family has a hard time seeing the value of developing a family legacy, while an enmeshed family has a harder time allowing members to individuate and generate the kind of diverse experience that will support an enduring legacy.

Because the FWTP process is about adapting the family wealth system to achieve family wealth continuity, the adaptability continuum is particularly important. Chaotic families have trouble making decisions about stewardship and defining a legacy, because these tasks require leadership and organization, both of which are often lacking in these families. These families also face challenges in the planning process itself, and especially in following through with FWTP, because of their lack of structure. The rigid family, on the other hand, may not be willing or able to adapt or change sufficiently. Rigid families may not be able to build into their plans sufficient flexibility to accommodate the inevitable changes that accompany movement through the individual, family, and business life cycles. Fortunately, however, each extreme characteristic may afford certain special capacities in the planning process. A chaotic family may be better able to stomach the kinds of changes required in FWTP than would its rigid counterpart, because change is so familiar to a chaotic family. A rigid family brings the capacity to both define and stick to FWTP.

The family characteristic of communication is embedded in each of the other continuums, as each family type brings with it a typical style of communication. But an adviser to a family in FWTP must also classify the productivity of communication itself within a family. Productive planning requires open communication within the family and the ability to cope with conflict productively. Understanding the family wealth system and designing a plan requires open and honest communication about the family and its individual members. Ideally, family members are frank about their needs and goals and allow communication of others' needs and goals. But few if any families are ideal. Family members may be cautious in sharing information, and there are likely some topics a family finds difficult to discuss at all. The adviser needs to find ways to open communication gradually by building trust in the process and in the people involved. If family members can be frank, when their needs and desires come into conflict the adviser can help them by finding ways to make this conflict productive.

Wealth Behavior Themes

The typology just described gives the adviser an overall sense of a family's general behavior. In FWTP, the next step is to discover how these characteristics manifest themselves in identifiable patterns of behavior relating to wealth. These themes play out over and over, often through generations, when wealth is at stake. For example, the theme of control and abdication draws from the adaptability continuum. An adviser who identifies a family as on the rigid end of the adaptability continuum will be on the lookout for control and abdication patterns of behavior in assessing the components of the family's wealth transition plan.

Some themes draw from the continuum of adaptability, others from the cohesion continuum. We have chosen here to illustrate only one communication theme: the family's ability to cope with conflict. This theme fundamentally affects a family's ability to understand its other behavior themes. Moreover, within almost every family, there is one meta-theme at work: trust and fear. Members of some families inherently trust one another, while members of others are fearful that if they are vulnerable to each other in any sphere of wealth, they will be hurt emotionally, financially, or in their connection to the family and others. It is not possible to change the level of trust within a family through FWTP (we leave that to family therapists), but the structures created within this process reflect the level of trust within the family. A fearful family, one that does not trust, needs a great deal of help in FWTP to build structures that begin to create a feedback loop of trust.

Figure 6.2 illustrates the connection between the typology of families and common wealth themes encountered in FWTP. Each major characteristic has its own attendant themes. Communication themes are

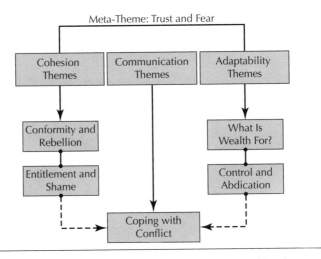

FIGURE **6.2**   How Family Typology Relates to Wealth Themes

embedded in each of the others, because how a family communicates, what it is able to communicate about, and how it approaches conflict are all critical to other themes. Overshadowing all themes is, of course, the meta-theme of trust and fear. For example, the degree of openness or reserve with which families relate to one another will affect their ability to resolve conflict, as will the way families manage the potentials for conflict between facts and the fantasies, which may be in conflict with those facts when family members don't communicate well with one another.

Needs, Capacities, and Constraints

Every pattern of wealth behavior brings with it certain needs that must be met in order to achieve family wealth continuity. Needs fall into three categories: tangible needs, emotional needs, and process needs. *Tangible* needs include financial wherewithal; *emotional* needs include the security that may accompany that financial wherewithal. *Process* needs are particularly important for the adviser. What kinds of processes should be created to produce a successful transition plan? Families of different types have very different process needs. Some families, for example, need a timetable, while others simply need time.

Although it is tempting to label certain wealth behavior patterns in a negative way, even the most frustrating of these patterns generates certain strengths, skills, and experiences (capacities) that the adviser can draw upon or develop to implement a plan. Playing to the strengths of a family rather than its weaknesses will make the process easier. The adviser can help the family draw upon its strengths by identifying and using these capacities, rather than letting the family become bogged down in facing its weaknesses.

Finally, patterns of behavior impose certain constraints that affect the FWTP process. Unless the process requires a family to conclude therapy successfully, it will not be possible to avoid these constraints. Sometimes, constraints can make what seems to be a perfectly plausible plan difficult or even impossible to implement. The role of the adviser is to help a family realistically assess its constraints and determine which are real and which are illusory. Often what appears to be a constraint is simply an unspoken need. An adviser can help a family use its existing or developing capacities to meet that need, and thereby remove the constraint.

The following sections discuss certain wealth behavior themes commonly encountered in wealth transition planning. Accompanying each theme is a chart summarizing the needs, capacities, and constraints that are characteristic of each theme. This discussion does not catalog every theme, and most advisers will identify, as they work with various families, other important themes that affect FWTP in important ways. Advisers can easily apply this methodology to newly discovered themes as a way to catalog the issues that a family will face as it comes to grips with its particular patterns of behavior.

Cohesion Themes: Conformity and Rebellion

Some families kick their young out at eighteen to find themselves, and take pride (perhaps secretly) in children striking out on their own path, even if that appears to be a rejection of family values. Other families assume that each child, or a designated child, will follow in the family business or conform to other expectations about where they live, what they do, and even whom they marry. As these children move through the next developmental stages of their families, they continue to struggle with separation and connection, and find ways to establish their own identities yet conform to family expectations sufficiently to be included in the core family system. Observing whether those who go into the family business do so willingly, reluctantly, or unmindfully will provide important clues into the issues of conformity and rebellion within the family.

During transition planning, the theme of rebellion and conformity raises structural questions that will be critical in developing a successful plan. An adviser can help a family explore questions about sharing wealth, such as how a child, whose journey toward greater individuation takes a completely different path, should equitably share the family's financial capital, particularly if those resources are generated through a family business. Does it matter whether that path was achieved through what family members view as rebellion? How does an individual who does not follow the expected course maintain a sense of connection to the family? How do differing levels of financial well-being affect the family's ability to stay closely connected if one family member or a branch of the family enjoys significantly less financial capital than the rest?

Advisers can help families that are caught up in the theme of conformity and rebellion by designing processes and structures that match the needs, capacities, and constraints summarized in *Figure 6.3*. The

FIGURE **6.3**   Conformity and Rebellion

Families or Family Members Who Value Rebellion		Families or Family Members Who Value Conformity
Need: • Support for experimentation • Acceptance that mistakes will be made • Multiple pathways to financial independence	NEEDS	*Need:* • Recognition of commitment to family • Process for keeping connections among family members intact • Ways to build and preserve wealth if roles change
Typically have: • Flexibility • Tolerance for differences • Different experiences, skills, and connections on which to draw	CAPACITIES	*Typically have:* • Tenaciousness • Family support for status quo • Familiarity with family processes
But may be constrained by: • Unwillingness to acknowledge family legacy • Unwillingness to participate or require participation • Being far away, physically or emotionally	CONSTRAINTS	*But may be constrained by:* • Fear of allowing mistakes, because consequences seem too dire • Obligation to family, whether real or illusory • Inflexibility in the face of potential rebellion

adviser can also remind the family of the never-ending cycles of change discussed in Chapter 5. The developmental task of individuation is inevitable, yet even the most rebellious family member is likely to yearn, at predictable stages of the cycle, for closer family connections and traditions. A family, therefore, must plan for structures that support both individuation and connection. For example, in a family wealth system marked by conformity, the transition plan must take into account the very real possibility that family members will veer off their expected course and someone else will need to take their place in management and ownership roles.

Cohesion Themes: Entitlement and Shame

—THE HERNÁNDEZ FAMILY—

José Hernández, age twenty-seven

I'm twenty-seven years old and my life is passing before my eyes: I am the No. 1 gofer for Hernández Hardware now and forever. I only get paid a manager's salary, even though I do all the work. Dad comes by a couple of times a week and yells at me about inventory—as if it's rocket science.

I live at home with him. Dad used be fun, like the time he brought home that vintage Chevy for me to restore. A few years ago, my girlfriend and I were making plans to move down to Los Angeles, go to art school together, and maybe even get married. But then my mother got cancer again. She died, and my grandmother died too. She was the only one who ever really got what was happening with me, even if she did call me Ramón half the time. Dad was so out of it I felt I needed to stick around. Luisa's not here, and Bart is such a robot I knew he wouldn't be any help to Dad. Anyway, Carolyn got tired of waiting for me and moved on. I don't blame her; she got a scholarship to the Rhode Island School of Design. We keep in touch some.

Even though I live at home, I'm old enough to come and go as I please. Sure, I smoke a little *mota* with my friends, but it's not like I'm into worse stuff, and we both know there's much worse stuff. Dad should just chill. He's finally quit walking around talking to himself at night. Now he needs to focus on what he wants for himself and quit trying to run my life.

Bart and Luisa are set for life. Bart runs a construction company, which I own half of, but you'd never know it from the way Bart acts. I offer to help, but we always get in fights. I can't help it if I have the vision of an artist and he, well, like I said, he's a robot. Me, I want to have a life, hang out, and have some fun. That's what I tell Luisa. She's always calling me up from her cushy doctor's office in Los Angeles saying, "José, when are you going to grow up?" If anyone else said that they would have a fight on their hands, but nobody can really be mad at Luisa. I tell her being a grown-up is pretty overrated. At least she has a life. She's the only one who's been able to escape this family and Fresno.

If there is one theme that is pervasive in planning for the transition of a family business, it is *entitlement*—the belief that some or all of the rights to wealth within the family wealth system inure to a family member because of a specific characteristic of that individual. These rights include the right to love and emotional support, the right to enjoy financial wealth in its various forms, the right to employment, the right to financial support, or the right to use family assets at will and without contributing to their maintenance. The essence of entitlement is a sense of the right to enjoy the benefits of wealth, without being subject to any external standards of behavior or performance.

Various members of the Hernández family have spoken about José's lack of motivation, and these stories reveal the family's displeasure at what it interprets as his sense of entitlement. José doesn't help matters by being less than appreciative of his manager's salary at the store, refusing to talk with his family about his true desires, and opting for pastimes such as "hanging out" and "smoking a little *mota*." Yet he also reveals his motivations for staying in Fresno, and is the only member of the family who appears to have insight into just how hard it was for Bart to lose Elena.

The pervasive entitlement belief in families of wealth is that birth into the family entitles a family member to enjoy all of the sources of family wealth. Certainly, this is common in estate planning. Children typically feel entitled to share in their parents' wealth after the parents' deaths, although most children will not talk freely before their parents die about this sense of entitlement. Many parents fully agree with this principle, and their estate plans reflect this belief. But there can be a divergence of beliefs about this entitlement as well. An estate plan that directs assets to charity, or to a second or third family of a parent, can come as quite a shock to children, especially if it is a secret until the parents' deaths. Rigid gender roles can also create a sense of entitlement, as when, for example, a family views men as more capable in business than women. The men in the family may become accustomed to preferential treatment and thereby feel entitled to control the family business. Likewise, entitlement may be tied to birthright, birth order, age, or any other characteristic linked to a family pattern of behavior.

Most family businesses have struggled with a family member's sense of entitlement to participate in the business, receiving not just profits in the form of distributions, but also special treatment at the office or on the shop floor, perks such as a car or fringe benefit plans, or even lifetime employment, regardless of performance. Many families find themselves in a situation in which a family member is underperforming in the family business, but because of the entitlement belief, no one can challenge that person's performance. The business suffers, and the family suffers too, both financially and emotionally. Family members dare not raise the issue, because they have no language in which to express the problem. Raising it feels extremely risky to family relationships. This is a classic situation of confusion of the different sources of family wealth. One can be legitimately entitled to enjoy the acceptance of family without being automatically entitled to share in family financial wealth because of one's DNA.

Some family members experience the opposite of entitlement: shame. *Shame* is the inherent belief that one is not entitled to share in family wealth in its various forms, not because of external standards, but because of what one is or is not. This can express itself in a number of ways, including the rejection of the family's wealth in all its forms, or an inability to participate in family endeavors. It is not guilt, which is tied to a belief that one has performed badly; it is a belief that one is inherently not entitled to participate. Again, family attitudes and patterns of behavior can give rise to long-standing patterns of shame.

Advisers to families struggling with issues of entitlement and shame will focus on the characteristics described in *Figure 6.4.* The remedy for a family that finds itself caught up in the entitlement/shame theme is to seek the middle ground of *empowerment*. Families who empower their members are able to manage wealth successfully, and they understand that capital in all its forms brings rights and responsibilities. Empowerment means accepting that a certain level of financial wealth may entitle the family to a comfortable lifestyle, but

FIGURE **6.4**   Entitlement and Shame

Families or Family Members with History or Attitude of Entitlement		Families or Family Members with History or Attitude of Shame
Need: • Externally imposed standards of behavior • Support (financial and other) • Education and experience with productive pursuits	NEEDS	*Need:* • Real permission (given and received) to participate in family wealth • Acceptance of differences • Education and experience with productive pursuits
Typically have: • Close family ties • Bravado in the face of uncertainty	CAPACITIES	*Typically have:* • Desire to participate • Desire to please family • Willingness to share wealth
But may be constrained by: • Unruliness • Ill defined roles • Illusion • Fear of honest appraisal • Lack of useful skills	CONSTRAINTS	*But may be constrained by:* • Feelings of low self-worth • Lack of experience in effective participation • Unwillingness to take risks • Continuing family attitudes toward certain members

it must be balanced by each individual's strong desire to perform consistently with externally set guidelines and to give back to society in a meaningful way. Family members may act responsibly by making gifts of their wealth to others, finding ways to empower others to participate in wealth-building activities, or saving most or all of the financial resources for future generations. It is helpful for families in the FWTP process to understand that heirs need to learn to be responsible for the financial assets left to them, and that this process is more likely to be successful if it begins long before the assets come their way. The growth of a family's human capital encourages the growth of its financial and social capital. When the financial capital comes from an operating company, families need to be clear that birth does not necessarily make a person a valued asset in the family business.

Worst-case outcomes can be avoided if families learn to communicate openly, recognize and appreciate their individual differences, and create appropriate boundaries between the family and its businesses.

Adaptability Themes: Control and Abdication

—THE WILLIAMS FAMILY—

Helen Weinstein Williams, age forty-eight

When my first husband was killed in Bosnia, I was a wreck. I just stopped—I couldn't work, couldn't go out, and could barely be a mother to Rebecca. My parents tried to help. They lent me their apartment and helped me with Rebecca and money and everything. After about six months my father sat me down and told me I had to go back to work. He was right, I guess. You know, you don't think you'll ever get over that kind of thing, but you do, somehow—and here I am now with four wonderful kids and John and a full and happy life. Anyway, I haven't been much involved in our—my and John's—family finances, so I can't really tell you exactly what we own. I do know we own our apartment; my parents gave us that as a wedding gift. We have the business and a good amount of savings for retirement. John and I had planned to sit down and go over this regularly when we married, but it always seemed to get put off. Then came the twins, then the business, then Lisa. Having John handle it all is fine with me, actually, because it's all I can do to keep up with the family. My father always took care of all these things, and as far as I could see, my mother didn't need to be involved—she was an artist, not an accountant. Now, though, I'm beginning to wonder if that's really what happened. She seems so on the ball with the investments in her trust, talking about diversification and betas and things like that. And John's bypass surgery last year made me think that I need to get a grip on all this, too. He won't tell you this, but he's not cutting back or watching his weight or doing anything that he's supposed to. He could drop dead tomorrow. I don't even know if he has any life insurance like he did when he worked for the firm.

During her marriage, Helen Williams abdicated almost all responsibility and accountability for the financial health of her nuclear family. Whether John welcomes the control his wife has abdicated is not clear, but he certainly has benefited from it in making his financial arrangements with Cindy.

Control and abdication issues permeate planning for the transition of financial wealth. A core event in any FWTP process will be the change in how this kind of wealth is managed, even if it simply means that another person will be making the decisions. Wealth founders often govern wealth unilaterally, and for them control is natural, so they take it for granted. A change in this governance structure requires an explicit paradigm shift, which is often difficult, particularly for business owners. Both control and abdication often arise from long-standing patterns of family behavior. This is the Williams situation, where Helen and John fell into a pattern of behavior by default, not explicit choice. It was easy for Helen to do this because she was imitating what she thought was her own family's approach to the management of financial wealth. (Whether she was correct or not is a different story.) Departing from these patterns will require an explicit change, and family support for that change.

Fortunately, control and abdication issues are often the easiest ones to identify when seeking to understand a family, except where a formal governance structure masks reality. Helen is puzzled that her mother seemed so uninvolved in financial matters, yet now seems knowledgeable. This anomaly, along with the trigger event of John's surgery, may act as a catalyst for Helen (and thereby John) to change. For the Williams family, Miriam is already modeling the necessary change, the antidote to both excessive control and excessive abdication. She is expressing the desire and the capacity to participate effectively in the management of her wealth. *Participation* requires learning how to manage capital in all its forms. Yet participation also means allowing room for others in making decisions, being honest about the facts, collaborating in joint decision making, and allowing others to make the inevitable mistakes that come with learning. In helping a family move toward participation and away from control/abdication, however, an adviser must pay careful attention to the needs, capacities, and constraints typical of this pattern of behavior, which are summarized in *Figure 6.5.*

Adaptability Themes: What Is Wealth For?

—THE WILLIAMS FAMILY—

Helen Weinstein Williams, age forty-eight

I saw my father's lawyers two days ago. They were being ever weirder than usual. They hemmed and hawed and finally gave me a letter from my father, along with all the trust documents. Then they hustled me out of there right away, and now I know why—I'm sure they didn't want to answer any of my questions. So I went down to the college library where I could have a little peace and quiet and not be disturbed. And, well, here it is.

FIGURE **6.5**   Control and Abdication

Families or Family Members for Whom Control Is Important		Families or Family Members with a History of Abdication
Need: • To find value in others' success • Faith that others can "step up" • Time to find and adjust to new roles	NEEDS	*Need:* • Willingness to educate themselves • Courage to take risks and make mistakes • Time and experience to accept new roles
Typically have: • Experience • Force of will • A plan in mind	CAPACITIES	*Typically have:* • Motivation after a trigger event occurs • Flexibility, because they are not attached to any particular plan • More influence than they think
But may be constrained by: • Fear that others may not be able to perform • Lack of alternative activities • Unwillingness to accept inevitability of trigger events	CONSTRAINTS	*But may be constrained by:* • Fear of alienating other family members • Fear of "not knowing how" • Continuing family attitudes toward those in control and those who abdicate

"Dear Helen:

"I wanted you to have this just in case I died before I found a way to talk to you about the trust I'm setting up for you. First of all, I want you to know that I love you. You have been the apple of my eye ever since you were a little girl. You weren't like all the other little girls around here. Barbie dolls? Forget it. Boys? Not a chance. All the time you were growing up, all you ever wanted to do was practice your cello. You begged us for lessons, trips to the Lincoln Center, and special bows. You could play like an angel, and I guess I'd say you have the heart of an artist, like your mother. All I ever wanted to do was make sure the two of you had a good life. I am so proud of you.

"When Steve died, I know it broke your heart. You got so quiet. We didn't know how to help you except with money. That might have been a mistake, but what's done is done. When you married John, you know I had my doubts at first. He was just too different from you, I thought.

I was wrong, though. We grew to love him and he took good care of you and Rebecca. You may remember that he and I had some words about the prenuptial agreement, and I want you to know I was just trying to protect you. I never thought it would be a real problem if the marriage lasted as long as it has.

"I'm not saying this very well, so I'll just come out and say it. John has a son with another woman, a woman named Cindy Jones who works with him at the bars. His name is Bradley Jones. I know this because I had a private investigator follow John, and I know you'll be angry with me about that. I'm quite sure the affair has been over a long time, or I would have found a way to tell you. You kept saying that John had to work late and couldn't join us for Shabbat. As it turned out, he really was working all those times, not seeing that woman. I didn't tell your mother, for obvious reasons. You will have to decide how much you want to tell her.

"So, I had intended to give you and John each a million dollars, but now I feel I have to protect you. I've put it all in a trust just for you. I want it to be available to you and my grandchildren, but not for John and his other family. If you don't want to stay with John, you won't have to. I've asked a banker friend to be the trustee, and to help you make decisions about how to use the money. I know I should have found a way to talk with you myself, but I just couldn't. I thought this news might send you back into that terrible depression. I'm sorry. I know you love John, but he's a *ligner* [liar] and it's my job to protect you. Please don't be angry with me. Take care of Mameh.

"I love you,

"Tateh"

What, exactly, is family wealth for? Does wealth have *intrinsic* value (meaning it is valued for its own sake), or only *instrumental* value (meaning it is valued for its usefulness to achieve other goals)? Scrooge, the central character in Charles Dickens' *A Christmas Carol*, exemplifies belief in the intrinsic value of financial capital (along with a total disregard for social and human capital). The wealthy playboy in the movie *Sabrina* is his opposite, exemplifying belief in the purely instrumental value of financial capital. Most families and their members are somewhere in between these two extremes, and within a family members may differ.

Jacob Weinstein believed that having a happy family is an end in itself, although it fosters other desirable goals as well. He would probably have labeled the development of human capital (particularly education) as being of intrinsic value. After all, he cultivated his daughter's early devotion to the cello rather than insisting that she conform to popular culture. It is clear he valued his wife and daughter, but we know little about his wider social connections, other than work. His daughter focuses on her busy family life, and obviously values it, at least so far. We know nothing of her philanthropy, if any.

And what about financial capital, such as portfolios of stocks and bonds or retirement plans? Many families will place financial wealth farther along the continuum toward having instrumental value: The function of money is to provide funds for a certain purpose. Jacob seems to suggest this perspective in his letter: "all he wanted" was to provide a good life for his wife and daughter.

The family business is the most difficult part of capital to categorize. For many families, and particularly founders of businesses, owning a business has intrinsic value, in addition to instrumental value. Families put their hearts and souls into a business, and they continue to do so every day. It is very often a central personal identifier: the business is "who they are," and the idea of not having the business threatens their very identity.

Exploring this theme helps define fundamental patterns of transition and suggests the legal structures that will be necessary to transfer wealth. It also begins to answer the "why" of FWTP. Why should this wealth be transferred at all? And why is one transition plan better than another?

Exploring the value of wealth can often reveal the fear in parents and grandparents that transferring too much wealth to the next generation may take away their initiative to work or undermine their self-confidence. In other words, these families believe the process of acquiring wealth on one's own is valuable. In some cases, wealth becomes a liability rather than an asset when people are not prepared sufficiently to manage it. Parents or grandparents may feel guilty about giving the next generation too much too soon. Young adults need to be able to balance quality of life and a desire for freedom with their parents' desire for them to be capable of earning a living, becoming productive members of society, and, eventually, managing inherited wealth. While their parents may have worked to get ahead, their children often take for granted the affluence that their parents have provided. Being aware of individual and family life cycles and exploring the theme of "what wealth is for" helps parents and grandparents appropriately transfer wealth to the younger generation.

When a family is unclear about what its wealth is for, it is unlikely to articulate its true goals during the transition of wealth. An adviser can help a family discover how wealth both defines and supports its members, and understand the relative importance of family relationships and family wealth. Generations within a family often have very different perspectives, which in turn reveal different needs and constraints (*Figure 6.6*). For example, a senior generation that views a family business as having intrinsic value may judge the next generation (whose members take a more instrumental approach) as lacking commitment to the business. A younger generation may be populated by playboys (or -girls), or by children who vow to spend more time with their kids than the founders/parents spent with them.

FIGURE **6.6** What is Wealth For?

Families or Family Members Who Believe Wealth Is of Intrinsic Value		Families or Family Members Who Believe Wealth Is of Instrumental Value
Need: • Income stream to support family • Confidence that other meaningful activities will be available • A family legacy independent of wealth story • Time and process to adjust to change	NEEDS	*Need:* • Income stream to support family and other activities • Process to hear other family members' perspectives on value of wealth
Typically have: • Tenaciousness and commitment • Influence in family • Cooperation of others • Motivation to protect family members and family	CAPACITIES	*Typically have:* • Objectivity • Ability to quantify needs accurately • Willingness to let go • Willingness to take action and involve outsiders in process
But may be constrained by: • Lack of objectivity • Need to "hold on" • Obligation to family, either real or illusory • Fear of loss	CONSTRAINTS	*But may be constrained by:* • Unwillingness to acknowledge family legacy • Irresponsibility • Not being on the same page as family

Communication Themes: Coping with Conflict

—THE MARSHALL FAMILY—
Billy Rob Marshall, age sixteen

One thing about Granddaddy is, you always know where you stand. You know if you're being smart or stupid or sinful, 'cause he'll tell you straight out. Then it's over and done. Or that's the way it used to be, anyhow. Like when Aunt Ruthie brought Pam home to the ranch for the first time. You know, I hadn't seen Ruthie in so long, and none of us had ever seen two women, like, married to each other. Granddaddy said to Aunt Ruthie and Pam, "I know that's not what the Bible had in mind about the sacred state of marriage." The next day Granddaddy and Ruthie went out to clean the barns. They were out there for a long time and they scared the horses with all their shouting. But when it came time for Sunday dinner, it was bless-our-family-and-welcome-Aunt-Pam-and-pass-the-biscuits-to-Pam-boy-where-are-your-manners, just like it always is when anyone joins up with the Marshalls. But like I said, that's the way it used to be. Now Grandpa blames my dad if any little thing goes wrong. Dad and Grandpa stalk around all the time. And Dad is drinking again. He thinks I don't know but I do. I can't talk to either of them anymore.

All families have a dominant communication style that will pervade the wealth transition planning process, although not every member may share that style. Some families have a certain ingrained openness. They are happy to talk, write e-mails, and attend meetings. They are willing to share personal information right away. They hash things through long into the night. They think they know everything about each other. They will fight in front of their advisers, or anyone else. These families speak of honesty, compassion, and integrity. They usually welcome new members warmly, and let them know what they think of them along the way. This is the kind of family the Marshalls seem to be, or at least have been in the past.

Other families are more reserved. They talk less. It takes longer to earn their trust and for them to share personal information. They fight behind closed doors. They learn about each other through back channels. They like memos. They want to think things through themselves before discussing anything with an adviser. These families speak of kindness, reflection, and integrity. They may take a wait-and-see attitude with newcomers, but are unfailingly polite during the examination period.

Adapting the family wealth system to foster family wealth continuity will inevitably lead to conflict, and each family has a style of approaching and managing conflict based on long-standing patterns of behavior. The adviser to a family will be alert to how the family's communication style relates to its ability to approach and resolve conflict and to the needs, capacities, and constraints of each style (see *Figure 6.7*). It is tempting to generalize that open families are better suited to conflict resolution than reserved ones, but that is not always the case. Many families who seem extremely reserved have time-honored ways of reaching an accord on difficult issues. However, the adviser must take into account each family's style of communication in choosing processes that will foster open and honest communication and will lead to productive, not merely painful, conflict.

Almost every family harbors at least one topic that is seemingly impossible to discuss. These are the topics that will stretch conflict resolution skills to the limit, because family members will be fighting their own unwillingness to approach issues. In the Marshall family, for example, Ruth and her father seem to have come to an understanding regarding her sexual

FIGURE 6.7   Coping with Conflict

Families or Family Members Whose Conflict Style Is Open		Families or Family Members Whose Conflict Style Is Reserved
Need: • Time and a forum to discuss issues and reach consensus • Focus and facilitation to allow them to make progress • Process to move from "talking about it" to "doing it"	NEEDS	*Need:* • Safe forum for discussion • Preparation exercises preceding discussion • Careful consideration of who is involved, and when
Typically have: • History of resolving conflict while preserving relationships • Storytelling abilities • Willingness to take risks in sharing ideas	CAPACITIES	*Typically have:* • History of working things out in a quiet way • Cordial relationships • Respect for others' privacy
But may be constrained by: • Too many cooks in the kitchen • Too much conflict to reach resolution • Inability to reach consensus	CONSTRAINTS	*But may be constrained by:* • Fear of hurting others or damaging family relationships • Hesitancy to share information • Inexperience with resolving conflict openly

orientation, but we sense that Billy Rob is in the dark about how that happened or what it means. With this family's inability to move beyond its catastrophic loss, the revelation of Arnie's drinking and Billy Rob's isolation from both his father and grandfather signal another taboo topic: the role of alcohol in the lives and deaths of its members. The adviser must find ways for this family to safely discuss what happened in 2004 and how patterns of family behavior, perhaps reaching back to before Johnny Ray's generation, will adversely impact family wealth continuity.

The Meta-Theme of Trust and Fear

Late at night, John Williams nurses a drink and muses:

> I know Helen will leave me and take the kids when she finds out. She should. Even if she could find it in her heart to accept Brad, the fact that I've kept it a secret all these years will be intolerable to her. It really was only a fling with Cindy, over for years now, but it happened right after Lisa was born with Down syndrome, when Helen was having such a hard time. She'd never understand why I kept Cindy on as manager and how she helps the business now. Keeping this secret has become torture.

While feeding the horses, Johnny Ray muses:

> We—the 112th Cavalry—we were the last to serve on horseback. We rode those Australian ponies over in the jungle, then the Army got rid of horses for good when we went to help the Seabees. Now I'm as outdated as those ponies were then. I can't handle all this at my age, and there's nobody to carry on after I go to my Maker. It all seemed so clear before that wreck…

Driving home from dinner at his dad's house, Bart, Jr. reflects:

> I know Dad's lonely. I know he feels he's earned the right to have some fun—and he has. I just know Samantha is a gold digger. She's thirty years younger. What could she possibly see in him except a meal ticket? I just can't see being partners with Luisa and José (and maybe even Samantha and her kids) in the store if Dad dies. Luisa will be a doctor to the rich and famous and it will be just José and me. It would be worse than the so-called partnership I've got with him now. I'm so tired I can't think straight.

"Trust versus fear" is a theme in the planning process that permeates most families' concerns. Even in the healthiest of families, parents and children, have fears about the future that come down to two fundamental questions:

❑ Do the transferors of wealth truly trust the transferees' ability and willingness to manage family wealth assets in ways that are consistent with the family's ideas of good stewardship, healthy family relationships, and the continuation of the family legacy?

❑ Do the transferees who will share wealth in the next generation truly trust each other to manage family wealth assets in ways that are consistent with the family's ideas of good stewardship, healthy family relationships, and the continuing creation of the family legacy?

Trust underlies all three components of family wealth continuity. It is central to healthy family relationships, the development of a positive family legacy, and stewardship of wealth.

But tackling trust issues is a risky business, for at least three reasons. First, there is no one definition of trust; people mean different things when they say, for example, "I trust my sister." It may mean they trust in her abilities, or trust in her values, or that she can be trusted to look out for the person extending trust. Or it could mean some combination of these attributes, but not all of them.[2] One sibling might trust another's ability (as José probably trusts Bart's ability), but not his or her benevolence. When a person trusts another, it means that he or she has a positive expectation of future interactions. Trust is built over time, through repeated interactions that allow for an assessment of abilities, values, and benevolence. Certain relationships assume trust: for example, Helen trusts (or at least trusted) her husband. A common problem in the planning process is that there is often a lack of experience in the areas in which trust is required. Moreover, this lack of experience may be masked by an assumption that the characteristics that a person exhibits in one wealth subsystem, such as the family subsystem, carry over into other realms.

Second, even if a family could agree on a definition of trust, how would it be measured? Family members may report trust or lack thereof, but these reports are notoriously inaccurate. There is no "trust-o-meter" to measure the quality of relationships among members of families, some of whom may not even be participating in the planning process.

If a family's communication is usually closed, it is challenging for family members to be completely honest about how much they do or don't trust each other and then share the same car home from the adviser's office. Inquiring about specific instances in which family members have taken business, investment, and other risks with one another may be helpful. Asking about the need for structures that act as a substitute for trust may test the waters as well. An adviser must be alert to the red flags that may indicate trust is an issue. For example, some members of a senior generation may have a strong desire to keep their wealth transition plan a secret until their deaths. Those clients usually love their families and want them to be safe and secure. But the unintentional message they can send with their secrecy is that they don't trust themselves or their heirs. An adviser could test the client's motivations for secrecy and show the client how this choice is intimately tied to trust issues. Perhaps the client doesn't know how to explain the choices that he or she is making, or is fearful of eliciting heirs' criticism or disappointment in those choices. Exploring other options for discussing all or part of the plan with heirs may prevent the situation in which, after death, it is too late to restore lost trust.

Finally, the FWTP process is necessarily about the future, when the situation will be different and people will be at different stages of their life cycles, responding to different developmental needs. At least some of the participants won't be around to monitor or control the situation, or to assess the trustworthiness of the others. The classic situation is a husband and wife discussing the disposition of their estate after the death of the first spouse. If they both agree that their children should inherit the estate left over after both their deaths, do the spouses trust one another not to squander family wealth on a second marriage or relationship after the first spouse's death? A wife may completely trust her husband today, but she has no way of knowing what he will be like five, ten, or fifteen years after her death. Asking her to trust that unknown person of the future is very different from asking her to trust the person she knows intimately today. However, husbands and wives are likely to be on the same life cycle path.

This situation is exacerbated for parents and children, because what masquerades as trust is more likely to be the capacity to let go of being able to monitor, control, or even influence people in the future. Family members vary widely in their ability to let go, and thus may require governance structures that allow a degree of control beyond the grave.

The opposite end of the trust continuum is not mistrust, but fear. Some people fear the FWTP process itself because of its complexity, its intrusiveness, and the likelihood that family secrets will be revealed. Fear looms large at the outset of the wealth transition planning process. Family members understandably fear losing all sorts of things: physical and mental capacity, power and control, financial wealth, status, the love of or access to other family members, or the illusions that they believe hold the family together. Johnny Ray Marshall illustrates this most poignantly in his fear that everything he built is "going to waste." Family members may not even be able to articulate their specific fears at this stage in the process.

The wealth transition process does not usually create these fears, but it does force participants to consider them realistically. Fear stymies. Fearful family members are unlikely to be able to communicate about what is really important, accept reality, let go of fantasies, take risks, and make and be confident in their decisions. If these fears overwhelm the participants, they may avoid planning altogether or may adopt ill-advised plans just to "get it over with." Yet fear also motivates family members to pursue a wealth transition plan, and to stick to the program when the going gets tough. If carefully planned and implemented, the wealth planning process itself offers ways to calm those fears and replace them with trust.

Loss of Autonomy

The wealth transition planning process can itself create one kind of fear: the fear of loss of autonomy, which can lead to dependence, shame, and doubt. A salient question is this: does the senior generation fear a loss of financial, physical, emotional, mental, or social autonomy if its members transfer assets and authority while still living? For example, while certain tax strategies may save significant estate taxes, the senior generation may be unwilling to sign off on them because of the potential for becoming dependent on others after a lifetime of independence.

Loss of autonomy may cut a wide swath, from losing the right to drive a vehicle, to losing the legal authority to manage investments, to losing the option to stay in the family home until death. Fear of lost autonomy may keep a client from implementing wealth transition strategies in a timely manner. That fear may be misunderstood by both family and adviser if open discussion and risk analysis of financial, legal, and quality of life variables are not possible.

Power and Control

It is impossible to talk about fear and trust without talking about power and control. The fear of abuse of power, being controlled, or being put in a situation in which one is powerless is anathema to the creation and maintenance of authentic trust. Because they are intimately tied to a family's tolerance for its members' individuation, as well as to family patterns about what behaviors are acceptable, one must consider how power and control are now and have been wielded in a family when creating a wealth transition plan. Is there a matriarch or patriarch who has exerted control over family members, financially or otherwise? How does the conflict style of the family reflect power and control issues? Are there screamers? Do some members seem silenced? Or is there a healthy peer-like relationship between parents and adult children?

A second question of power and control involves those who will share wealth after the transition. Are there fears that one or more of them will try to control wealth inappropriately, or exert other kinds of control or power over the others? Do they seem to trust each other? Do they have experience with one another to justify that trust? Do they seem content to defer to the expertise of one or more of them?

The adviser's goal is not to create trust. That task is impossible in the context of a wealth transition process, because one learns the fundamental ability to trust in the first years of life and practices it daily thereafter. Instead, the adviser's task is to move the family away from fear and toward the trust end of the continuum. An important part of this movement is the alleviation of fear through processes of safe communication and decision making. This can happen if families acquire the language to discuss trust and fear issues without blame. For families without a good storehouse of built-in trust to draw upon, the adviser can provide ideas for structures and processes that are "trust substitutes." In such a case, even if a family member cannot trust another member directly, he or she can trust a process or structure that replaces trust with accountability.

Implications of Patterns of Behavior for Business Families

Every family will have one or two dominant wealth themes that the adviser must take into account when developing a FWTP process. By identifying these themes and exploring how they play out in a family, the FWTP adviser can begin to understand the needs of the family, the constraints within which the adviser must develop the plan, and the capacities of those family members who are available to assist in the process.

These patterns of wealth behavior also inform plan design. Patterns of wealth behavior evolve through feedback loops that often repeat over generations. The specific components of FWTP should take these into consideration and develop interventions and structures that will support desired outcomes. For example, if it becomes clear that siblings do not trust each other to manage wealth, a governance system must be put in place that will serve as a substitute for trust until true trust is developed. A family that struggles with control and abdication will have to understand how these two characteristics feed upon each other and accentuate the worst of both. Role development plans may assist them in interrupting that cycle and moving toward genuine participation.

Of all of the various aspects of the family wealth system, it is the patterns of behavior that are most likely to derail a FWTP process. Most planners deal adequately with the components of the family wealth system, even though they give short shrift to certain nonfinancial forms of wealth. Many are alert to the connections among these components, and to how life cycle changes affect a plan's deployment. It is more difficult to deal with wealth behavior patterns. These are largely invisible to the outsider, and families may not be willing to admit to certain wealth behavior patterns because of their negative connotations. But when perfectly good estate plans are not implemented, the culprit is often patterns of wealth behavior that the process failed to address.

CHAPTER NOTES

1. See generally, David H. Olson, Candayce S. Russell, and Douglas H. Sprenkel, eds., *The Circumplex Model: Systemic Assessment and Treatment of Families* (Haworth Press, 1989).

2. Harvard researchers Kacie LaChapelle and Louis B. Barnes have identified four useful components that create a climate of trust in family-owned business:

- ❏ Character (integrity, honesty, credibility)

- ❏ Competency (skills, expertise, performance in the context of decision making and judgment)

- ❏ Predictability (kept promises, consistent responses and behavior)

- ❏ Caring (empathy, understanding)

See their "The Trust Catalyst in Family-Owned Businesses," *Family Business Review,* Vol. XI, No. 1 (March 1998), pp. 1–17.

CHAPTER 7

THE EXTERNAL ENVIRONMENT

A FUNDAMENTAL CHARACTERISTIC of the family wealth system is its *openness*. Multiple forces outside the system penetrate its boundaries, with the potential to affect its components deeply for good or ill. This chapter focuses on the impact of those forces.

External forces present themselves in a variety of forms, from people to ideas, from government regulation to industry competitors. Families accept new members through marriages, partnerships, births, adoptions, and new friendships, each of which inevitably changes the family wealth system by increasing its complexity. Families also draw upon outside expertise in solving problems. New people, new ideas, and new processes work constantly to change the family wealth system. Family wealth transition planning (FWTP) advisers are themselves an important external force at work within the system.

General economic conditions, such as interest rates, economic growth, energy costs, and inflation buffet families no matter how great their financial wealth. Business trends in general, as well as those specific to an industry, affect families with a significant stake in operating businesses. Governmental regulation may also influence the family wealth system. Regulation is more or less a given in any business, but families with significant philanthropic goals must also contend with Congress's cyclical focus on private foundations and public charities, the latest round of which came in 2006.[1] Many of these external influences shape the family wealth system in ways that are not congruent with a family's needs or capacities.

As the planning process evolves, new structures will be introduced, which must complement existing arrangements or replace them, and which must adequately deal with the external forces continually at work on the system.

External Threats and Opportunities: The Evolution of Legal Entities

—THE MARSHALL FAMILY—
Arnold (Arnie) Marshall, age fifty-nine

Our lawyers over in Dallas had told us for years that we should have a whole herd of little corporations to do all the things we do around here, instead of one corporation. They kept at us about liability and lawsuits and all that. Dad always pooh-poohed it, and mostly he just ignored the one corporation we had. Well, we should have listened. When that accident happened, my son was out driving one of the ranch trucks. He was supposed to be bringing some feed back from San Angelo, but instead he had a gang of his friends with him and they were all drinking. Anyhow, you know the rest, and it seems like everybody in the world is suing all of us. Sure, Mom and Dad nod when the lawyers talk tough, but they were really close to the families of those kids that were killed or hurt. They wouldn't be able to hold their heads up around here if they truly fought the lawsuits. The lawyers told us that the only thing we did right was set up those retirement plans, which was not the right thing to say to Dad. Me, I don't know what to say without trashing my son's memory. So I don't say much.

Most business families embark on the FWTP process with some legal entities or arrangements already in place. Their lawyers and accountants have recommended corporations, limited liability companies (LLCs), trusts, and perhaps even more exotic legal devices to contend with potential threats from outsiders. For an entity to achieve these benefits, state law imposes certain requirements. For example, when using the corporate form, a business must observe corporate formalities: the owners must treat the entity as a separate legal person, governed by its board, and not as the owners' alter ego or checkbook. The price of violating this rule may be a piercing of the corporate veil, which is apparently what happened in the Marshall situation. The principle of maintaining a separate entity is not limited to corporations, of course. In trusts, a trustee's violation of the rules of the road, such as prohibitions on using trust assets for personal purposes and on mixing personal and trust assets, may lead to the imposition of personal liability on the trustee for trust obligations.

A legal entity created for defensive purposes perfectly illustrates the potential for clashes between internal and external forces within the family wealth system. Because these entities evolve within a family wealth system as a response to external (nonfamily) forces, they do not necessarily serve internal (family) goals. Often, externally imposed requirements collide with existing patterns within the family wealth system, which explains why families often fail to meet basic requirements that their lawyers have characterized as essential.

In the Marshall family, the lawsuits and their effect on family wealth are important clues into the patterns of wealth behavior in the family. In families like the Marshalls, where a patriarch exercises a high degree of control, compliance with externally imposed standards may collide with the autonomy he requires. That person may actively rebel against the use of these entities. In addition, the Marshall family demonstrates how entitlement and shame issues affect family decisions. A family that believes it is special may not truly believe that they need these kinds of defensive legal entities for their activities, even in high-risk environments. After the accident, the family's shame contributed to the decision to attempt to compensate the injured families, which greatly complicated settlement of the lawsuits.

This clash between internal needs and external forces is not limited to the creation of defensive legal entities. These entities also evolve to take advantage of opportunities. Proper use of legal entities helps in identifying the people and assets that can benefit from some special advantage, such as a tax benefit or regulatory exemption. For example, if proper procedures are followed, tax deferral or deductions may arise from the use of qualified retirement plans, education savings vehicles, public charities, and charitable trusts, to name just a few devices. Families are less likely to rebel against requirements that bestow some value on them, but may still struggle with implementing the specific requirements for qualification. Chaotic families in particular are less likely than other families to follow through with ongoing compliance requirements and other formalities.

At the outset of the engagement, the FWTP adviser must deal with existing legal entities that became part of the family wealth system to protect it against outsiders or to allow the family to take advantage of special benefits. In some situations, an entity may be around for reasons that no one can remember and that serve no current purpose. Or an entity may appear to serve no purpose, but in fact be the cash drawer for some family members. The FWTP adviser must assess both the continuing viability of these entities and the family's ability to use them, given the internal workings of the family wealth system. Moreover, the FWTP process is likely to result in the creation of new legal entities, which must coordinate with existing entities. In the design of wealth transfer structures, the adviser must be aware of those patterns of wealth behavior within a family that affect its ability to maintain these entities and use them to full advantage.

The Impact of Income Taxes on the Family Wealth System

—THE HERNÁNDEZ FAMILY—

Luisa Hernández, age thirty-three

Growing up, all us kids worked at the hardware store. When I turned thirteen, I think, Papá put an advertisement for a cleaning crew on the refrigerator. My brother Bart told me he'd been through all this, and what I was supposed to do was find a few friends who wanted to do this, then apply for the job. Papá interviewed us really seriously, like he didn't even know me—I don't know how he kept a straight face with us giggling girls, we were so silly. He set high standards, for sure, and we worked hard. He made me treat it like a business and one year I got all tangled up in the taxes, and had to borrow money from him to get it cleared up. Mostly that same group of girls and I worked together all through high school. All of us just had to have the latest clothes and working for Papá, we sure made more money that we would've made flipping burgers. When José came along, he did the same thing, but for him it was gas money and art supplies. Oh yeah, I forgot, Papá made us set up those individual retirement accounts (IRAs). That was one of those things with him if any of us wanted to work there. That's why he overpaid us, I guess. When I'm home, my

friends and I sometimes laugh about this now, and we're really glad we
couldn't spend everything we earned on clothes.

The typical business family will have incorporated many income tax
planning mechanisms into its family wealth system long before it begins
FWTP. Family members often view income taxes as more important
than transfer taxes, because income taxes are a burden right now, but
transfer taxes will not be a burden until many years in the future—and
maybe never.

Income tax planning for families relies heavily on systems analysis.
Families have the opportunity to reduce income taxes within the family wealth system as a whole and to optimize their overall income tax
situation, rather than focusing on the taxes generated by any one subsystem or component of the system. Rearranging financial and human
capital within the system using the strategies discussed later in this
chapter can often result in reduced income taxes. A family's inclination
to take advantage of these is directly tied to its levels of cohesiveness
and adaptability.

Luisa's story demonstrates the special capacity that business families
have for using income tax strategies to minimize taxes within the family
wealth system as a whole. Owning a business provides many opportunities to funnel the benefit of income to family members in a tax-exempt,
tax-deductible, or tax-deferred manner or to direct income to family
members in the lowest tax bracket. For example, the Hernández family understands the benefits of directing income toward younger family
members, who are in a lower tax bracket than their elders. When Bart
employed his children and their friends, he not only generated a deduction, but also ensured that the young people's income would be taxed
at a lower rate than his own. This arrangement generates a deduction
while directing income to family members, and also generates earned
income for the junior family members. Earned income does not trigger
the kiddie tax, discussed below, as passive income does. This strategy
also qualifies the young workers to establish retirement vehicles such
as regular or Roth IRAs, although their part-time status probably prevents their participation in any company-sponsored retirement plan.
Given the number of years until these junior family members retire,
they are likely to benefit greatly from this early contribution. Of course,
families do not have unfettered discretion to take advantage of these

strategies. They are constrained by both case law and statutes, as well as by the IRS's vigilance in ferreting out abuses.

These tax-saving opportunities warp the shape of the family wealth system by introducing certain tax structures that would otherwise never become part of the system. Qualified plans, fringe benefits, large salaries, and fractionalized ownership are all income tax structures that would likely not exist within the family wealth system but for their tax benefits. When it is time to transfer wealth, by either sale to outsiders or transfer to family members, these strategies complicate the transition. If a sale to an outsider is the desired structure, these "perks" must be extracted in determining the value of the company, because family members must either do without them in the future or find a substitute. If the transfer of wealth is within the family, structures such as inflated salaries for family members or questionable fringe benefits have a direct impact on the perception of whether wealth is equitably shared among transferees who have different relationships to the business.

Fortunately, no matter how complicated an income tax plan may be, it will be motivated by one or more of the following four basic income tax planning strategies:

❑ Receive assets, whether as cash or otherwise, such as company-provided health insurance, that is excluded from gross income for tax purposes.
❑ Defer income into the future, taking advantage of the time value of money, through techniques such as investment in real estate, which allows the tax on appreciation to be deferred until sale.
❑ Maximize current deductions, such as compensation paid to family members.
❑ Use strategies under which net income will be taxed at the lowest possible rates, such as selling stock in a family company (rather than corporate assets) in order to give the seller capital gains treatment.

A full discussion of these strategies is beyond the scope of this book. *Figure 7.1* summarizes the tax structures that incorporate the strategies that are most important in FWTP planning: exclusion, deferral, deduction, and tax rate.

FIGURE **7.1** Income Tax Strategies Important in FWTP Planning

Exclusion Strategies	Deferral Strategies	Deduction Strategies	Tax Rate Strategies
• Gifts and bequests • Life insurance • Delaying sale of gain property until death so basis is fair market value at date of death • Sec. 1202 exclusion on sale of stock • Fringe benefits	• Delaying sale of gain property • Transferring property to entities in tax-free contributions • Sec. 1031 exchanges • Installment sales • Low-interest loans • Deferred compensation (qualified and nonqualified) • Employee stock option plans (ESOPs)	• Compensation (current and deferred) paid to family members • Rent for buildings and equipment • Charitable deductions (outright and in trust) • Fringe benefits • Sec. 1244 stock • ESOPs	• Choice of business entity (pass-through or C corporation) • Design of trusts (grantor, simple, complex) • Assignment of income • Transformation of ordinary income to capital gain

The Impact of Transfer Taxes on the Family Wealth System

—THE HERNÁNDEZ FAMILY—

Clara Hernández Paz, age fifty-one

When Elena came down with cancer again, we were all so broken up. We didn't even think about estate taxes or anything like that. Afterward, Bart checked with the accountants, and told us that it turned out okay, because everything went to him and so he didn't have to pay any estate taxes. They told him the tax problem will come when he dies—and it will be a big one. They gave him some ideas, but Bart ignored them because he said they were too complicated for now. I know people who own all their real estate in these partnerships with their kids, and they say it's the only way to beat the estate tax. I know Bart's young, and I shouldn't worry, but he should be planning for these things, if for nothing else than to put his kids' minds at ease. I foresee a wedding on the horizon, and that's going to send Bart and José into orbit, so he'd better get this taken care of.

The federal estate, gift, and generation-skipping taxes (and their state counterparts) change the shape of the family wealth system by inducing taxpayers to create certain structures to save taxes. These structures would never exist but for transfer taxes. For example, had the Hernández family been able to do estate planning before Elena's death, the family wealth system would have likely included a credit shelter trust, a marital trust, and possibly a few family-owned limited partnerships or limited liability companies (LLCs) to hold real estate. It is easy to believe Clara's statement, "we didn't even think about estate planning," but it is unlikely to be the case in this sophisticated business family. This family knew there was a transfer tax problem, but made a decision to spend their time and energy during Elena's last days focusing on her, not on estate planning. This decision has likely created an unnecessary tax in the future, but is an important clue as to the values of this family: people are more important than money. Any wealth transfer structure that is created in FWTP must implement this value. Now, however, Bart is again ignoring the warning about estate taxes. He might say that there is plenty of time to deal with this later. Or he might say he's still thinking about what to do. Maybe he suspects that implementing an estate plan will negatively affect how he wants to organize and run his businesses.

Business families have a special capacity for achieving transfer tax savings. By dividing ownership of their businesses among family members, they can take advantage of significant reductions in the value of the gross estate, for example. They can also, within limits, reduce the value of the taxable estate through the use of family foundations and similar charities. Of course, they do not enjoy unfettered discretion to implement these structures. Not only do laws and regulations constrain them, but they often face a very difficult choice: they must let go of control of wealth in order to take advantage of these strategies. This may be fundamentally inconsistent with the family's wealth behavior patterns, and if so, proper implementation of the strategies will be difficult. Specific structures and the problems that arise with them are discussed in Chapter 8.

No matter how complex an estate plan may be, it is based on achieving one or more of a limited number of objectives:

❑ Reducing the value of the gross estate through strategies such as giving property away during life to family or charities
❑ Reducing the value of the taxable estate through proper use of the marital and charitable deductions

❑ Avoiding or reducing transfer taxes in the succeeding generation through optimal use of the generation-skipping tax exemption

❑ Paying transfer taxes in a way that will preserve family wealth

Figure 7.2 summarizes the major transfer tax planning provisions that are important in FWTP planning. We will discuss these in more detail in the following sections.

Reducing the Value of the Gross Estate

The smaller the *gross estate*, the less estate tax is due. There are two methods of going about reducing the gross estate: moving assets out of the estate, and depressing the value of the remaining assets. In many situations, these are two sides of the same coin. Thus, these transfer taxes create an incentive for transferors to make gifts to donees earlier than they might otherwise have made such gifts, all other things being equal.

FIGURE **7.2**   Strategies to Reduce Transfer Taxes

Strategies to Reduce the Value of the Gross Estate	Strategies to Reduce the Value of the Taxable Estate	Strategies to Avoid Tax in Succeeding Generations	Strategies for Paying the Tax
• Outright gifts of appreciating property • Annual exclusion gifts • Gifts for medical and educational purposes • Crummey trusts • Irrevocable life insurance trusts (ILITs) • Grantor retained annuity trusts (GRATs) • Grantor retained unitrusts (GRUTs) • Charitable gifts • Outright gifts • Charitable remainder unitrusts (CRUTs) • Charitable remainder annuity trusts (CRATs) • Fractionalizing interests in property of the estate	• Marital deduction • Outright gifts • Gifts in trust • Life estates • Charitable deduction • Outright gifts • CRATs • CRUTs	• Maximum use of the generation-skipping trust (GST) exemption • Dynasty trusts	• Savings • Insurance • Sec. 6166 election • Sec. 303 redemption

A *gift* is any transaction in which an interest in property is gratuitously passed or conferred upon another, regardless of the means or device employed.[2] Outright gifts, gifts in trust, bargain sales, and indirect gifts all are gifts subject to the transfer tax.

Exceptions to the Definition of "Gift"

Fortunately, some transfers are excluded from the definition of *taxable gifts*. These include transfers made for tuition or medical expenses of the donee[3] if the tuition is paid directly to the university, and does not include amounts for books, fees, or room and board.

The most commonly used exclusion is the so-called *annual exclusion gift*. Internal Revenue Code Sec. 2503(b)(1) allows an individual to transfer up to a certain amount ($13,000 in 2009) to any donee per year.[4] Married couples may join together in making annual exclusion gifts, so that in 2009 they could transfer $26,000 to each donee. An important limitation on this exception is that the gift must be of a present interest, meaning the donee must receive a current right to enjoy the benefit of the gifted property. When the donor ties up the gift too tightly (such as to protect it from a young donee's bad judgment), the gift may fail to qualify for the annual exclusion because the beneficiary does not have a current right to the property. Several vehicles remedy this problem:

❏ Section 2503(c) specifically provides that a properly structured trust for minors, which must distribute the property to the minor upon his or her attaining age twenty-one, is a gift of a present interest. While many transferors do not use the Sec. 2503(c) trust because of their unwillingness to give the donee the unfettered right to the property at age twenty-one, it may be a suitable vehicle for funds the donor earmarks for a specific purpose, such as education.

❏ The Crummey trust requires that beneficiaries be given notice once a year of their right to withdraw from the trust amounts contributed to the trust. This right lasts for a number of days. If the trust is properly structured and implemented, contributions to the trust constitute gifts to the beneficiaries that qualify for the annual exclusion.[5]

❏ Contributions to 529 plans are gifts of a present interest, even though the beneficiary might not use the funds for many years.[6] Moreover, if the amount of the contributions exceeds the annual exclusion, the donor can elect to treat the aggregate amount as contributed ratably over a five-year period.[7]

Questions have recently arisen about whether gifts of interests in entities are present interests that qualify for the annual exclusion.[8] In using the annual exclusion for these gifts, advisers must take care to ensure that the transferee has some reasonable expectation of a current benefit from the transferred property.

Grantor Retained Trusts

Because gifts generate an actual gift tax when a donor's lifetime transfers exceed $1 million, as compared to the threshold for estate tax ($3.5 million in 2009), it is important to use the gift tax exclusion wisely. Making a gift of property before it appreciates in value is one technique. Another is to depress the value of what is given, so that the donor uses up less of the $1 million with any particular gift. The primary way to accomplish this is to give a gift in trust in which the grantor retains an interest that qualifies under IRC Sec. 2701 as a qualified payment.

Fractional Ownership

As Clara points out, one way to reduce the value of the gross estate is to ensure that the decedent's estate includes a minority interest in assets or business entities. This objective is achieved by fractionalizing ownership of real estate and making gifts that were sales of equity interests in business entities, a technique discussed more fully in Chapter 8.

Reducing the Value of the Taxable Estate

The estate tax is levied on a decedent's taxable estate. The *taxable estate* is determined by adding up the total value of the property in which the decedent held (or was deemed to hold) certain property interests at death (the gross estate) and subtracting all available deductions.

The gross estate is reduced by a variety of deductions, including a portion of state inheritance taxes, administrative expenses, charitable contributions, and transfers to a spouse. Of these, transfers to spouses and charitable contributions are the most important in FWTP.

Marital Deduction Planning

The most basic estate tax planning for a married couple seeks to ensure that each spouse takes advantage of the lifetime exclusion amount so that it is not wasted upon the death of the first spouse to die. (This is what apparently happened upon Elena Hernandez's death.) At the death of the first spouse, a portion of the property included in the deceased's estate is placed into an irrevocable trust (called a "bypass trust," "credit shelter trust," or "exclusion trust") to which the surviving spouse has access for support, subject to an ascertainable standard, such as health, education, support, and maintenance. The rest of the property passes to the surviving spouse, either in trust or outright, in a manner that ensures that this transfer qualifies for the marital deduction. These trusts also serve to direct assets to the desired recipients in situations such as blended families and second or third marriages. There are volumes of commentary on the proper way to structure these trusts, fund them, and provide for a surviving spouse, all of which are beyond the scope of this discussion. If properly implemented, these dual trust arrangements can allow each married couple to shelter $7 million (in 2009) from federal estate tax, but they warp the shape of the family wealth system in ways that many families find undesirable.

Charitable Deduction Planning

The federal estate tax provides an unlimited charitable deduction for qualifying gifts.[9] Thus, the charitable deduction can completely eliminate the estate tax by reducing the taxable estate below the applicable exclusion amount.

Outright gifts are the most common form of charitable deduction. For large estates, however, *split-interest gifts*, in which property is bequeathed to the trustee of a trust with both charitable and noncharitable beneficiaries, are common.

In a *charitable lead trust* (CLT), the charitable beneficiaries enjoy the income stream for a number of years, and at the termination of the trust, the corpus is distributed to the noncharitable beneficiaries. In a *charitable remainder trust* (CRT), the noncharitable beneficiaries enjoy the income stream from the trust for a number of years or for the lifetime of a beneficiary, and at the termination of the trust the corpus remaining is distributed to the charities named in the trust agreement.

A properly structured CRT is exempt from income tax, although the noncharitable beneficiaries pay tax on their distributions.

A split-interest trust can be structured as an annuity trust or a unitrust. In an annuity trust, the amount payable to the current income beneficiaries is measured as a percentage (not less than 5 percent or more than 50 percent) of the initial value of property contributed to the trust. In these trusts, no additional contributions can be made because the payout is tied to the initial value of the trust. These are particularly useful for property that is expensive to value, such as real estate. The payout of a unitrust is tied to the value of the property each year. Unitrusts can accept additional contributions, and are appropriate for trust property that is easy to value annually, such as stock or securities. Unitrusts also protect the value of the payout to current beneficiaries from the ravages of inflation. If inflation causes the value of the property to increase, the payout to current beneficiaries will also increase.

The value of the deduction is the present value of the gift to charity, computed under IRS tables. The uses of this technique are discussed more fully in Chapter 8.

Reducing the Estate Tax in Succeeding Generations

Some of the strategies described in this chapter also serve to reduce estate tax in succeeding generations. Fractionalized ownership, for example, depresses the value of property in the hands of the recipient for transfer tax purposes, just as it does for the portion retained by the transferor. The primary vehicle for reducing estate tax in succeeding generations, however, is the proper use of the generation-skipping trust (GST) exemption.

In theory, the estate tax is to be imposed once per generation. However, judicious use of the GST exemption allows a transfer of this amount to skip persons (those two or more generations below the transferor) without incurring this additional tax. The GST exemption may be allocated to outright gifts or gifts in trust, and given the relative ages of many transferors and their children or grandchildren, gifts in trust are an attractive option.

Many owners of businesses are curious about so-called *dynasty trusts*, which are irrevocable trusts organized in jurisdictions that have abolished the rule against perpetuities (which requires trusts to terminate after a certain number of years) so that a trust can literally last forever. The trust agreement describes the future beneficiaries and the standard by which the trustee may make distributions to or for the benefit of these beneficiaries. Because the transferors have allocated their GST exemptions to the trust, distributions to beneficiaries do not trigger the GST tax.

Family wealth transition planning advisers usually have strong beliefs about the advisability of dynasty trusts. Some view them as an essential vehicle for wealthy families. This kind of irrevocable trust can ensure that the benevolent wishes of a settlor carry forward into the future. Proponents also point out that when assets are held in a trust, and the trustee has a hand on the spigot, creditors of beneficiaries as well as divorcing spouses have a hard time reaching those assets. Other FWTP advisers view dynasty trusts as a dangerous addition to the family wealth system, pointing out that there are good reasons for the rule against perpetuities. The family wealth system is always in flux, and a vehicle that cannot adapt to an unpredictable future, or even be dissolved, is likely to make the family wealth system less adaptable to achieving family wealth continuity.

Payment of the Transfer Tax

In the usual situation, the federal estate tax is due nine months after the death of the decedent. A fear of many business families is that they will have to sell the family business in order to pay the estate tax on that schedule, which leads them to take steps to ensure liquidity in the form of savings or insurance (particularly second-to-die insurance). However, business families may be able to pay the tax in ten annual installments if the value of the family business exceeds 35 percent of the value of the adjusted gross estate.[10] A special low interest rate of 2 percent applies to the first $1,330,000 (in 2009) of value,[11] and the interest rate on the rest is 45 percent of the applicable federal rate.[12] In many cases, it will make sense for a business family to take advantage of this low-interest loan, but it comes at a price. The IRS may require the family to post a bond to secure the tax,[13] and a missed payment can accelerate the entire tax.

In addition, a business family may be able to take advantage of IRC Sec. 303, which treats the redemption of stock to pay estate tax as a sale or exchange, even if it would otherwise be treated as a dividend. As with Sec. 6166, this provision is only available if the value of the stock exceeds 35 percent of the gross estate, minus indebtedness, expenses, taxes, and losses. In the current tax environment, in which qualified dividend income and capital gains are subject to the same rate of tax, the distinction between a redemption that is a sale or exchange and one that is a dividend is usually of minor importance. However, because the decedent shareholder's stock receives a basis equal to its fair market value on the date of death, Sec. 303 creates an advantage: only amounts distributed in excess of that basis will be subject to tax.

Use of these tax rules, which lessen the burden of payment of tax, re-quires advance planning. The 35-percent thresholds are strict, and the FWTP adviser must coordinate other aspects of the wealth transition plan that are designed to reduce the value of the closely held business interests in the gross estate of the decedent (gifting of fractionalized interests, for example) to ensure that they do not work at cross-purposes with the desire to take advantage of these provisions. Moreover, in the case of an IRC Sec. 6166 election, the FWTP adviser must consider the family's ability to post a bond, and its likely compliance with the require-ments of an extended payment period, in light of the family's patterns of wealth behavior.

The Impact of Liquidity and Credit on FWTP

A major (but often invisible) external force at work on the family wealth system is the overall availability of credit and the relative ease with which the family can, if necessary, generate liquid assets for business expansion, family needs, or paying taxes. These factors ebb and flow with general economic conditions, and family wealth systems will differ greatly in their sensitivity to economic conditions due to each family's unique mix of assets.

In the initial stages of FWTP, the advisory team must evaluate the current credit situation of the family and discover the amount of out-standing loans, which assets are subject to pledges or similar restriction, and which family members are debtors or guarantors of debt. The ten-tacles of debt can reach over multiple subsystems and their components in complicated family wealth systems, and it is not uncommon for senior generation family members to make guarantees for the benefit of junior generations. These arrangements can outlive their efficacy to the family, in light of the changing life cycles of the individuals and businesses involved. The transition process often involves changing arrangements with creditors. Therefore, involving lending institutions at appropriate stages of the plan is critical. In certain situations, the external force of credit availability may block what might otherwise seem a sensible plan.

At the outset of a planning engagement, many advisers perform an initial projection of the probable amount of transfer taxes. In many cases, the family discovers that it does not have sufficient cash with which to pay taxes without liquidating important assets. Or liquid assets within the family wealth system may be earmarked for other purposes, such as business expansion or emergencies. It is not uncommon for family members to disagree on the earmarking of assets. Some family members may assume that their long-standing relationship with a bank or other institution will result in easy credit and may minimize the potential impact of changes in the overall credit market on a family's ability to pay the tax.

Implications of the Open Family Wealth System for Business Families

The FWTP adviser must never forget that he or she is an external force at work on the family wealth system. The adviser balances the objectivity that comes from being outside the system with empathy for how a family actually operates its wealth system (and why) in order to introduce new ideas and processes to people inside the system. The common goal of the planner and the family is *change:* adapting the system to make it more likely to produce family wealth continuity.

The adviser's first task is to take stock of the existing arrangements that the family has developed to deal with external forces. Every family commencing the FWTP process will arrive with certain entities, such as partnerships, corporations, and prenuptial agreements, that they have developed to deal with the vicissitudes of the outside world. The FWTP adviser must catalog these arrangements and evaluate their current usefulness. Some may be artifacts: the forces that inspired their creation may no longer be around. Others may continue to play an important role in business planning, income tax planning, relationship planning, or estate planning.

The FWTP adviser will recommend certain adaptations of the system to deal with external forces, especially taxes. These changes will necessarily affect the family's existing arrangements, the results of which must be predicted and taken into account. Merely grafting these new arrangements onto an existing system, without more careful study, is likely to lead to failure. As discussed in Chapter 8, the adviser must select new arrangements, such as trusts, entities, and other kinds of wealth transfer structures, to match the needs, capacities, and constraints of each family. Then these arrangements must be nested within the family wealth system with the appropriate governance systems and role development plans to ensure their success.

CHAPTER NOTES

1. Pension Protection Act of 2006, Pub. L. No. 109-1280, 120 Stat. 780 (2006).

2. Treas. Reg. Sec. 25.2511-1(c).

3. IRC Sec. 2503(c).

4. IRC Sec. 2503(b).

5. See *Crummey v. Commissioner*, 397 F.2d 82 (9th Cir. 1968).

6. IRC Sec. 529(c)(2)(A)(i).

7. IRC Sec. 529(c)(2)(B).

8. See *Hackl v. Commissioner*, 335 F.3d 664 (7th Cir. Jul. 11, 2003), *aff'g* 118 T.C. 279 (2002).

9. IRC Sec. 2055(a).

10. IRC Sec. 6166(a). The adjusted gross estate is the gross estate less administrative expenses, indebtedness, taxes, and losses. IRC Sec. 6166(d)(6).

11. IRC Sec. 6166(j).

12. IRC Sec. 6166(j)(1)(B).

13. The IRS determines whether a bond will be required on a case-by-case basis. IRC Sec. 6166(k)(1).

CHAPTER 8

WEALTH TRANSITION
STRUCTURES

FOR ALL FAMILIES, the ultimate goal is the same: to create and implement a transition plan that will support family wealth continuity for generations to come. But because each family will have different needs, capacities, and constraints, each family's constellation of plan components, and the design of each component, will be different.

The three essential components of a successful family wealth transition plan are wealth transition structures, role clarity/development plans, and governance systems. Of the three components, family wealth transition planning (FWTP) advisers are most familiar with wealth transition structures, whose function is to provide answers to the four big questions of wealth transition:

❏ What is being transferred—financial, human, or social capital?
❏ Who is transferring, and who is receiving, wealth?
❏ When will the transition take place—now or later, suddenly or gradually?
❏ How will the transition take place—by gift, sale, or both; what conditions are imposed on the transition; will sharing be required; and if so, how will it occur?

Wealth transition structures include traditional legal structures such as trusts, gifts, and sales, but are not limited to these kinds of arrangements. They also include a wide variety of nonlegal structures with very different forms, functions, and legal effects. Traditional wealth transition structures were first developed to transfer financial capital and evolved into forms that also transfer human and social capital. Transferring any kind of capital in unusual circumstances may require adaptation of these forms and the creation of new structures matched to the needs, capacities, and constraints of each family.

Estate planning lawyers usually recommend legal transition structures that are inspired by the external forces at work on families of wealth, such as potential income tax or estate tax liability. Yet the traditional approach of recommending legal structures inspired by external forces works well only when these structures complement the needs, capacities, and constraints of the family wealth system. When the requirements and effects of those structures are fundamentally inconsistent with the family wealth system, a successful family wealth transition plan is not possible. Thus, the adviser must understand the inner workings of a family wealth system in order to choose the right wealth transition structures and avoid using the wrong ones.

The great variety within family wealth systems makes it impossible to cite any hard-and-fast rules about the selection of wealth transition structures. It is the FWTP adviser's job to filter the information gleaned about a family through a process of discussion and reflection, in which the family and its advisers explore meanings drawn from information about the family wealth system; tease out the assumptions family members make about the four big questions; and examine their beliefs about family and wealth. This process is nonlinear; family wealth transition conversations will mix these issues as the proper wealth transition structures emerge.

This chapter focuses on transitions of wealth in the operating business subsystem, and on how reverberations from that transition echo throughout the entire family wealth system. Although the focus is on the transition of an operating business, its methodology can be adapted for transitions within any of the subsystems of the family wealth system.

The Relationship of Wealth Transition Structures to Other Wealth Transition Plan Components

Viewing wealth transition structures in isolation would be a mistake, because this component of the plan is inextricably tied to the other two components: role clarity/development and governance systems. In fact, choosing a wealth transition structure often constitutes an implicit or explicit choice about roles and governance systems. All wealth transition structures require people to fill roles to make them work, which in turn requires clarity (about what roles are required) and planning (to develop new roles). Similarly, many wealth transition structures bring with them specific governance systems, with varying suitability to a family's particular needs.

Governance systems and role development plans build capacities within families, and help adapt the family wealth system to manage wealth better as it is transferred. For example, building trust within a family with a history of distrust may be an impossible task, but building a governance system for wealth, which acts as a substitute for trust, is an achievable goal. Governance systems and role development plans can also alleviate the impact of conflicts between external forces and internal needs and constraints. For example, a family may need a trust to achieve some transition tax objectives, but beneficiaries may chafe under the restrictions of a trust. Educating trustees and beneficiaries about their respective roles leads to better selection of trustees, informed enjoyment of wealth by beneficiaries, and the avoidance of future litigation caused by nasty surprises. Thus, the three components of a wealth transition plan are inextricably entwined. Beginning with wealth transition structures, however, creates a starting place in the familiar practice of estate planning.

Changing Existing Patterns Within the Operating Business Subsystem

A core attribute of business families is that various family members generate shared wealth by contributing different kinds of inputs to an enterprise, in exchange for different kinds of benefits. The allocation of those inputs and benefits among participants will vary significantly over time. The family wealth system has a memory, so the current allocation pattern will reflect the system's needs, capacities, and constraints at some point in the past.

Whatever the established pattern of allocating the fruits of the enterprise among participants may be, in terms of financial capital (salaries, distributions, fringe benefits, rent, and other kinds of payments), as well as human and social capital (recognition, opportunities, or acceptance), the FWTP process will change that pattern. At a minimum, the process will cause family members to examine how the pattern of allocation came into being and how and why they chose a particular pattern of allocation of inputs and benefits. Simply looking at the pattern often creates change, because most families' wealth systems include a few *artifacts*: structures created to respond to stimuli long absent from the family system. The FWTP process is all about creating a new pattern, one that will promote family wealth continuity given the new demands within the system.

When making these choices, the process must address who will have the authority to make future changes in those patterns, and how they will exercise that authority. This authority is the essence of *control*, a concept that has an enormous impact on planning. Properly structuring the transition of control is perhaps the most challenging aspect of creating FWTP, because it involves all three components: a wealth transition structure, a governance system, and a plan for role clarity and development.

What Kinds of Wealth Will Be Transferred?

—JOY SASAKI, CERTIFIED PUBLIC ACCOUNTANT—
Consultant to Helen Weinstein Williams, age fifty-two

Helen Williams hired me to look over her family finances when she discovered that her husband had a child from an affair that she didn't know about. Man, was she a wreck. I would be one too if I was in her shoes. She didn't know the first thing about her family's money, not even how to start up Quicken on her home computer. She's smart, though, that's for sure. I didn't have to tell her twice how to do anything. You know, John Williams is something of a celebrity around here. I remember when they did a big spread on him as one of the new breed who gave up corporate life for entrepreneurship and more time with family. Then I found out the truth. He took a huge amount of money—$500,000—from his retirement account (he used to be a big deal with an ad agency) without her knowledge, and apparently used it to buy a co-op for his honey. I couldn't tell if he owns it or she does. I didn't get into the details with Helen, because she was upset enough. But he would have had to forge her signature somehow because a spouse has to consent to this kind of withdrawal. And it would have resulted in hefty penalties for early withdrawal, because he's young. I think their savings are pretty much gone. It's interesting that her husband didn't try to hide any of this, not like some I've seen. He didn't even password-protect the file. It's almost like he wanted to get caught.

A fundamental question in wealth transition for businesses is determining what wealth is to be transferred in the FWTP process. The family wealth system teaches us that there is much more to the picture than financial capital. For most families, the family operating business subsystem is a storehouse of human and social capital as well as financial capital, all in varying degrees of importance. In the Williams family, for example, Helen is discovering that many sources of capital she had unthinkingly relied upon have simply evaporated. It is not enough that a large portion of the retirement plan accumulated in the couple's pre–Jazz Jive lives has apparently vanished. Even more important, her trust in her husband is under assault with each new discovery. It may turn out that the Jazz Jive bars are more important to Helen's financial future than she had ever anticipated.

Helen is likely now inspired to take an inventory of her family's sources of capital. For any family, the process of mapping all of these kinds of capital may be challenging. *Figure 8.1* summarizes the

FIGURE **8.1** Capital Within Operating Business Subsystem for Which Wealth Transition Structures Must Be Created

Financial Capital	Human Capital	Social Capital
• Equity interests in business	• Education or experiences that will benefit business	• Governance system that works
• Tangible business assets	• Ability to understand, set, and implement business goals	• Good relations with employees, union
• Intellectual property		• Relationships with customers, vendors, and others that provide inputs
• Goodwill and going concern value	• Ability to make decisions	
• Employment contracts/ salaries/wages	• Ability to allocate resources within business to achieve goals	• Good relations with regulatory agencies
• Favorable leases and other contracts for inputs		• Productive relationships with advisers: lawyers, CPAs, etc.
• Real estate used in business	• Ability to manage people	
• Loans to/from company, guarantees, other credit support	• Technical skills	• Good banking relationships
	• Salesmanship	• Existing buy–sell agreements
• Insurance (e.g., key person or split-dollar)	• Understanding use of debt	
• Fringe benefits	• Ability to share wealth with others, including charities, community, and other family members	• Community connections, charitable activities
• Qualified plans and nonqualified deferred compensation plans		• Good credit rating

common kinds of capital within the operating business subsystem. It is not an exhaustive list, and no bright lines delineate the categories of human, social, and financial capital within the operating business subsystem. This list simply prompts consideration of the different kinds of capital that are relevant to building wealth transition structures for a family. Every business family will have its own forms of each kind of capital that FWTP advisers must take into consideration.

Thinking of the operating business as a system nested within the larger family system generates a second lesson about choosing wealth transition structures for the FWTP adviser: the connections between the assets that must be transferred are as important as the assets themselves. Transferring any capital without attending to those connections will likely fail. For example, preserving the good credit rating of a company is usually an important goal in the FWTP process. The rating depends not only on the financial experience of a company, but also its management and its relationship with banks and others that provide credit support. A good transition plan will require investigation into the sources of that rating and how the three kinds of capital connect to produce it. The adviser must map and attend to each relationship that is a source of wealth for the family. The wealth transition structures the adviser chooses must incorporate the transition of each of these relationships.

Who Will Be Transferring Wealth, and to Whom?

Given all the kinds of wealth we have described in earlier chapters, it is unlikely that a single person, or even a couple of individuals, control all of them for a particular family. In fact, some cannot be "owned" at all. A challenge of the planning process is identifying (1) who has the ability to transfer wealth and (2) how the transfer might happen. An example is the *goodwill* of a business (the expectation that customers will patronize the business in the future as they have in the past). In some businesses, the transfer of goodwill is likely to be only partially successful unless there is a plan for ensuring that customers are comfortable dealing with the new owners or managers. The legal documents of transfer may provide for goodwill, but without a plan for implementation, they are not a wealth transition structure.

The process of identifying this wealth also leads to the issue of determining the proper recipients of this wealth. There likely will be different recipients for different kinds of wealth, because the current transferees are probably more diverse than their predecessors were. Many transferors of wealth begin FWTP with their ideas solidified as to who should receive wealth, but with some reservations about their readiness. Many others will not have examined the transferors' and transferees' overlapping life cycles or the family patterns of behavior that affect those choices. Transferors need some mechanism with which to evaluate the readiness of heirs to receive wealth of any kind, and particularly wealth in the form of control of a family business. This process is tied to a plan for clarity and role development; the selection of a wealth transition structure takes a back seat.

In many situations, the first recipient of transferred wealth, including interests in closely held businesses, is not the next generation, but instead the marital or bypass trusts created as part of the estate plan. The plan must take into consideration the intervening years when trustees will manage all or part of the business.

When Will Wealth Be Transferred?

The question of when wealth will be transferred is largely dependent on the overlapping life cycles within the family wealth system, which in turn are influenced by external forces and the particular family's wealth behavior patterns. Many wealth transition structures for business families have two parallel timelines: a "just in case" one and an evolutionary one. Usually, the first plan to be put into place is on the "just in case" timeline. A family able to accept the inevitability of change and the likelihood that trigger events will occur is usually open to having a plan for worst-case scenarios such as sudden or multiple deaths or incapacity.

A wealth transition plan will involve all the usual aspects of estate planning, including a trust or will with tax planning provisions that takes advantage of the exclusion for each spouse and provides for disposition of the estate to the intended beneficiaries. Insurance (life, health, disability, and long-term care) may also feature prominently. Wise business families go a step further and create a plan for managing the business in an emergency situation. During a crisis, having clear lines of authority and a plan of action is critical. Many families discover too late that in a crisis of management they lack even the most basic of tools: the right computer passwords.[1]

Business families are busy people, and once this first timeline is in place, they have the natural human tendency to stop planning. Overcoming this natural aversion requires FWTP advisers to shift the family's focus from contemplating trigger events to considering the transferors' desires for family wealth continuity. Creating a worst-case scenario plan is *good* stewardship of business assets, but it is not the *best* stewardship. Nor does it achieve the other goals of family wealth continuity: healthy family relationships and the creation of a family legacy. The second timeline, by comparison, incorporates wealth transition structures that will meet all of these goals more gradually than will the dramatic "just in case" timeline.

The Conflict Between External and Internal Forces in Transferring Ownership

The tax system creates an enormous incentive for owners of closely held businesses to transfer interests and control in the business to younger generations well before death. If the value of the business increases over time, the estate of a decedent who hoarded these interests until death, just to transfer the interests to the younger generation at that time, generally pays more in transfer taxes than the estate of a decedent who transferred appreciated interests to the younger generation during life. Moreover, valuation discounts significantly reduce the value of the interests retained in the decedent's estate, if the decedent previously gave up control. Finally, transfer of equity ownership to the younger generation may direct income away from the transferor generation and to the transferee generation, which in turn may save income taxes.

Certain forces at work within many family wealth systems amplify this tendency to transfer assets during life. Transferring interests to children may serve the nontax interests of transferors, who may use these transitions to recognize the contributions of children who work in the business, see those interests as a source of financial security for children, or recognize that those children who do work in the business will not do so indefinitely without an equity stake. Other transferors may be motivated by purposes that reflect less attractive family wealth behavior patterns, such as gifts that further enmesh a family or tie a child into the family legacy. Moreover, transferees exert pressures on transferors to start the capital transition process before death. Those working in the business likely *expect* a transfer of capital. Each family will have its own combination of external and internal forces that create an incentive to transfer financial wealth in businesses before death.

Yet, in many families, three kinds of issues create a strong opposing force, causing business owners to retain ownership of business interests until death.

First, control of a business carries with it the ability to allocate the rewards of that business among participants, both within and outside the family. A transition of control inevitably means a change in that allocation. Rigid families find it very difficult to adapt to change, while chaotic ones may not be able to find a durable pattern of allocating wealth. The more closely a family is enmeshed, the more difficult it will likely find this process.

Second, overlapping cycles of change among families, individuals, and businesses create barriers to transition. For example, during the start-up phase of a business, giving interests to the younger generation is relatively easy and cheap, because the business has little value at that time. Yet during this phase, founders may not view shared ownership as practical, because it may impede the nimbleness they require in this stage of the business life cycle and the founders may not respect any form of shared governance. Later in the business cycle, it is more expensive to give interests, both because the company is more valuable, and because gifting may require complex arrangements.

Lastly, family patterns of behavior can strongly influence transferors to delay any transition of wealth. Transferors may fear generating a sense of entitlement in their children or grandchildren. The biggest problem, however, may be one of trust. Transferors may not trust transferees to make the "right" allocations of the benefits of the enterprise or the other family stakeholders, or they may fear that they themselves will be left with insufficient resources, either financial or in terms of the meaning they derive from work.

When a family does not resolve these competing influences to retain or transfer control of a business, it tends to procrastinate in making the decision. This often becomes a decision in itself. The result is that

182   Family Wealth Transition Planning

transitions occur, pursuant to the "just in case" plan, after transferors die
or become incapacitated. Or the transfers are made without due consideration by the family, or in ways that smack solely of tax planning and
thereby invite audit. The FWTP adviser's job is to help a family resolve
these competing influences and to keep it focused on the question of
how they can be the best stewards of their wealth.

How Will Wealth Be Transferred?

Determining how a family will transfer the inherent wealth in a family
business requires answers to three important questions:

❑ Will the transfer be by sale or by gift?
❑ What conditions will be imposed on the transfer?
❑ Will the recipients be sharing the wealth, or will it be divided among
   them in ways that allow them to be good independent stewards?

Sales can be to insiders or outsiders, or to a combination of the two.
Gifts, of course, are usually to family members, but the definition of
family can vary widely. Gifts are often loaded with legal or moral conditions, restrictions, and stipulations. These can be articulated through
trust agreements, governance documents, or implicit expectations communicated through the steely eyes of a transferor.

Perhaps the most important question to ask during the transfer of
a family business is whether multiple recipients will share the wealth
(in all its forms) created by the business. In many situations, the family business is the kind of asset that cannot be divided and still retain
its value. If it is to be shared, how is that to occur? How will the
recipients work together as good stewards of this wealth while building healthy family relationships? The wealth transition structure that
is created will have an enormous impact on the sharing of wealth.
Governance/role issues come to the forefront when transferees share
business wealth.

Figure 8.2 summarizes common wealth transfer structures for the
financial, human, and social capital represented by a family business.
Not all are legal structures. This list is not intended to be exhaustive,
but to spark ideas about how to structure the transfer of various kinds of
capital using traditional as well as nontraditional methods.

FIGURE **8.2** Common Wealth Transition Structures in the Operating Business Subsystem

Financial Capital	Human Capital	Social Capital
• Gifts of equity interests outright	• Formal educational programs	• Governance documents of all kinds
• Gifts in trust (such as qualified subchapter S trusts, electing small business trusts, or grantor retained annuity trusts)	• Internship programs	• Family councils
	• Mentorship programs	• Family constitutions
	• Employment agreements	• Governance training
	• Consulting contracts	• Retirement celebrations
• Sales of equity interests	• Guaranteed board seats	• Split-interest gifts
• Bargain sales		• Family foundations
• Reorganizations (split-ups, freezes)	• Voting trusts	• Charitable work by family members
• Employee stock option plans	• Trustees and trusteeships	• Community involvement
• Gifts to charity	• Retiree health insurance	
• Split-interest trusts (charitable remainder annuity trusts and unitrusts)	• Introducing "Junior" to vendors, customers, and others, and communicating confidence in Junior's abilities	
• Family foundations		
• Deferred compensation programs (qualified and nonqualified)		
• Retiree health insurance		
• Disability insurance		
• Bankruptcy		
• Closing the business		

Sale to Outsiders

While many families are happy to "take the money and run," some families find it difficult to accept that sale to an outsider is the right result for transfer of a business. This result can feel like a family failure, and the prospect of such a sale may induce family members to continue the business even though their individual life cycles demand a different path. These are the families that view the business as an important part of their legacy.

For these families, the FWTP adviser's job is to help them see that sale of the business may be the most responsible exercise of stewardship. In many cases, it is the natural result of the overlapping life cycles of individuals, families, and the business, which prevent an easy transfer within the family. Frequently, the needs of a business as it moves from one stage to the next are inconsistent with the capacities of individuals within the family wealth system, given their stages of individual and family development.

Sometimes the line between "insiders" and "outsiders" is not so clear. At times, selling to nonfamily employees, either individually or as a group, is the obvious choice when there are no family members interested in taking on an ownership role. Employee stock ownership plans (ESOPs) may be an appropriate choice for some family businesses. An ESOP is a mechanism to place all or part of the ownership of a company into the hands of employees through a trust arrangement that purchases shares for the retirement accounts of the employees. A sale of stock to an ESOP can have particularly advantageous tax consequences to the seller and the company,[2] and an ESOP structure can help a family liquidate its ownership interests while rewarding long-time employees who have contributed to the growth of the family's capital. Sharing the wealth with those who created it helps a family come to terms with their good fortune and also contributes to the family legacy.

Moreover, because a sale to an outsider can take many forms, this kind of sale is a *transformation* of wealth: it moves assets from one subsystem to another. When the sellers continue as shareholders of the buyer, there may be opportunities for board seats or other involvement at a high level. Alternatively, family members may continue as consultants or employees. Sale of an operating business creates an influx of financial capital into the investment subsystem. Managing it requires developing a different set of human capital skills than those needed to manage an operating business. If the sale results in the seller's retaining liabilities, these must be allocated within the family system.[3] Family members may have become accustomed to drawing fat salaries and benefits from the company rather than receiving dividends; family charitable efforts may rely heavily on company support; and the family business may be the main source of meaning and values within the family. Untangling these connections takes time and thought, yet negotiation of a sale to an outsider typically occurs at a pace that does not lend itself to careful consideration of these issues. If sale of the family business is a likely stewardship option for a family, an important role of the FWTP team is to prepare the family and its business for the sale by initiating contingency planning about the impact of such a sale well before a potential buyer opens up negotiations.

Sales to Insiders

In some situations, an owner of a business may prefer to sell the business to the younger generation instead of making a gift. Life cycles and financial need may require a sale, for example, when the sellers depend on the income for retirement. Parents sometimes use this approach to achieve parity among all the children when fewer than all children have an interest in continuing the business. In many cases, family patterns of wealth behavior make a sale the logical choice because a sale sends a very different message than a gift. Sellers concerned about entitlement issues may structure the transfer of at least some portion as a sale. For other sellers and buyers, a sale may help mark boundaries that would otherwise remain fuzzy. If owners have a difficult time letting go of control, a sale transaction may allow them a graceful exit. The lone control freak in a chaotic family may insist on purchasing the business in order to clarify "who's in charge" or to prevent later arguments about obligations to other family members. Thus, the choice to sell a business to family members is informed as much by family patterns of behavior as by financial concerns.

When an intrafamily transaction is structured as a sale, it almost always takes the form of a sale of equity interests, in contrast to the asset sale structure most commonly used in sales to outsiders. This typically generates tax savings to the transferor generation in the form of capital gains on the sale, but at a tax cost to transferees. In an intrafamily sale, a portion of the purchase price will likely be allocated to an ongoing consulting or employment arrangement for the previous owner. This will result in a tax deduction for the company and ordinary income, subject to employment or self-employment taxes, for the former owner. Structuring this as an employment contract allows the seller a longer period to adjust to ending participation in fringe benefit plans. In the intrafamily context, consulting or employment arrangements are preferable to covenants not to compete, because covenants not to compete are amortized on a fifteen-year schedule,[4] while employment and consulting arrangements provide an immediate deduction. This arrangement also reflects the reality that both buyers and sellers generally want the seller to continue to participate in the business.

Alternatively, if both the sellers and the buyers are current owners of the business, the company may *redeem* (purchase) the sellers' interests. Redeeming corporate stock is easier to do today than in the past from a tax perspective, because even if the proceeds are treated as a dividend, they receive favorable tax treatment as qualified dividend income.

Installment Sales

In an intrafamily sale, a large portion of the purchase price is almost always paid with an installment note. This raises various planning opportunities and pitfalls. The intrafamily installment note must bear a minimum rate of interest.[5] This rate will almost always be lower than the rate the buyer would have to pay to borrow funds commercially, which preserves wealth in the hands of the purchasers and reduces the estate of the transferors. In some cases, it may make sense to structure the installment note as a self-canceling installment note (SCIN). This will further reduce the value of the estate of the transferors, albeit at a potential tax cost, since the estate may realize taxable income upon the note's cancellation.

Setting the Price

Before settling on the structure of an intrafamily sale, the family and its FWTP adviser must carefully consider how to establish the purchase price and how to allocate that price among equity interests, employment and consulting arrangements, and covenants not to compete. In intrafamily transactions, competing family wealth behavior patterns tend to amplify these problems.

The value of the company lies in the eyes of the beholder, at least until the company's market value is established. Owners typically overvalue their companies at the outset, but outside buyers offer up a healthy dose of reality with their discussions of the company's earnings, valuation formulas, and all the warts that appear during the due diligence period. That level of frankness is largely absent in intrafamily sales, and indeed family buyers often view intense negotiation as unseemly. As a result, conversations about price tend to focus on two topics: (1) what the owners "need" in retirement and (2) what payments the company can support. The former is not relevant to value, and the latter depends upon the length of the payment plan and interest rate, so neither helps much in setting a price. Yet families regularly allow purchase prices to be set by reference to these issues, which can lead to a serious under- or overvaluation of the business.

The obvious remedy is an appraisal, an approach families often reject as an unnecessary expense in an intrafamily sale. A FWTP adviser faced with stiff resistance to an appraisal may want to consider the family's wealth behavior patterns. An important role for a FWTP adviser is to help a family see how its own patterns of wealth behavior interfere with good stewardship by blocking them from obtaining adequate information upon which to base decisions. A family that prefers fantasy to facts may know that it will not be able to accept an appraisal, no matter what the appraisal says, so introducing these "facts" is likely to lead to conflict. Patterns that interfere with seeking appropriate information include the following:

❑ How well owners understand the difference between their personal and business roles has measurable impact. An entrepreneurial couple experiencing a divorce may believe that the divorce won't change the dynamics of the divorcing couple as business partners and so may resist either selling the business outright or buying the other's interest.

❑ How much the owners trust in (or fear) their own financial future will inform what they feel they need and the price at which they are willing to sell.

❑ A family that has operated under rigid controls may be unwilling to challenge the opinion of the owners as to value, even by reference to a neutral outside party.

❑ A family with a history of substance abuse may refuse to acknowledge patterns of enabling behavior such as making a lot of financial capital available after a sale when a family member with substance abuse issues repeatedly returns to substance abuse behavior after going through rehab.

A family embarking upon a sale structure usually has multiple motivations, which often include benevolent goals. They know intuitively that fair market value is a range, not a number, and they would prefer that their children enjoy the lower end of that range.

Closing the Business

In some situations, closing a business is the only responsible form of stewardship. A FWTP advisory team may quickly perceive that the family business is a black hole that devours family financial, human, and social capital. Or the business may be marginally profitable, creating cash flow only for its owners, who are happy to spend countless hours working on a labor of love. It may be obvious to the FWTP advisory team, but not to the family, that keeping this kind of business alive is a decision to transfer wealth gradually outside the family wealth system. An adviser who has reached this conclusion must collect the relevant financial facts about what it would take to create and continue a profitable business, focus the family on the likely consequences of continuing on the current path (bankruptcy or transfer of an impossible situation to the next generation), and try to create options for closing the business.

Some families are open to this process, but most have been exposed to this information before, and either have been unable to see it or have rejected it as inaccurate, to the frustration of advisers and other family members. To overcome these barriers, the FWTP advisory team must unearth the patterns of family wealth behavior that create these kinds of blinders. For example, an extreme view that the family business is of intrinsic (not instrumental) value may block realistic wealth transfer options because fantasy over facts can combine to allow a family to deceive itself for years about the profitability of its business. Unless the family addresses the underlying assumptions that play out in their wealth behavior patterns, the family's penchant for fantasy may impede the FWTP process for years.

Gifting Interests in Entities to Family Members — Fractional Ownership

—THE MARSHALL FAMILY—

Robert L. (Bobbie Lee) Marshall, age forty-seven

The Christmas I turned sixteen, there was a shirt box under the tree for each of us kids. They were wrapped up like my mother always did, but they were light, like nothing was in there. It wasn't the usual Sunday shirt and tie for us boys, that's for sure. Our dad took a stack of crisp $100 bills from his wallet and said, "I'll give each of you $500 for your box." I was ready to sign right up for that deal—$500 would buy a new engine for the Ford I was fixing up and whatever was in the box couldn't be better than that. But Ruthie—she was always the one who could read the truth in anyone's eyes—hissed at us, "Say no, no matter what he offers!" Dad upped the ante to $1,000, then $2,000, even an unbearable $5,000, saying, "All you have to do, boys, is hand over the box, unopened." Eddie didn't know what was going on, really, and he flapped around the room like he does when he feels the tension in the air. Ruthie made all of us say, "No way, we'll stick with the box," and even Arnie hung tough when his wife (not Betty, one of those crazy earlier ones) shouted, "Take the cash, honey, we could really use it." When I opened my box, I thought Dad had gotten us again with one of his practical jokes, because the only thing in there was a piece of paper—a stock certificate for Marshall Enterprises. And for a measly 3.3 shares! But Dad said, "Y'all did right, listening to your sister. Those shares are worth more than you know, and a lot more than a new engine for an old pickup. Welcome to the family business."

Robert Marshall's experience is common among families with significant business or investment holdings. The owners of these assets typically contribute them to an entity, such as a corporation, in exchange for ownership interests. Over time, the owner makes gifts of interests to family members. At death, the estate of the original owner of the business, investments, or other assets holds only a partial interest, perhaps only a minority interest, in the entity.

This can achieve three interrelated goals in the FWTP process. First, it can provide a gradual transition of governance from one generation to another. Second, it can allow income from property to be directed among family members who are owners.[6] Finally, this structure can save significant gift and estate taxes, which rely on the theory of *minority discounts*.

These discounts reflect the concept that the value of a fractional interest in an entity will be less than a comparable percentage of the entity's underlying assets. Two factors reduce the fair market value of these interests compared to that of the underlying property. The first is lack of marketability. There simply isn't a market for fractional interests in closely held entities like there is for those of publicly traded entities. The second is lack of control. If the interest represents a minority interest, the minority owner cannot (absent exceptional circumstances) control the destiny of the entity. The minority owner also cannot ensure that the entity will distribute any money, much less control the timing of that distribution. Because the value of an interest depends in large part on the free cash flow that the interest generates, if there is no market for the interest or there is the possibility that no cash will be distributed, the value drops. These two factors, taken together, result in the value of a minority interest in an entity being significantly less than the value of a proportionate share of the underlying assets—sometimes 40 to 60 percent less.

Valuation discounts are not restricted to interests in entities. Any fractional interest in property will carry a discount for lack of marketability. For example, an undivided interest in real property is less valuable than the percentage of the value of the entire property, because, at the very least, partition and its costs are a predicate to sale on the market.[7] However, the discounts that apply to interests in entities are likely to be greater, because the restrictions found in state law and in an entity's governing documents may impose higher barriers to marketability than do the laws relating to co-ownership of property.

The existence of minority discounts creates three opportunities for reducing gift and estate taxes. First, the value of a gift of a minority interest in an entity will be significantly lower than its percentage share of the entity's assets, which allows gifting at a relatively low tax cost. Second, if the transferor holds only a minority interest in the entity at death, the discounts significantly reduce the value of the transferor's estate below what it would be if the transferor owned the underlying assets. Finally, if the entity's assets increase in value, this appreciation has already been removed from the estate of the transferor.

Of course, the IRS stands ready to challenge these strategies. It typically uses two counterstrategies. The first focuses on what happens at the time the gift is made. Taxpayers try to depress the value of the gift, but the IRS can challenge that valuation using traditional valuation methodology, the special tax code provisions that were enacted to restrict estate tax freezes (IRC Secs. 2701–2704), or even the argument that the entity is a sham. The second counterstrategy is triggered at death. Once the transferor dies, the IRS may seek to increase the value of the property in the transferor's estate by bringing the gift back into the estate.

These are not mutually exclusive strategies: The IRS can challenge the value of the gift *and* the value of the estate. It has many opportunities to do so, because most of these strategies require the filing of a gift tax return, and the estate tax return now specifically asks whether any valuation discounts have been claimed. Legislative initiatives also periodically threaten the use of valuation discounts for some types of assets or transactions.

Valuation Discount Principles and Family Patterns

Given the likelihood of an IRS challenge, families should proceed with caution when using valuation discount strategies. While a discussion of the technical aspects of minority and lack of marketability discounts is beyond the scope of this book, advisers to business families should be aware of the key legal principles that provide the foundation for these FWTP structures. An adviser must evaluate a family's capacities and constraints with respect to these principles before recommending use of these strategies. There are three overarching legal principles that inform successful structures.

A Valid Business Purpose

It is a fundamental principle of valuation discount planning that a family must be able to articulate, and demonstrate the reality of, one or more reasons for forming the entity that are independent of tax concerns.

Fortunately, entities that operate active businesses rarely encounter difficulty with this requirement. For entities that hold investment assets, however, the task can be more challenging. The purpose must pass the blush test: liability protection for an eighty-eight–year-old woman in a nursing home just won't work.[8] But preparing for a corporate liquidity event, ensuring multigenerational governance, or imposing a particular investment strategy might well serve a valid business purpose. Moreover, the approach to the family wealth system described in this book provides a methodology for developing a robust business purpose by examining (1) internal needs of the family wealth system that are tied to goals of family wealth continuity; (2) internal and external forces that must be taken into account in developing ways to meet these goals; and (3) the family's special needs, capacities, and constraints. A FWTP adviser can help a family by guiding it through the process, because simply going through this process bolsters the business purpose.

Businesslike Operations

The family must respect the legal requirements for operating the entity and treat it as a separate and independent business in every respect. All prospective owners should negotiate the governance agreements (such as limited liability company [LLC] operating agreements) at the outset. Minutes must be kept, all transactions must be at arm's length, and personal assets must be kept separate from business assets. To the extent possible, governance agreements should look like those typically negotiated among nonfamily business associates. The operation of the entity should mimic as closely as possible the ways strangers pool their resources to generate wealth. A family that can show that the property they contributed to the entity was managed differently after creation of the entity than it was before will be more likely to prevail in litigation than the family for whom nothing changed in the management of the property. The FWTP adviser can assist the family by helping them create checklists, calendars, and other tools to make sure that it respects business formalities.

Truly Letting Go

The most difficult of the three principles is the requirement that a transferor who makes a gift must truly let go of control over the property, relinquishing it to the transferee. Of course, defining "letting go" in the context of a governance system can be difficult. If a transferor retains the right to direct the use or distribution of assets, or to claim them at will, it is clear that the transferor has retained control. Even in the absence of an explicit retained interest, a transferor may be treated as having kept control if factors such as these exist:

❑ Continued occupation of real estate transferred
❑ Commingling of personal and business assets
❑ Distributions that are disproportionate to ownership
❑ Use of entity funds for personal expenses
❑ Transferring the majority of the transferor's assets to the entity

By paying attention to these three principles, the FWTP adviser will help the client family address the most important factors when passing family operating companies from one generation to the next.

A Fourth Principle?

Experienced FWTP advisers will suggest a fourth principle: *don't get too cute*. Limited liability companies created by transferors on their deathbeds, and overly complex plans that no family member understands, are examples of tempting structures that may ultimately lead to disaster. Here, as well as with the three other principles, the FWTP adviser can assist a family by providing a reality check on proposed structures and assessing whether the plan meets the spirit of the three principles we have articulated.

Family Wealth Patterns

Choosing to use a valuation discount entity illustrates a basic principle of the FWTP process: the adviser must carefully consider how closely a family's capacities and constraints match up with the legal requirements for such an entity. This is not limited, of course, to valuation discount entities. The principle is equally applicable to structures such as credit shelter trusts or family foundations. Whether a particular structure will work for a family depends not just on legal principles but on the components of the family wealth system, the family's wealth patterns, and its life cycles.

For example, in developing a business purpose for creating an entity, a chaotic family faces particular challenges because of its inability to define and stick to goals and strategies. The overlapping cycles of change within the family wealth system also affect a family's ability to develop a business purpose. Deathbed transfers hardly ever succeed. The individual life cycle stage of the transferor and the life cycle stage of the business have a huge impact on the viability of business purposes.

Both chaotic and enmeshed families may have difficulty in following through with the requirements to respect all formalities, or to treat an entity as separate from its owners. A pattern of rebellion within a family may also undermine the family's capacity to follow through with these requirements in the long run.

Family patterns regarding control and abdication of control become particularly important in a valuation discount strategy, even if it does not appear as a red flag in the adviser's initial evaluation of the family. A family marked by extreme patterns of control and abdication of control will not be a good candidate for this strategy because it will continue this pattern of behavior after creation of the entity. A transferor bent on controlling the entity will not likely succeed in truly "letting go" in a legal sense. Family wealth transition planning cannot change this pattern of behavior, and governance systems can only mitigate its effects to a certain degree. By contrast, a family with a history of flexible roles, adaptable leadership, and empowerment is much more likely to succeed using this strategy.

Holding Business Ownership Interests in Trust

The usefulness of trusts to hold ownership interests in family businesses cannot be overstated. The most common use of trusts, of course, is to provide a wealth management device that can help ensure that transferees successfully navigate certain life cycle stages prior to inheriting wealth. These trusts contemplate that at some point in time, usually defined by age or accomplishments, the beneficiary will be ready to manage wealth and the trust will terminate. Of course, some family members may never be able to navigate these life stages, and for them, a vehicle such as a special needs trust is critical.

Trusts are also useful in managing accountability when some transferees manage a family business while others are passive investors. In order to manage effectively, those involved in the business must be able to rely on their investor counterparts to be responsible investors and not to meddle excessively in business operations. For families that can predict that this will be a problem, there are several solutions. The manager may receive voting stock, while the other owners receive nonvoting stock. This might not prevent meddling, however, as the legalities of stock voting rights rarely prevent late-night phone calls from distraught relatives. Or a family might separate the wealth entirely, giving the business interests to the managers and other kinds of wealth to those not involved in the business. If this is not practical, a buy–sell agreement or similar mechanism may allow the manager to buy out the investors if they become too intractable.

When the interests are held by the investor transferees in trust, the trustee interacts with the family managers and acts as an intermediary between family members who are involved in management and those who are not. A trust arrangement can be sufficiently flexible to accommodate changes in family members' roles. When properly structured, it is also a mechanism to educate both managers and investors about accountability structures. It allows them to practice and learn about what does and does not work for their family business. The trustee selected should be familiar with the role of a responsible investor in a family business. If a trustee doesn't understand the dynamics of the operating company and its need to take risk in order to remain strategically competitive, an unintended consequence of this trust structure may be suboptimal performance or even the sale of the company.

Patterns of wealth behavior can also inform the choice of a trust as a suitable wealth transition structure. Certain families favor trusts because of their special characteristics. Because a trust offers centralized management through a trustee, it is a particularly useful wealth transition structure for chaotic families and for family members who are content to abdicate their responsibility for management of financial capital. The power to mandate management and distributions in ways that other kinds of entities (such as corporations or LLCs) cannot is also attractive to certain transferors, particularly those in rigid families or families that struggle with control/abdication or conformity/rebellion issues.

Families struggling with these issues often choose trusts as an easy way to continue a pattern of behavior rather than doing the hard work of moving toward a more functional pattern. Using trusts may cause detrimental patterns to repeat in future generations, and even can exacerbate the problems. The centralized power of the trustee, and the trustee's duty to carry out the trustor's intentions, do not necessarily support the evolution of the beneficiary from child to young adult to highly functioning adult, nor do they encourage the entrepreneurship that often provided the original source of the family's wealth.

An entrepreneur's approach to risk is often very different from a trustee's. As wealth held in trust moves from the first generation to subsequent generations, an increasingly greater percentage of the beneficiaries' financial capital tends to be held in trust. This structure may have a significant impact on individual family members and the family as a whole, because it affects their willingness and ability to take risks and make decisions about their wealth. It may also affect the sustainability of the family's financial well-being, because family size may increase faster than the financial capital the family needs to sustain its members for generations.

To counteract the potential unintended consequences that trusts create in family members' development and relationships, some families use a trust as a "just in case" structure while they work on making long-term changes. Trusts also emphasize the trustee's role as mentor to the beneficiaries as they learn how to assess risk and make effective decisions in all areas of their lives.

Specific Trusts for Family Businesses

Most owners of family businesses employ revocable living trusts as their basic wealth transition structure in order to avoid difficulties such as lengthy probate proceedings.

Unless the transferors have fully implemented their transition plan prior to death, it is likely that the first transition of ownership interests in a business will be to the credit shelter and marital trusts upon the passing of the first spouse to die. This raises the perennial question of how to structure the funding of these trusts when a significant asset of the estate is an interest in a closely held business. Proper valuation of ownership interests becomes critical now, since astute division of the ownership interests can create minority discounts useful in planning for the second spouse's death. Similarly, allocating a majority of ownership to a trust may create a control premium. These must be considered in funding any marital gift.

The death of the first spouse may be the first time that the family gets an accurate picture of the value of the business, because an appraisal of the business (and possibly of a fractional share of it) will be required. Depending on the funding formula chosen, an update to that appraisal may also be needed when the trust is funded. It is important to get expert advice about the appropriate valuation model to employ.

Owners of corporations that have made a subchapter S election face special challenges when transferring equity interests to trusts. The S corporation is supposed to be a simple structure, so only certain kinds of trusts, specially blessed by the tax code, qualify as S corporation shareholders. These include grantor trusts, qualified subchapter S trusts (QSSTs), and electing small business trusts (ESBTs). These trusts are not as flexible as many trusts, and in order to protect the S election, the advisory team must take special care to ensure that a trust both meets the needs of the family's situation and qualifies as an S corporation shareholder.

Wealth Transition Linkages
to the Family Subsystem

When family wealth transition planning involves the transfer of a family business, the FWTP adviser must manage the inevitable reverberations of the transition throughout the family wealth system. In order to achieve the goal of wealth continuity, the adviser must analyze the linkages between the business subsystem and the family subsystem and be prepared to replace or repair those linkages as part of the process.

Linkages are as varied as families, but the following are some common linkages meant to inspire inquiry within the FWTP advisory team:

❑ Did the business provide the impetus for family gatherings through board meetings or even ordinary meetings? Will that continue after transition, or does the family need to create a new impetus?

❑ Did the family use the business as a training ground for values? Did children tend to work in the business and absorb family attitudes and history through that experience? If so, will this continue? Does the family want it to continue? If not, how will children be taught history and values?

❑ If the business is staying in the family, how will relationships change after the transition? What assumptions about roles need to be considered as part of this process? For example, if the former owner is now to be a consultant, how will that change day-to-day interactions?

❑ Did the business meet an individual need of the transferor that remains critical to that individual's quality of life? Businesses provide a sense of meaning, an assurance of independence, and "something to do." They also provide a place to "be the boss," whereas the family subsystem often feels like the opposite.

Attending to these linkages will implicate the other components of a wealth transition plan: role clarity/development and governance systems.

Wealth Transition Structures Within the Family Subsystem

Just as wealth transition structures in the operating business subsystem affect the family subsystem, wealth transition structures in the family subsystem have important effects elsewhere in the system. The very idea of transferring wealth within the family subsystem is alien to many families, because the family subsystem isn't usually populated with "assets" in the traditional sense. Instead, the assets of the family subsystem are intangibles: belonging, memories, emotions, acceptance, support, traditions, and values. Many FWTP advisers shy away from discussing the transition of wealth in the family subsystem, because these assets are impossible to capture on a balance sheet, and every family has unique ways of passing these assets along. Yet attending to these transitions is an important component of creating wealth transition structures within the overall family wealth system.

Wealth Transition Linkages to the Investment/Office Subsystem

When the time comes for the transition of a family business, the advisory team must explore linkages between the transition and the investment/office system prior to implementing the transition. If the transition is by sale, for example, this will result in a sudden influx of liquidity into the investment/office system. Families whose wealth has primarily been in the form of an operating business will need new skills to manage this wealth, from investment skills to knowing how to select new advisers to learning a new form of budgeting.

If the business was family operated, yet the equity ownership was concentrated in one generation prior to sale, conflict can arise if the proceeds are not shared in ways that reflect the various contributions of family members. Many families' transition processes have been derailed by a liquidity event that occurs prior to promised gifts being made. Once an offer is on the table, it is difficult if not impossible to make gifts at an acceptable tax cost. Assignment-of-income principles, too, may prevent effective income tax planning.

Every business family has a few obvious linkages, and even more hidden ones, between their investment and operating subsystems. The FWTP adviser must ferret these out and manage them appropriately. A few to consider are:

❑ Real estate leased to the operating company by the transferor, through a different entity. Will this arrangement continue, and if so, how will lease rates be set?
❑ Qualified retirement plans that offer much higher contribution levels than individual retirement accounts (IRAs) or similar vehicles. A sale of a business will likely result in termination of the plan and rollover

of funds into an IRA. A transfer may also adversely affect the ability of the transferor to participate in the plan. How will these changes affect the transferor's ability to save, and how important is that to the transferor?

❏ Fringe benefits, such as health insurance, life insurance, an automobile, or the services of a bookkeeper. Will these benefits continue? If not, how will these needs be met?

❏ The "deductible slush fund" for expenses such as football tickets, fishing trips, or box seats at the opera. Will these types of expenses be viewed as "appropriate" by the investment/office or other subsystem, now that there isn't a shred of hope of deducting them?

Wealth Transition Structures Within the Investment/Office Subsystem

The essential function of the investment/office subsystem is to accumulate and manage assets for family stewardship of wealth. This subsystem must address financial needs, and also human capital needs: education and the ability to plan for an uncertain future, set and achieve goals, manage investments, and save and spend wisely. Training youngsters in saving and spending habits, investing, and dealing with uncertainty is an important component of human capital within this subsystem.

Wealth Transition Linkages to the Philanthropic Subsystem

The closing, sale, or gift of an operating business potentially has an enormous impact on the philanthropic subsystem. The essential difference between the philanthropic subsystem and the other subsystems within the family wealth system is that philanthropy moves financial capital away from the personal use of family members and toward the greater community in which the family lives. This transition has the potential to build an even greater amount of human and social capital within the family wealth system, which in turn will form a strong base for the family's legacy. However, this exchange can generate particularly strong ripple effects throughout the system. Managing these effects requires rigorous planning and a long-term view in creating and implementing transition structures. A FWTP process must accommodate those reverberations, both good and bad.

Wealth Transition Structures Within the Philanthropic Subsystem

Most transferors of wealth would say that, given the choice, they would rather transfer financial capital to a charity than to the government. Yet many charitable gifts that would otherwise make sense are never made because of certain internal dynamics within the family wealth system relating to cycles of change and family patterns of behavior.

Overlapping cycles of individual and family development often pull transferors in opposite directions regarding making a charitable gift. Aging transferors may have both the capacity for and interest in charitable giving, while younger family members' attention is focused inward, on spending time with young children and building their own family's wealth. The antidote to this, inoculating all family members with the values of generosity and benevolence, requires a long-term commitment by other family members to consistently exemplify those values and provide meaningful opportunities for their practice.

Coordinating Wealth Transition Structures Within the Operating Business and Philanthropic Subsystems

The sale or transfer of a family business can often be coordinated with charitable giving strategies that will soften the tax blow of such transitions or make the transfers "cheaper" for the transferees. All of these strategies result in the transfer of value outside the family system, and many require substantial liquidity. When transactions involve a sale, whether to a family member or an outsider, these strategies are particularly helpful. The FWTP advisory team must carefully analyze various options and their impact on the family if this type of transfer is to work.

CHAPTER NOTES

1. See Bonnie Brown Hartley, *Sudden Death: A Fire Drill for Building Strength and Flexibility in Families* (Cambio Press, 2006).

2. See IRC Sec. 1042 (seller deferral of gain on sale to ESOP if reinvested in securities). See generally Martin Staubus, David Binn, and Ron Bernstein, *Transitioning Ownership in the Private Corporation: The ESOP Solution*, 2nd ed. (The Beyster Institute, 2005); Scott Rodrick, *Leveraged ESOPs & Employee Buyouts* (National Center for Employee Ownership, 2005).

3. In the typical asset sale, the selling entity will retain liability arising from presale events, such as product liability claims. Because it is likely that the sales price will be distributed to the owners of the seller, this liability is often personally guaranteed or otherwise provided for through a reserve. The selling family, accustomed to the liability protection afforded by a corporate entity, may be surprised by this personal liability.

4. See IRC Sec. 197.

5. See IRC Secs. 483 and 7872. There are limited exceptions to the requirement of a market rate of interest. IRC Sec. 7872(d) allows the imputed interest on a gift loan of less than $100,000 between individuals to be limited to the borrower's net investment income.

6. Of course, the family partnership rules of IRC Sec. 704(e) must be considered.

7. See, e.g., *Shepherd v. Commissioner*, 283 F.3d 1258 (11th Cir. 2002), *aff'g* 115 T.C. 376 (2000).

8. See, e.g., *Rosen v. Commissioner*, TC Memo 2006-115.

CHAPTER 9

GOVERNANCE SYSTEMS

THE SECOND CORE element of a successful family wealth transition is a mechanism for making decisions about shared wealth that will lead to family wealth continuity. Finding the right way for a diverse group of stakeholders to make decisions about wealth is an important aspect of stewardship of that wealth. Properly structured, these mechanisms support existing family relationships and help build even better ones by overcoming patterns of wealth behavior that breed mistrust, rebellion, and chaos.

Governance systems are critically important in family wealth transition planning (FWTP) because of the paradox of the successful family. The more successful a family is in empowering its members to move naturally through their individual and family life cycles, the more diverse the family becomes. This creates a core challenge for families and their FWTP advisers when wealth is transferred: finding new ways in which wealth transferees, who likely will have very different perspectives from their forebears and peers, can share wealth productively. It is not possible to rely on the common expectation of a transferor that the transferees will "just work it out." A governance system, properly structured and implemented, is more likely to shape the family wealth system in ways that support the goals of family wealth continuity.

The role of the FWTP process in relation to governance systems is threefold. First, the planning process requires an assessment of the current governance systems operating within the family wealth system, and especially those relating to the business and existing wealth management structures.

Second, the adviser must identify the needs of the family in order to design a governance system that will fit them. Boilerplate wealth transition structures are a good starting place for designing governance systems, but most families will want to adjust various aspects of these systems to meet their particular needs.

Third, the adviser should assist a family in practicing its new governance system well before a trigger event requires it. This will require attention to the definition and development of roles.

The Core Governance Problem
for Family Businesses

Families often struggle with choosing a governance system, or a number of governance structures, to manage their family wealth system. In most families, each successive generation increases the total size of the family. New members differentiate themselves from their families in fascinating ways. The diversity of experiences, interests, skills, and abilities within families typically increases, rather than decreases, over time. Paradoxically, the more successful a family has been in encouraging the individuation of its members, the more it needs a governance system in order to share wealth productively.

Consider a business founded by the transferor generation that involved just a few family members, all of whom worked in the business. The small number of stakeholders helped in the decision-making process. The stakeholders' shared experiences allowed them to arrive at a common understanding of the role of the business in the family wealth system. Over years of making decisions together, the founders created an implicit governance system that likely bore little resemblance to the legally required governance system of whatever legal entity they adopted. That didn't matter. They were fully able to accomplish the core job of governance: allocating the benefits and burdens of the operating business subsystem among all of the participants in the business.

Over the years, the transferors established a pattern of sharing the wealth created by the business with stakeholders that reflected the state of the family wealth system and the external forces at work upon it. Individual, family, and business life cycles and patterns of wealth behavior, as well as business exigencies, economic conditions, and tax laws affected the transferors' choices of how to allocate the benefits and burdens of the business. The transferors created a governance system to establish how to make those allocations, whether they involved how to set salaries or make distributions, or whether a grandchild could have a summer job in the business. They neither called it a governance system, nor operated it in accordance with formal legal rules. It was likely a nimble, autocratic system involving, to a greater or lesser degree, all those who owned the business, plus their spouses.

This generation may choose to transfer the ownership of the business to transferees who must share this wealth. From the transferors' perspective, dividing the business would mean killing the goose that laid the golden egg. Choosing one child instead of others doesn't seem quite fair, even if one child has a closer connection to the business than others do. Sharing ownership of the business may be the only way to ensure that transferees benefit fully from this source of wealth.

The relationship of these transferees to the business is likely to be very different than their predecessors' was. Some may work in the business; others may be involved in professions or even be perpetual students. Some may rely on the business for a livelihood, while others may view it as an investment. Some will live close at hand and others far away. Some may believe the best approach is to continue the business; others may wish to sell.

These transferees cannot rely on years of shared business experiences, or on years of making decisions together and living with the results. They cannot even expect to share a common view of the world.

The result of all this diversity is that the governance system of their predecessors will not work for them, because that governance system is implicit and depends upon particular people and their experiences. They need a different approach.

Some transferors anticipate this problem and look to their FWTP advisers for ways to help the next generation share this wealth responsibly. But others deny that this problem could ever exist. They expect the transferees to "get along"; after all, the transferors made it work, despite their differences. More fundamentally, the idea that sharing wealth is something new doesn't ring true for many transferors, who truly *have* been sharing the wealth from the business for years with various family stakeholders. These transferors need to understand how wealth transitions will change this dynamic if they are to grasp the need for a governance system.

This complexity changes the map of stakeholders in the family operating business subsystem. In the founders' generation, everyone who made decisions about the business worked there. By the third generation, that is rarely the case. Owner/managers and owner/investors will have divergent interests with very real practical effects. A new class of owner/investors will create a demand for distributions because they do not receive their wealth from the company through salaries and benefits. Moreover, as the map of stakeholders changes, the pattern of sharing that the transferor generation established will change. Maybe not right away, and maybe incrementally, but it *will* change The stakeholders need a rational way to decide how to accommodate these changes, given their diversity of experience, interests, and involvement with the business. Even more important, the absence of a good governance system is likely to undermine both family relationships and the creation of a family legacy.

Thus, the central problem of governance in FWTP is designing a way for a diverse group of family members to share wealth in ways that foster family wealth continuity. Increasing complexity in the family wealth system is likely to lead to some sort of centralized management, in which a subset of the stakeholders will make decisions for the larger group. This likely represents a fundamental change from the way that the previous generation made decisions, and it may feel risky for family members because it implicates all of a family's trust, control, and adaptability issues.

As part of these big changes in the family wealth system, the family must develop a governance system that will build, rather than destroy, healthy family relationships and encourage responsible stewardship of wealth.

Components of a Good Governance System

—THE MARSHALL FAMILY—
Ruthie Ann Marshall, age fifty-three

All us kids, we gave my mother and father a fiftieth wedding anniversary party. People came from all over, 'cause everybody knows them and everybody loves them. When Daddy got up to make his speech, somebody shouted out, "Hey, Johnny Ray, what's the secret to a happy marriage?" Daddy didn't miss a beat. He winked at Mama and said to the whole crowd, "Oh, that's easy. Me, I just do as I'm told." Everybody roared with laughter.

Family members are often surprised to hear that they have a family governance system in place. But all business families do have some mechanism in place to make decisions about the management of wealth. Ideally, these mechanisms have one primary task: to involve the right people in the right way about decisions concerning aspects of family wealth continuity, through a rational, predictable, and sustainable process. How well they succeed in this mission, of course, varies greatly.

A governance system is necessary only when more than one person has a legitimate claim to the benefits of a component of the family wealth system. If a family doesn't need to share wealth, each person will govern his or her own share and no governance system will be necessary.

Most families commence FWTP with some governance systems in place. Many of these will be implicit and others are part of a legal component of the family wealth system. As part of the process, FWTP advisers must evaluate how these systems are actually used as compared to their legal forms. They must evaluate both explicit and implicit systems to determine their continued utility within the family system after wealth transition.

The FWTP process will import new wealth transition structures into the family wealth system. Some of these incorporate specific governance systems. Yet in too many transition processes, families adopt boilerplate systems in response to external forces, without careful thought or adaptation to the needs of the family. To create a successful wealth transition plan, these wealth transition structures should be tailored to meet the family's particular needs.

Understanding existing governance systems is an essential part of mapping the components and connections within a family wealth system. In evaluating these governance mechanisms, and designing new ones, the adviser can consider three essential elements:

❏ Identifying legitimate stakeholders
❏ Defining appropriate involvement
❏ Creating a rational, sustainable process

Who Has a Legitimate Stake in Outcomes?

While legally recognized rights (stock ownership, cotenancy, community property) are a component of the family wealth system, they are rarely the most important kind of rights for families. The critical question is whether the family views a person as having a legitimate claim to share in the wealth created by a form of capital within the family. If so, that person has a stake in the outcome of at least some decisions made with respect to that asset.

The stakeholder analysis discussed is a good tool for determining who, within and without the family, has a stake in the outcome of decisions. As the family tests its assumptions about individual family members' rights, roles, and responsibilities, the places of family members as stakeholders may change. Stakeholders will change with the inevitable cycles of change and equilibrium at work within the family wealth system.

What Is Appropriate Involvement in Decision Making?

A governance structure must clarify who has the right to participate in making decisions. This has both an internal and an external purpose. Internally, it lets the participants in the venture know who can and will make which decisions. Externally, it allows third parties to rely on the decisions made by those with authority.

Appropriate involvement in decision making can range from highly participatory, in which all stakeholders participate in decision making, to highly centralized, in which a few people (i.e., managers) try to make decisions in the best interests of a larger group of stakeholders. One pattern is clear: as families become more complex, they evolve toward centralized management methods of ownership, particularly in business.

What Is a Rational, Predictable, and Sustainable Process?

A governance system provides the rules of the road for making decisions. A good governance system should have three characteristics: rationality, predictability, and sustainability. If any one of these three elements is missing, a governance system is likely to be unable to support family wealth continuity.

Rationality

First, the system must be rational. *Rationality* in this sense does not mean the absence of emotions. It means that the decision-making process is sensible. Its processes must relate rationally to the ends at hand, whether the decision is about selling an operating business, distributing charitable funds, or use of the family vacation home. The governance structure should provide a decision-making process that adequately gathers relevant information, analyzes it, produces a decision, and monitors the effect of that decision.

Predictability

Second, a good governance system must be *predictable*, in the sense that the family members who are expected to use it understand the rules and can access them easily. A secret process is unlikely to support any of the goals of family wealth continuity, and an overly complicated one will never be used.

Sustainability

Third, the process must be *sustainable*, in two ways. It must be self-perpetuating, so that it can survive the departure of the specific people involved at the outset and endure under the stress of trigger events such as divorce, death, or business disappointments. It must be flexible enough to evolve with the needs of the family. Moreover, it must not be unduly inefficient: It must not impose unnecessary transaction costs on those who use it.

The Trend Toward Centralized Management

—THE HERNÁNDEZ FAMILY—

Ramón Hernández, age twenty-two

I'm not going to tell tales about my mother—that's Clara—and grandmother and aunt because they were so good to me my whole life. But if you were a fly on the wall of their shop when they first started, you'd run for your life, you really would. They would argue and shout at each other; they would carry on about whether this design was stupid or that fabric was impossible, and if there was even a dime missing in the books they would stay up all night looking for it. What I mean is that was the way it was when I was little. By the time they had turned it into really something wonderful—and it really was, people still say my mother is the best designer they've ever met—my grandmother was getting older and my Tía Elena had cancer. My mother was actually running things by then. But it wasn't like she could ever get away with anything. All three of them went to Mass together three times a week, and on the first Wednesday of every month, right after Mass, Mamá always had to go to "Second Confession." I don't mean to any priest, either, but to Grandma and Tía Elena. Mamá always said that confessing to her mother and Elena was worse than to a priest, because at least with a priest you knew you'd get absolution, but with those ladies, you were never quite sure. Mamá would take the books over to Tía Elena's house and they would pore over them, and they'd talk about employee problems and new lines of kiddie clothes. The other ladies would give their advice and sometimes Mamá would take it, sometimes not. Occasionally, Uncle Bart would sit in, but he usually kept pretty quiet. I remember when I was fourteen asking Mamá why she put up with this confession business; after all, she knew a lot more about the business than they did. She said, *"Ay m'hijo, no entiendes nada de nada."* (Oh, son, you don't know anything about anything.)

The Hernández clothing business illustrates the natural evolution of governance systems toward centralized management.[1] As the situations of the three women became more complex, they moved from equal participation in management to relying on Clara as manager. But Clara clearly understood that she was accountable to her partners. The women set up a system of accountability early on with which all three women were comfortable. All three had access to the financial records. María and Elena gave advice, but Clara did not necessarily have to follow it. Apparently the system worked well, as the women ultimately sold the business for a tidy sum.

The need for centralized management emerges when the family wealth system starts to get complicated. Complexity also arises naturally as the business, the family, and its individual members move through their respective life cycles.

This experience illustrates the central concern of governance structures in which not all stakeholders are equally involved in decision making: striking the right balance between the autonomy granted to decision makers and the accountability owed to stakeholders. Managers need discretion, yet too much discretion can breed inappropriate behavior, or the suspicion of it. So the stakeholders create some sort of oversight system, such as a board of directors or an advisers' committee. Some managers may chafe under this oversight, complaining of micromanagement. Some owners may complain of alleged mismanagement. If the governance system is a good one, it will provide a process to balance discretion and accountability that will satisfy both groups' needs. A family may choose familiar governance structures, such as trusts or corporations, or may invent their own, as did the Hernández women.

In a family business, not everyone with a financial or emotional stake in the enterprise is suited to or interested in management. There may not be a place at the top for everyone. When investors in a public company are unhappy, they can just sell their investments, but in a closely held enterprise, this is rarely practical or even possible. The Hernández women were fortunate to find a buyer for their relatively risky enterprise. Moreover, unresolved conflict about what comprises a healthy balance of discretion and accountability can undermine family relationships. Since a fundamental goal of transition planning is supporting healthy, loving family relationships, avoiding this predictable source of conflict is critical to the process.

Striking the right balance is particularly challenging in the family context, for several reasons. First, it is not clear just who is entitled to participate in oversight. Membership in any stakeholder group changes as family members and the family as a whole move through their respective life cycles. When Ramón was fourteen, his mother did not view him as a legitimate stakeholder, but if the women had kept the business, Clara might have changed her mind. Moreover, membership in stakeholder groups varies among wealth subsystems. Bart's role as a stakeholder is unclear. Was he invited to sit in on Second Confession because he had lent money to the business? Or because of his important role in the family? Why did he "mostly keep quiet?" These ambiguities underscore the need for careful stakeholder analysis. In this analysis, the FWTP adviser must take care not to fall under the spell of traditional models, in which managers are charged with operating a business solely on behalf of its owners. Not only does modern corporate law theory challenge this premise, but it is also clearly inaccurate in many family-owned businesses. The stakeholders to whom managers are accountable include more than just owners. This group potentially includes spouses of owners, family members employed by the business, lessors of property, and anyone whom the family views as a legitimate stakeholder, as well as those with recognizable legal claims.

Elements of Accountability

—THE WILLIAMS FAMILY—
Helen Weinstein Williams, age forty-eight

One thing my father always told me was never to react in anger, but only in knowledge. So, once I found out about John's affair and child, I decided to stay quiet and take a look at our whole financial situation. You were very helpful in recommending that accountant. The accountant sent someone over to our house, and she downloaded all of the records from the computer onto a tiny little computer thing. She said John hadn't even protected the computer with a password, which just goes to show you how confident he was that I would stay totally in the dark. A week or so later, the accountant called and asked me to stop by for a visit. I especially wanted to know if John was paying any money to Cindy. He's not, but I don't know if that's good news or bad, because the accountant said he (and I!) might owe her a lot of back child support. But she also told me that in 2002 John made a huge withdrawal—over $500,000—from his retirement account. The accountant says we probably had to pay a lot of tax penalties because of that withdrawal, but I don't remember seeing penalties on the tax return, which I signed but didn't read very carefully, I suppose. The check was to a title company, and there's a notation, "C's co-op." I'm not stupid—just blind—and I can sure guess what this is. Everyone knows you can't buy a co-op for half a million, so I'll bet there's more bad news to come. I put my accountant's bill on John's desk with a little note—"Be sure to pay this!"

Helen Williams is well on her way to renegotiating the governance structure of her family wealth system. She has embarked upon a journey of learning about family finances as well as demanding more accountability from John.

Helen has begun with the basic tool of accountability: access to information, or *transparency*. This is one of three tools she may ultimately employ, the others being *review of decision making* (the power to have a decision reviewed or changed) and *transformation* (the ability to fundamentally change the relationship).

Transparency of Information

Transparency allows stakeholders access to information about decisions made by managers, including not only the decision itself, but also the underlying data on which managers rely in making decisions. State or federal law establishes default rules for many legal arrangements so that the parties know what information various stakeholders are entitled to receive and the way in which managers must share it. Private arrangements may vary this pattern. When Helen wanted information, she was able to obtain it easily, raising the question of whether John really wanted to keep his secret.

Almost every business entity must make some sort of report to its stakeholders. Tax returns provide information to nonfamily stakeholders. A publicly traded corporation must file regular reports with the Securities and Exchange Commission. State law usually gives equity participants in a venture the right to certain information about the activities and decisions made for an entity. Shareholders have the right to inspect the books and records of a corporation. This right is unlimited for some information, such as the identity of other owners. But for other information, the shareholder must have a proper purpose for making the request. It is not only businesses that must be transparent, however. A charity must make its tax returns and certain other documents available to the public. State law usually gives a trust beneficiary the right to inspect the trust agreement and typically requires the trustee to provide an annual accounting of income and disbursements to each beneficiary.

Contracts between an entity and a participant may grant information rights that are unavailable under state law. Banks loaning money may require the borrower to meet income ratios, and require regular reports or audits to ensure compliance. When an installment sale of stock in a closely held corporation occurs, the seller is often given the right to inspect any and all records, accounts, and other information about the business, and the right to audit those accounts.

The governance documents of an entity may give stakeholders much more extensive information rights than those granted under state law. An agent acting under a power of attorney may be required to provide annual reports to named persons as a condition of the granting of the power. Families themselves often have implicit rules that determine how open they will be about information. In some families, parents never share any aspect of their plan for wealth transition before their deaths; in others, everyone knows exactly what will happen and why. Most families are somewhere in between.

Responsible stewardship of wealth requires that both managers and stakeholders understand their respective roles in sharing and receiving information. Helen and John's system made Helen vulnerable to all kinds of trigger events, such as John's sudden death or incapacity, or the discovery of a secret. Helen had completely abdicated her role in keeping up with family finances to John's control, who implicitly agreed to Helen's abdication.

Many stakeholders genuinely desire information, because they want to ensure that the manager is acting in their best interests, but do not understand what information is appropriate to share, or what to do with information they receive. Some stakeholders suffer from the myth of perfect information: an expectation that a manager will share *all* information, with the accompanying belief that a perfect decision could be made if only the right information were considered.

Sometimes, stakeholders confuse transparency in decision making with higher levels of accountability. When this happens, the sharing of information can easily turn into second-guessing the manager's decisions. This can trigger a cycle of distrust, in which managers resist even reasonable requests for information, which causes suspicion among stakeholders, which in turn generates greater resistance. Transparency processes simply give stakeholders the power to know about certain managerial decisions. What transparency processes don't do, however, is provide a remedy if stakeholders object to a decision. That requires the next layer of accountability.

Review of Decisions

Proper accountability incorporates opportunities for decisions to be reviewed and potentially overridden, modified, or remanded for further consideration. Again, these processes can be a function of state or federal law, or private arrangements. Helen and John Williams, for example, are likely to struggle with John's decision to buy a co-op for Cindy and Brad. Helen's options for challenging this decision are few, and she may ultimately ask the divorce court to provide a remedy.

In business entities, some decisions are usually reserved for some subgroup of stakeholders. Shareholders must generally vote on merger, sale of all assets, and other major corporate moves, although managers have discovered processes by which voting can be bypassed. Bylaws and other governance documents may expand the universe of these decisions, potentially removing a great deal of discretion from managers and reserving decisions to owners. This has a tendency to undermine the benefits of centralized decision making, but may be necessary to create trust between managers and stakeholders.

State law usually provides a mechanism for a court to review decisions made by managers, whether they are boards, managers of a limited liability company (LLC), or trustees. The difficulty of obtaining review often depends on the type of decision and how it was made. Most business entities have special rules for conflict-of-interest transactions, requiring approval for transactions in which managers might benefit at the expense of other stakeholders. Managers' decisions are often protected by the business judgment rule, so that even getting into court is difficult, and prevailing there is even more so. Trustees, however, are subject to more stringent oversight, and typically cannot rely on the business judgment rule. Therefore, it is easier for stakeholders to challenge their actions.

The ultimate check on the discretion of managers is the power of stakeholders to remove and replace them with individuals more amenable to the interests of the stakeholders. In some instances, removal is easy and painless. A principal who has granted an agency under a power of attorney can simply remove the agent, revoking the unilateral power—at least while the principal still has the capacity to do so. At the other end of the spectrum, it is quite unusual for trust beneficiaries to have the power to remove or replace trustees, absent some wrongdoing or a grant of that power by the trustor. Business entities lie somewhere in between: state law usually provides a mechanism for equity owners to elect or appoint managers, but it is an unwieldy process.

Transformation

The third level of accountability is *transformation*, or the ability to change the structure itself or alter the relationships within it in fundamental ways. If the other processes of accountability don't work, and those with a stake in the outcome are still not satisfied with the arrangement, they may be able to either "take their toys and go home," or eliminate the governance relationship entirely. This is the nuclear bomb of accountability, and as such, it is usually reserved for situations in which the other tools have failed. When a process of transformation is absent, the only practical alternative may be protracted, expensive, and painful litigation.

Entities and arrangements used in FWTP vary significantly in terms of the participants' ability to fundamentally alter the structure or relationships within it. Some families evidence a pattern of cutting off family ties, creating a fundamental shift in the relationships in the core family subsystem. Divorce is obviously the most common method for changing these relationships, and pre- and postnuptial agreements are intended to serve as a tool of transformation. Helen and John's prenuptial agreement was intended to be this kind of structure, but if they seek a divorce, John's actions with respect to Cindy and Brad and the co-op are likely to trigger heated controversy.

State law provides a variety of mechanisms to transform structures. Owners of a corporation or LLC may, for example, seek judicial dissolution of the entity if malfeasance or deadlock occurs, but judicial dissolution is an unwieldy tool that families are especially hesitant to employ for fear of airing their dirty laundry. Families are more likely to seek private arrangements to meet this need for a transformation structure. Family members enter into buy–sell agreements, employment contracts, prenuptial agreements, and similar contractual arrangements in order to provide a process that includes sensible checks on the ability of members to invoke it. These arrangements must also be consistent with the ongoing wealth accumulation and management plan of the family.

Wealth Transition Structures as Governance Systems

Before deciding to use any wealth transition structure, a family and its FWTP advisers should analyze the fit between the structure's governance system and the family's needs. Each of these structures provides a different governance system, through state law rules that apply in the governance arena. Many of these rules can be altered by agreement of the parties, although a few are immutable, such as the fiduciary duty of a trustee.

Each of these structures expresses a different combination of governance characteristics along three dimensions:

❑ Participation (versus centralized management)
❑ Accountability
❑ Transaction costs

For entities marked by *high participation* in governance, those with a stake in the outcome have the right to be involved in decision making. Because of participation by stakeholders, the need for accountability systems is low. In a member-managed LLC, the right of members to obtain information and participate in management eases the need for highly developed fiduciary duties of one member to another. Structures at this end of the spectrum tend to have high transaction costs. Since there is an expectation that all participants will take part in decision making, the governance process is likely to take time, effort, and expense.

At the other extreme, families may choose to create entities with the highest degree of centralized management and the most highly developed accountability systems. For example, in both trusts and conservatorships, the manager (the trustee or conservator) makes decisions, often without any participation by the beneficiary or protected person. As a corollary, highly developed rules of accountability bind these managers, including the entire realm of fiduciary duties as well as mandatory processes for sharing information with beneficiaries and the courts. The access that a beneficiary has to trust information is defined by statute. In a trust, the opportunity for review of a trustee's actions is limited and transformation is difficult.

Between the two extremes are entities that incorporate a blend of participation and centralized management. The corporate form prescribes limited participation for shareholders, and as a corollary imposes fiduciary duties on directors to act on the shareholders' best interests. For example, shareholders must usually vote on the board of directors' recommendation to sell all or substantially all of the corporate assets. Moving along the continuum, a common wealth transition structure involves limiting participation by some shareholders by creating voting and nonvoting stock. Yet a shareholder holding voting stock can still rely on the fiduciary duty of the board of directors and other shareholders for protection.

Any of these models can be modified to vary the participation of owners, the accountability of management to owners, or the transaction costs. The standard corporate model may be modified by giving shareholders additional rights to participate in governance. This is done by reserving to the shareholders certain decisions that would normally be made by the board.[2] Sometimes these variances are incorporated into the legal documents establishing the entity. Other variances require supplementary documents and enforcement mechanisms. A shareholders' agreement, which may supplement the articles and bylaws of a closely held corporation, can address many of the accountability issues discussed later in this chapter.

Designing the Right Kind of Governance System for a Family

The fundamental governance design question in the FWTP process is how stakeholders will participate in the management of wealth. The design of a governance system will depend on a number of interrelated factors: the kind of business, the existing systems, the choices of wealth transition structures, and underlying family patterns of behavior. The more active the business, the more thought must be given to governance systems, but even passive investments require a formal, rational governance system, a feature that is even more important given IRS challenges to valuation discounts.[3]

The transition process is about adapting the family wealth system in ways that will support family wealth continuity. Thus, the governance system for the operating business subsystem should create feedback loops that support the goals of family wealth continuity and interrupt or dampen existing feedback loops that don't support these goals. Every governance system will facilitate shared participation in decision making, but each kind of family has a different core need that the governance system must fulfill. Unfortunately, the governance systems that a family finds attractive may not be what they need to adapt their family wealth system.

Some families have special needs for governance systems. For example, a rigid family's patterns of wealth behavior likely involve amplifying feedback loops of control and abdication. Exercise of control induces abdication, which in turn provides the justification for more control. But this pattern of wealth behavior is not likely to support either good stewardship of business assets or a family legacy. This family's challenge is to learn to share participation in decision making and to interrupt the control/abdication pattern by using a governance system with participatory characteristics. These families are attracted to models of governance that involve highly centralized management, but discover in the FWTP process that moving toward a model of shared participation supports family wealth continuity. To have any realistic chance of success, this governance system must include two other features. *Role development* for those with a history of abdication will be a critical element, because shared participation in governance requires better education about this kind of decision making. A strong *accountability structure* within the governance system will also be necessary to induce those in control to try the new system.

On the other hand, many families, in particular enmeshed and chaotic ones, are initially attracted to a fully participatory model. It may be familiar; it's the way the transferor generation made decisions. Transferors may try to use it to "bring the kids together" to maintain the illusion of a cohesive family. And, for families in which fear trumps trust, a fully participatory system may seem the only way to ensure protection of each person's interests. This approach may be appropriate for a few families who share a relatively passive form of financial capital, but it has the potential to stymie the operations of any business with a diverse set of stakeholders. While attractive in theory, the idea of involving all the stakeholders in complicated decisions simply doesn't work in business. The only practical approach for almost every family in which financial wealth will be shared is a form of centralized management in which a smaller group than the whole will be making decisions, but will be subject to proper accountability structures.

Families must begin their quest for a governance system with preferences that are consistent with their patterns of wealth behavior. Adaptation of a family wealth system to support good stewardship, healthy relationships, and a family legacy requires a governance system that moves them part of the way along the continuum. For rigid and disengaged families, the core challenge is finding ways to share decision making. The core challenge for chaotic and enmeshed families is finding ways to bring structure to their decision making. To do this, FWTP advisers adapt the common forms of business organization by including features that increase the participatory or centralized management aspects of the governance system.

The Implications of Trust and Fear

Assessing the degree of trust and fear[4] in the family is fundamental to determining the attention that the FWTP adviser must pay to the design of a governance system. When FWTP advisers hear drumbeats of fear within a family, they know that this family will require particularly close attention to the design of a governance system. It is tempting for the FWTP adviser to try to build trust through the process aspects of FWTP, but this may be futile because trust cannot develop so quickly. Instead, if properly structured and implemented, a well designed governance system will allow trust to replace fear as the family acquires a history of good experiences with decision making in the sharing of wealth. In the meantime, it acts as a substitute for real trust.

A family with a high degree of trust can adopt simple decision-making and accountability systems because its members bring to FWTP the capacity for belief in each other's good intentions. They believe at a fundamental level that those in charge will act in their best interests, as well as those of the family as a whole. Therefore, it is tempting for the family to adopt boilerplate systems that are inherent in the wealth transition structures chosen as part of the FWTP process, and move on to the third component of a successful wealth transition plan: role clarity and development. But even these families should invest some energy in the creation of a governance system that meets their particular needs and takes advantage of their particular capacities.

Some families appear neutral regarding trust and fear. These family members may not have enough experience in making decisions together to accurately assess how much they trust each other on wealth matters, but they are not ruled by fear. Disengaged families are often of this type, as are successive generations who have not participated in business decisions with their predecessors. For these families, investing in a governance system allows them to make conscious decisions about the degree of participation they want to take on, and put in place explicit rules about accountability.

Implications of Entitlement and Shame

A family with a history of entitlement and shame[5] requires greater attention to governance systems than other families. However, for these families, ideas about what entitles a person to participate in decision making create special problems. Those who wear the entitlement mantle expect to inherit control, yet may be torn between claiming their place in the sun and rebelling against family expectations. Those who are not "entitled" often rebel or abdicate all responsibility for decision making. These families must come to grips with the idea that shared wealth means each participant will make some sort of contribution, and that it may not be in the interests of family wealth continuity for the patterns of the transferor generation to continue.

Varying Participation Features to Find the Right Blend

In the FWTP process, wealth transition structures are often selected in response to external forces, such as tax or liability issues. The structure will establish the legal parameters for participation in governance. Selection of a corporate vehicle, an LLC, or some sort of trust will import specific default rules of law relating to governance, and specifically to the relative rights of stakeholders to participate in management. Some families may choose to adopt these rules as their governance system. Yet these rules are not optimal for most families, because they represent a compromise struck by lawmakers—a default solution designed to work in most situations. These rules, particularly in the corporate and LLC context, were not designed for family endeavors. The adviser can use these rules to avoid reinventing the wheel, but should help a family adjust each structure to meet its needs more effectively.

Varying the degree of participation and centralized management within a business entity such as a corporation or an LLC is a relatively simple matter. Some are obvious, such as the use of a manager- or member-managed LLC. *Figure 9.1* summarizes other variables that the FWTP adviser can consider to move a business entity toward greater participation or more centralized management. Some of these variables,

FIGURE **9.1**   Variables Changing the Mix of Participation and Centralized Management

	Attributes Creating More Participation	Attributes Creating More Centralized Management
Corporation (can be adapted for LLC)	• Use of only voting stock • Reserving more decisions for shareholders than required under state law • High quorum requirements • Supermajority requirements for certain votes • Preemptive rights • Use of voting trusts or voting agreements to ensure board membership is representative of all shareholders • Prohibition on proxies • Put rights	• Use of nonvoting stock • Extensive use of proxies • Call rights • Low quorum requirements • Minimum voting requirements for shareholder votes (e.g., majority instead of supermajority) • Staggered board terms • Voting trusts
LLC-specific	• Member management • Required annual (or more frequent) meetings of members	• Manager management • Relaxed fiduciary duties of managers

such as requiring annual meetings for an LLC, also figure prominently in the design of accountability features, but these variables also function independently to blend participation and centralized management.

A trust potentially represents the ultimate in centralized management, where the trustee acts on behalf of the trustor to the benefit of the beneficiary. Opportunities for participation by the trustor or the beneficiary are fraught with danger. Thus, it is critical at this juncture for the FWTP adviser to ensure a family understands that trusts are a fundamentally different choice of governance system than business entities.

Varying Accountability Features to Accommodate Family Needs

Following adoption of any form of centralized management, it is necessary to put in place some rules of accountability to ensure that the managers are acting in the best interests of the stakeholders. Traditional governance systems provide some features of accountability, but they rarely, if ever, provide the right kind of accountability for any particular family.

What accountability features actually do is (1) give those playing the oversight role information about the managers' management of wealth, and (2) give managers feedback about how well they are doing in terms of meeting the needs of stakeholders. When it works properly, accountability generates *amplifying* feedback loops that build trust and *dampening* feedback loops that dispel fear. Particularly when governance systems are in flux, as they are in a FWTP process, family members may misinterpret even innocuous events because they fear the impact of these changes. That misinterpretation can undermine trust in the manager's future activities. Even the tamest of accountability structures, such as a phone call, can interrupt this cycle and create a feedback loop that dampens fear and builds trust. The more fearful the family, the more attention accountability will require.

It is possible to vary each of the three features of accountability discussed earlier—transparency of information, review of decisions, and transformation—to increase or decrease accountability within a governance system. Designing a good governance system may require variance of one, two, or all three in order to meet the needs of a family and take advantage of its particular capacities.

Transparency of Information

As discussed above, as participation in decision making increases, so does the transparency of information, because participants must have the proper information in order to make wise decisions. While transparency of information decreases with centralization of management, no system is devoid of a way to give information to stakeholders. For example, while a trust can be viewed as a highly centralized form of management, the trend is toward more transparency of information. The law has long required trustees to provide an annual accounting, and the Model Trust Code increases transparency by clarifying that a beneficiary is entitled to examine the trust document and requiring that notice be sent to beneficiaries upon the occurrence of certain events.[6] Once a family adopts any of the wealth transition structures defined by law, it knowingly or unknowingly adopts a methodology of sharing information. Once they understand the default state law rules, most families are shocked at how little information certain stakeholders are entitled to receive, and most want to clarify that family stakeholders have rights to more information.

Varying from state law by requiring additional information is one way to meet particular needs of a family when designing governance systems. For example, under state law shareholders are entitled to examine only certain records of a corporation, and only for certain purposes. These laws strike a balance between giving shareholders the information they need, so they can be responsible investors and exercise appropriate oversight, and protecting the corporation from inappropriate disclosure of information and interference from meddling shareholders. The state law default is a compromise that is unlikely to fit the needs of most families. Examining a family's need for information, as revealed by its wealth behavior patterns, is critical in deciding to vary from state law provisions regarding transparency of information.

Two examples of family communication patterns of wealth behavior should prompt the FWTP adviser to consider such an approach: extreme orientations to either openness or reserve and extreme orientations to either fact or fantasy. Two common patterns of wealth behavior should prompt the FWTP adviser to consider such an approach: the openness/reserve and fantasy/facts continuums. First, the family's patterns of openness and reserve will inform their need for information. A family whose members are reserved with one another about business matters may prefer less, rather than more, transparency. This may have served them well before wealth transition, but when the next generation of transferees must share wealth, this reluctance to share information may breed distrust. The FWTP adviser should respect their belief in the need to protect information from inappropriate disclosure by putting in place protocols for what kinds of information will be shared, in what form, when, and with whom, with appropriate consequences for inappropriate disclosure.

On the other hand, a family with a history of open communication about business matters will be more inclined to share information. These families may also view this issue as an unnecessary conversation. They say, "Well, of course we will share information, what's the big deal? Let's move on." However, these open families need to be made aware of why certain information is not shared as a matter of course with all stakeholders, and that the level of information to be shared triggers a need to design confidentiality provisions. As the family diversifies, implicit understandings as to the use of information must be made explicit in the form of shareholder or member agreements.

Another clue to the level of transparency in a family's communication is how they distinguish between facts and fantasies when they communicate with one another.[7] Families who prefer fantasy to facts will face special issues in sharing wealth after transition. In many families, it is tempting for those not involved in the business to assign it an improbable value, to view the salaries paid to insiders as unreasonable, and to be unrealistic about the practicality of business opportunities. In other families, those involved in the business maintain fantasies about its value and importance within the family wealth system. This can easily lead to conflict between those involved in the business and those not involved in the business. Building protocols about sharing a higher level of information may provide a basic level of factual information to avoid this conflict.

To tailor the transparency of information within a governance system, stakeholders should explicitly agree about the following:

❏ What kinds of information are stakeholders entitled to under state law? These typically include shareholder lists, shareholder meeting minutes, and the vague "books and records" required by law to be kept.

❏ What additional information is desirable, and why? Possibilities might include financial statements, strategic plans, organizational charts, employee compensation information, or minutes of board meetings.

❏ Who will be entitled to what information? Shareholders, creditors, and lessors are likely candidates. It may be necessary to clarify expectations regarding the access of spouses and partners to this information.

❏ When will that information be provided? Will it be available on demand, distributed at annual meetings, or posted on an intranet?

❏ In what format will that information be provided? Finding ways to make financial information accessible to stakeholders requires creativity and education.

❏ What restrictions will be imposed on recipients' use of the information? Legally enforceable confidentiality agreements are essential.

The goal of developing such a protocol is to create a feedback loop that enhances the goals of family wealth continuity. Increased levels of information build trust, which in turn fosters the goal of healthy family relationships. On the other hand, if recipients react to additional information by micromanaging those involved in the business, the decision to increase transparency will undermine both the goal of good stewardship of wealth and the goal of healthy family relationships. Therefore, any decision about the level of transparency requires an answer to the next question: what are recipients of information supposed to do with that information? This answer lies in role clarity and development plans, which we will discuss in Chapter 10.

Review of Decisions

The second feature of accountability is a forum and process for review of decisions made by those charged with making them. Governing law usually puts in place a specific review process, such as mandating that a court review the actions of a trustee upon application by a beneficiary or other "interested party."[8] These laws give some outside authority the right to review and affirm, overturn, or revise those decisions. State law provides owners with the opportunity to create their own mechanisms for review of decisions. Bylaws may allow shareholders to make proposals to take the company in a particular direction.

State and federal law rules offer default solutions designed for strangers, not family members. Most families dread airing their dirty laundry in public. They have heard horror stories about family-owned businesses crumbling under the weight of litigation, a process that forever changes family relationships. What these families desire is to make the family system less open to the external forces that accompany litigation. Yet, at the same time, there must be some forum for reviewing decisions if family members are to share wealth.

Certain patterns of wealth behavior signal a need for special attention to this issue. Disengaged families may be more litigation prone than connected ones, because the former have less to lose in terms of family relationships. Assessing a family's level of cohesion, then, becomes critical in designing this feature of accountability. Family patterns of control and abdication figure prominently in this element of plan design. A need for control will signal the likelihood that special decision-making processes are needed, including a way that the family can review decisions that managers of a business make.

These issues implicate accountability in three important ways. First, at a minimum, deciding on a forum and process for resolving disputes is a critical piece of designing a governance system. Arbitration, mediation, and combination methods are appropriate candidates. A family may choose to submit any dispute to an experienced family systems mediator for a first crack at resolving it. However, a few families may believe that resorting to the court system is so expensive and public that it acts as a suitable deterrent to conflict.

Second, a governance system may seek to change the duties owed among the participants of a venture. The default systems of state and federal law import specific duties into the relationship between those that make decisions and their stakeholders. For example, a board of directors is under a fiduciary duty to shareholders; a trustee owes a fiduciary duty to beneficiaries. While the exact extent of fiduciary duties within LLCs is not clear, it appears that a manager of a manager-managed LLC owes a duty to members as a general partner owes to limited partners, while in a member-managed LLC the fiduciary duties members owe one another are more likely akin to those of general partners.[9] In some situations, of which the LLC is the primary example, fiduciary duties in some states may be relaxed so that managers can carry on their duties without fear of a lawsuit. In a trusting family, this may be an appropriate way to relieve those willing to take on managerial responsibilities of the added worry that they will commit a breach of fiduciary duty. However, such an approach should be taken only when there is no danger of an IRS attack, and when the family and its advisers are confident that the level of trust, as well as the needs of the business for nimble action, justifies it.

Third, a governance system may provide an internal review of the substance of certain decisions, placing that review in the hands of all or some stakeholders who, under the default rules of state law, would not have any input into the decision at all. For example, in the Hernández family, Bart Sr. wants to make sure that every Hernández family member has the opportunity to work in the construction business that he financed. Yet his sons are locked in conflict. A family faced with such a situation may choose to place responsibility for the decision to hire, or terminate the employment of, a family member on a group of stakeholders that is larger than the set of officers or directors of the company.

Most families are able to identify a few decisions with which they have special concerns. Common areas for concern, and therefore reasons for altering the review process, include:

❏ Employment of family members.
❏ Taking on certain levels of debt.
❏ Changes in strategic direction.
❏ Decisions to make distributions rather than investing excess funds in the business.

Changing the decision-making group necessarily involves changing the landscape of information as well. If, for example, the three Hernández siblings, Bart Jr., Luisa, and José, are to make decisions about José's employment, all three will need information about the position, José's capabilities, and the financial condition of the business. This increases the transaction costs of the process, but achieves the family goal of inclusion.

Transformation

The third feature that can be altered to create more or less accountability is *transformation*—the ability to change the structure itself or alter the relationships within it in fundamental ways. These include, among others, renegotiating the relationship, exiting the subsystem, and substituting someone else in a particular role. Many family businesses already have some transformation mechanism in place in their buy–sell agreements. But many more have implicit agreements, which most family members understand patchily if at all.

Buy–sell and similar agreements help a family face trigger events and a future full of overlapping changes in individual, family, and business life cycles. But they also become an accountability feature in a governance system where not all stakeholders are involved in management. If nothing else works, transformation processes give family members a way out.

A couple of patterns of behavior are clues for FWTP advisers that transformative processes will be particularly important for a family.

When a family struggles with issues of conformity and rebellion, they will likely need a predictable exit strategy, giving rebels a way out with minimum family pain, and dampening others' use of the family business to impose conformity. This is as true when multiple generations own a business together as it is when members of the same generation share ownership. Moreover, when family members disagree as to the instrumental or intrinsic value of wealth involved in a family business, an exit strategy is critical to avoiding prolonged family conflict. Those that view ownership as an investment like any other will want to be able to get out of this investment and into another. Given the liquidity issues most family businesses face, this will be a challenge to those who view ownership as having intrinsic value.

In any transformative process, the following questions must be resolved:

❏ Under what circumstances will individuals have a right to put their interests in the company or other stakeholders up for purchase?
❏ Under what circumstances will the company or another stakeholder have the right to acquire a person's interest?
❏ What will be the price and terms or payment?

Helping families understand how different trusts are from business entities in the transformation department is critical. "Irrevocable" really does mean irrevocable, or revocable only with high transaction costs. Trusts can be designed to be unassailable in perpetuity in certain jurisdictions. Transformation must be built into trusts at the outset, and state law does not provide a great deal of flexibility once a trust becomes irrevocable. Use of a trust adviser or trust protector can assist in this process, but families should understand that there are limits to using these roles to provide flexibility should circumstances change.

Role Clarity and Development and Governance Systems

Adapting the family wealth system by introducing new governance systems will create new challenges for each participant in the family wealth system, and even the most beautifully designed system will fail if these challenges go unacknowledged and unaddressed. Family members must take on new roles that require them to act in unfamiliar ways. While some family members may take to their new roles naturally, many will likely feel awkward and unsure of themselves. It is easy to abandon the idea of a new governance system because of these reactions.

A family can meet many of these challenges through a process of defining new roles within the family wealth system and developing the expertise and experience to fill those roles. For example, moving to a shared participation model from an autocratic one will require education as to how one participates appropriately in the governance system. Moreover, practicing these new roles before a trigger event occurs is critical to success.

The process of developing wealth transition structures, governance systems, and role clarity/development plans is presented in a linear fashion in this book, but this is not the case in any real planning situation. Wealth transition structures and governance systems are intimately related, and the family's capacity for role definition and development must be considered when making judgments about governance systems.

CHAPTER NOTES

1. The natural evolution of governance structures toward centralized management has become an accepted part of corporate law theory. R. Coase began a revolution by observing, "In order to carry out a market transaction it is necessary to discover who it is that one wishes to deal with, to inform people that one wishes to deal with and on what terms, to conduct negotiations leading up to a bargain, to draw up the contract, to undertake the inspection needed to make sure that the terms of the contract are being observed, and so on." At some point, the costs of doing all this become large, and a "firm" springs up. This firm is an agreement among participants (who would otherwise act autonomously) to abide by the decisions of a manager to coordinate their joint efforts. A firm arises whenever the costs of engaging a manager (both direct costs and costs of oversight) are less than the costs of each participant in the venture or market making a contract with every other participant. When a manager is engaged, of course, a need emerges to make sure that the manager, as agent, is working in the best interests of the principal. The cost of oversight is a special kind of transaction cost called *agency costs*, and these costs must be figured as part of the equation. Infinite variations of oversight structures exist, of course, and balancing the discretion of the managers against their accountability to other participants is often called the central question of corporate law.

The "firm" described by Coase and others is not any particular entity: it is a system in which various people have contributed inputs (expertise, capital, labor, or property) in exchange for an expected return, measured differently depending on the contribution (salary or wages, rent, or residual profits) and someone (or a group of someones) makes decisions about the allocation of those inputs. Modern corporate law theorists, extending the Coase theory, have dubbed the firm a "nexus of contracts" among all of the various participants in the venture: shareholders, who provide capital in exchange for profit; employees, who sell their labor in exchange for a wage or salary; lessors, who provide property in exchange for rent; even communities, which provide tax relief or other capital infusions in exchange for jobs for their citizens.

While a complete discussion of the nexus of contracts theory is beyond the scope of this book, one of its most interesting premises is that there is no overarching reason that the managers of a firm (a system) should operate it to maximize the return to equity investors. In the nexus of contract theory, equity investors are just one group of contracts in this web of contracts, and no one contract automatically trumps another. Who gets the best return among the mix of contracts will vary from time to time, depending on the market for a particular input. Just who will receive which benefits will also vary from time to time.

2. The Model Business Corporation Act Sec. (Sec. 7.32) allows shareholder agreements that retain for the shareholders actions that would otherwise be within the domain of the directors. The Delaware close corporation laws allow a corporation's business to be conducted by shareholders rather than by a board of directors (DGCL Sec. 351) and allows a majority of the shareholders to bind the parties with a shareholders' agreement (DGCL Sec. 350).

3. See Chapter 8.

4. See Chapter 6.

5. See Chapter 6.

6. See Kevin D. Millard, "The Trustee's Duty to Inform and Report Under the Uniform Trust Code," *Real Property, Probate and Trusts Journal* (Summer 2005).

7. See Chapter 6.

8. See Section 1001 of the Uniform Trust Code, which specifies the remedies that a court might order for breach of trust.

9. See L.E. Ribstein & R.R. Keatinge, Limited Liability Companies sec. 9.1 (Thomsen West, 2008). As the authors point out, however, these analogies are not exact, and the differences between LLCs, corporations, and partnerships must be taken into account in assessing fiduciary duties. Id.

CHAPTER 10

ROLE CLARITY AND DEVELOPMENT

IMPLEMENTING THE RIGHT wealth transition structures and governance systems helps families manage the complexity of the family wealth system as well as adapt it in positive ways. But these elements of a wealth transition plan are merely intellectual exercises without the third component of a successful wealth transition plan clarifying existing roles and developing new roles. This component is unlike the other two in a couple of ways. First, role clarity/development takes a longer-term perspective than the creation of wealth transition structures and governance systems. It potentially requires lifelong learning for families as they let go of old roles, adopt new ones, and adapt to a changing family wealth system. Second, if successful, this is the component of transition planning that most families find to be most enjoyable and gratifying. Many families will suffer through selection of wealth transition structures because they know tax savings and protective devices will result. They indulge their advisors in the design of dull governance systems if they believe that this will help the business stay on track when trigger events strike. Some parts of achieving role clarity can be awkward, gut-wrenching, and even terrifying. But most families take unabashed joy in furthering their knowledge about wealth and stewardship plans for all their generations. Directing wealth toward the development of human capital is what family wealth transition planning (FWTP) is all about.

The wealth transition structures and governance systems a family adopts provide the skeleton of a role clarity and development plan, because the family must choose these structures with a view to its special needs, capacities, and constraints. Each component brings the need to adapt existing roles and develop new ones. Without role clarity/development plans, however, neither wealth transition structures nor governance systems can achieve their potential in fostering family wealth continuity. A governance system may lay out the rules of the road for making decisions, but these rules don't tell family members how to fulfill these decision-making roles: they don't provide the nitty-gritty of what to do, what to say (and not say), how to act, and how to interact with each other to make the governance system work. A role development plan provides education, training, and practice that create new kinds of feedback loops within the family wealth system—connections that bolster family wealth continuity instead of undermining it.

Many family wealth transition plans fail because they end with execution of the estate planning documents that create wealth transition structures and conceptualization of appropriate governance systems. By failing to add the third component—role clarity and development—family members do not learn to use the wealth transition structures and governance systems the plan contemplates. They understand the new roles as an intellectual matter only. If they fail to invest in education about the new roles they must play, or do not have the opportunity to practice those roles prior to the destabilizing effect of a trigger event, they are likely to view these structures and systems as failures.

Clarifying existing roles is important because the family wealth system often comes to rely on certain critical roles played by family and nonfamily members. These roles have developed over time, and the family has come to rely on them and on the people filling them. Other family members have adjusted their roles to complement the system, in both positive and negative ways. This explains why family members may play opposing roles in patterns of wealth behavior. For example, one person's controlling behavior can create a feedback loop of abdication in another family member. If the FWTP process is to alter these roles in order to make the family wealth system more adaptable to family wealth continuity, it is necessary to consider the ripple effects of role change throughout the system. If someone gives up a role, who fills it? How? Or will it be abandoned? Are there ways to slice and dice a role so that multiple people fill it? Does the role need to be filled at all, or is it an artifact of an earlier need within the family wealth system or of the particular expertise or personality of a family member at a prior time?

Once roles are clarified, a plan for role development is usually critical to designing an enduring process. Developing roles is intimately tied to the selection of appropriate governance systems, because the success of these systems requires that family members practice new roles of governance. Advisers must not assume that family members are familiar with any particular governance role, even if they have had a specific legal entity in place for years, because it is rare that a family's governance system as it currently exists matches the legal ideal of governance of any particular entity. Instead, family members must learn collaborative roles of management and oversight for the family business, and more general stewardship skills for other kinds of wealth. Developing new roles means retaining and creating sufficient wealth management competencies to be good stewards, and as their wealth changes, family members must develop new competencies to remain good stewards. Evaluating each competency is an inherently subjective affair. The first step is to assess its human capital: the information, skills, and experiences that are necessary to develop and manage a particular kind of wealth. Then, a family can assess its level of competency and identify areas for additional development as well as their own priorities for doing so.

What Is a Role?

A *role* within a family wealth system is a position within that system that is integral to carrying out the particular function of a subsystem. Mothers, fathers, children, and extended family play central roles in the family subsystem. Founders, family employees, and even grandchildren with summer jobs play roles in the business subsystem. Because the family wealth system is an open system, nonfamily members such as spiritual advisors, financial consultants, charities, and even the IRS, to name just a few, play critical roles in various subsystems. During transition planning, role clarity and development of family members is critical, because family members fill multiple interconnected roles throughout the system, and these roles change over time.

Defining a role requires explicitly communicating what the role is (and what it is not) so that the person filling the role can succeed in it and others can interact with it productively. Defining a role requires several tasks:

- ❑ **Articulating Its Function or Purpose:** What is a person in this role supposed to accomplish? What's not in his or her job function? How would you know that the person is successful? Does the role have identifiable, measurable outcomes?
- ❑ **Describing the Tasks That Lead to That Function or Purpose:** What is a person in this role supposed to do (and not do)?
- ❑ **Ensuring That the Person Knows How Those Tasks Are to Be Carried Out, at Least in General Terms:** How is this job done?
- ❑ **Tracing How the Role Connects with Others' Roles:** With whom does the person work and how? What are the communication pathways that ensure an effective collaboration between this role and other family members' roles?

The capacity of a family to articulate these characteristics often varies in proportion to its degrees of openness and reserve.[1] Communication skills are critical in articulating these characteristics of a role, and in particular, in designing the collaboration among roles.

Families who routinely accomplish all these steps with nonfamily employees may be stymied when it comes to describing the new roles of governance for family members. A wise FWTP adviser team expects role confusion (and even role misbehavior) and helps a family learn from these experiences instead of throwing out the governance system, saying, "This obviously won't work!" As always, practice makes perfect.

Identifying Current Roles
in the Family Wealth System

—THE HERNÁNDEZ FAMILY—

Bartolomé (Bart) Hernandez Sr., age sixty-two

Luisa called me up the other day and told me she's sending me a check to repay the loan I made her so she could go out on her own, with interest, she said! She sounded so happy—she said things are really going well and finally, now that she's out of that big group of doctors, she can do things her way. I don't need her money. I don't want it. But if I don't take it she'll feel disrespected—she's a proud woman like my sister. Clara insisted on giving me a share of her sale price just because I made that loan at the start to her and Elena. *¡Qué cosa!* It got me thinking. I lent Bart and José that money to start the remodeling business. Bart's paid back some of it, but nowhere near the whole amount. Now I've put some land deals together with Bart and I've guaranteed his debt to the bank. I don't want to think about how much I've lent José over the years. I want to be fair, but how am I ever going to square this with all three of my children—and Samantha?

While Bart's question is framed as an issue of financial fairness among his children, it also reveals a significant role clarity and development problem. Bart plays a wide variety of explicit roles throughout the Hernández family wealth system: lender (to almost everyone); adviser to his wife and sister's business, a role that apparently turned into being an unwitting investor; guarantor of loans; owner of businesses; father; brother; grandfather; and intimate partner with Samantha. He also plays important *implicit* roles—those that the family may not be as willing to identify. He may be the enforcer of conformity, the solver of all problems, and the person whose approval family members crave (or whose disapproval they dread).

The client in a FWTP engagement is often the "Bart" of a family. This person serves multiple overlapping roles, and tends to exert control over the direction of the family wealth system. In many situations, a "Bart" fulfills his or her multiple roles in ways that are invisible to others within a family. In the course of his day, Bart may be negotiating leases and loans, agreeing to make a charitable donation, trying to make Luisa keep her money, and negotiating with José about taking inventory. He probably couldn't describe "a day in the life of Bart" because to him it is all one fabric. This illustrates that transferors don't necessarily differentiate or separate roles, which can make it difficult for the next generation to really see how those different functions are accomplished and how they might fulfill these different roles, particularly if more than one member of the next generation are to assume leadership roles.

Roles are a compendium of human capital connected with other components within a family wealth system. Genograms provide important information as to family relationships and highlight patterns that repeat through generations. Stakeholder analysis places family and nonfamily members within the various subsystems and helps family members identify where they believe that they have a stake in the outcome of decisions, whether or not they have a legally recognized status therein. Cycles of individual, family, and business change show how these relationships have changed and are likely to continue to change over time. It is helpful to use the language of the cycles of change to help families talk about how they see their roles changing.

Family members often enjoy mapping the various explicit roles they play within the family wealth system. But mapping implicit roles is more difficult. For example, although the Hernández family is enmeshed, it seems to be fairly structured, neither particularly chaotic nor rigid. Yet something is going on with Bart and his children. Does Bart control things, or is he an enforcer of conformity? Is José a rebel, or is he motivated by other emotions?

A person in Bart's position may also suffer from role overload, a problem that may come to light only when there is a trigger event. Life cycle changes may affect a person's willingness to continue to serve in certain roles. Yet untangling these roles can be difficult for any number of reasons, and particularly for the transferor client who is the owner of a family business. The transferor may seem so critical to a successful operation that there is no time to allow others to get up to speed; the transferor may not trust others to do a good job; or the sheer complexity is overwhelming.

The Fundamental Challenge of Role Clarity and Development for Family Business

Although wealth transition structures may transfer ownership of assets, true ownership is not just having one's name on stock certificates or sitting at the desk where the buck stops. True ownership is developing a way of thinking about how to build wealth of all kinds throughout the family wealth system and how to best allocate the benefits and burdens of the wealth, both to family members and to others. This is what creates good stewardship of wealth, healthy family relationships, and a family legacy.

A governance system sets forth the rules of the road about how that thinking will take place: who participates in it, how they participate, and what happens when disagreements arise. In successive generations, the power to decide on proper allocation of the benefits and burdens of wealth among all the stakeholders falls to increasingly diverse groups of individuals. To accommodate that diversity, each family in each generation strikes a new balance between having stakeholders participate in decision making and having stakeholders rely on others, after properly equipping themselves with tools of accountability. The fundamental challenge of role clarity and development in governance is how to participate in this new decision-making system in ways that promote family wealth continuity. Anyone who has worked with board governance knows the mantra: those in an oversight function (a board, for example) *set* policy; management *implements* it. The reality, however, is never quite so clear.

Governance Roles in the Family Business

The governance systems families adopt differ, and each governance system requires that family members serve different roles, which are often unfamiliar to them. No family has an innate ability to do this. Their members develop the ability through education and practice.

The Management Role

Those who serve in the management role are intimately involved in operational decision making for the business. They are most familiar with the business and its needs, capacities, and constraints. They may be working on the floor, in the warehouse, or in an office, or they may be taking less of an operational role and more of a leadership role. These are the people who say, "The buck stops here." They may have the title of CEO, president, or manager, or no title at all. They are the ones responsible for getting results. They may be family members or, as we will find in Marshall Trucking, trusted nonfamily members.

Managers are made, not born. In many business families, the founders worked every day in the business, and learned to manage it by trial and error. Their successors may take the same route. In today's world of business families, however, younger family members often bring education in a technical or professional field or experience with an outside company to the manager role. This can either create conflict or build expertise, depending on how the family views this form of human capital.

As business wealth passes through generations, it becomes increasingly unlikely that there will be a place in management for every family member that might want to serve in this role. They must develop a process for training, evaluating, and promoting those on a management track that creates and rewards skill and results, not DNA. There must be nonmanagement tracks available to family members. Sometimes achieving role clarity means very little change for some family members.

The technical expertise required of a manager is beyond the scope of this book, as it will vary widely by position and industry. What is critical in planning, however, is developing a manager's ability to work with those in oversight roles. The governance system defines the right blend of discretion and oversight, but fleshing this out requires establishment of certain communication pathways that both the manager and those in an oversight role can rely upon. A manager must develop specific skills to make this work. Some managers seem to do this effortlessly, while others chafe under oversight restrictions or fail to claim their rightful arenas of unilateral action. Managers can develop a number of skills that will increase their competence in this collaboration, including:

❑ How to present financial and operational information in accessible ways.
❑ How to respond to questions.
❑ When to call upon the expertise of those in an oversight role.
❑ When to let those in an oversight role know of specific developments.
❑ When and how to appropriately claim the right to act without input.
❑ How to be open to the different perspectives of those in oversight roles.

The Oversight Role

Acting responsibly in the oversight role requires a clear understanding of the function of this role as compared to the management role. It is easier to explain what oversight isn't than what it is: it is neither micromanagement nor meddling, nor asking the loaded question over

Thanksgiving dinner, nor constant criticism, nor the arched eyebrow. Oversight is asking the right questions in the right ways at the right times. It is acting responsibly with information by promptly reviewing it and seeking help in understanding it. It is preparing for meetings using that information, and seeking to understand the manager's perspective before criticizing. Properly structured and implemented, the oversight function ensures that the ways in which the family creates and allocates wealth are consistent with the best interests of the stakeholders in the family wealth system.

Those in an oversight role have important functions to accomplish in the two core tasks of governance in a family business: keeping the business on track to create wealth and allocating the benefits and burdens within the family wealth system. They must take a bird's-eye view of how the business is doing. For many families in transition, it is tempting to get involved in the daily operational decisions, but that is not the oversight role. Instead, those serving in oversight roles must look to key performance indicators that allow them to understand how the business is doing compared to its peers, given the economic context in which it operates. Those in an oversight role rely on those in management to provide that information on a regular basis.

Family members serving in an oversight role bear the lion's share of responsibility for allocating within the family wealth system the benefits and burdens of the wealth created through the family business. They must keep track of the kinds of wealth that are generated through the business, and make decisions about the allocation of this wealth.

Some families may wish to allocate to the oversight role certain decisions that, under the default rules of business governance, would be part of the management role.[2] These might include whether and how to hire and fire family members, whether to pursue certain strategic opportunities, or whether to take on debt. In these situations, it is important to prepare those in an oversight role to make these decisions without overstepping the boundaries of their role. For example, in order to evaluate whether and how to employ family members, those in an oversight role would need more detailed information about employees, skill sets, compensation arrangements, and chains of authority than those in an oversight role would normally have. It is important that this information not empower them to meddle in other employment affairs for which those in a management role remain responsible.

Moreover, those in an oversight role have the responsibility of keeping track of the changing constellation of stakeholders whom they represent. The FWTP process provides an opportunity to articulate this responsibility, perhaps for the first time. There remains the need to periodically reevaluate whether the people doing the core work of governing the family business are the right ones for that task, if the governance system is to be sustainable.

Family members who serve in an oversight role can develop a number of specific skills to increase their competency in this role. These include:

- ❏ Knowledge of and experience in making decisions, including a recognition of the mistakes that groups frequently make when trying to reach a decision as a group.
- ❏ Willingness to engage in conflict, rather than to avoid it, while at the same time ensuring that conflict is productive, even if painful.
- ❏ Understanding the key performance indicators of the business, how they are measured within the industry, and how the family business compares to industry averages with respect to these key indicators.
- ❏ Understanding financial statements, including profit and loss statements, balance sheets, and cash flow statements.
- ❏ Understanding of and willingness to participate in the strategic planning process for the business.
- ❏ Understanding the stakeholders of the family wealth system and being open to change in those stakeholders.
- ❏ Willingness to trust the manager to carry out the plans agreed upon through the day-to-day functioning of the business.

The Impact of Life Cycles on Role Clarity and Development: Letting Go and Taking On

—The Hernández Family—

Bart Hernández Jr., age forty

Susan told me last night that if I went ahead with buying my father's hardware business, it would be the end of us. I know she's been telling me I don't spend enough time with her and María Elena, and I tell her I'm just trying to provide for her and our daughter and give them a good life. We've gone round and round about this kind of thing for a couple of years. She says she's done with hearing all that, that we are doing just fine, and if I buy it (she called it "that dying business," which really ticked me off) she would leave. She says I just don't have time with night school and the construction business and all and it's time for me to focus on my own family, not everybody else in this family. She said she waited a long time to have María, because I said I wanted us to be set in life before having children. "It's now or never for more kids," she says, she's not getting any younger.

Life cycles are the most important variable that affects the timing of role clarity and development as a component of the FWTP process. Knowing the respective cycles of individual, family, and business development is a critical step in developing any plan. These stages of development inform not only an individual's ability and willingness to let go of old roles and adopt new ones, but the possible contours of those roles as well. As role clarity and development plans often play out over a longer period of time than traditional estate plans, there is time to accommodate these variables.

Susan and Bart Jr. find themselves at an important crossroads of individual, family, and business development. Bart Jr. is probably right that something must be done about the hardware store, which is probably not as profitable as it once was. Susan is placing in stark relief the joys and burdens of families with young children. Thus, the needs and constraints of being a Stage Three family are in direct conflict with Bart Jr.'s initial thoughts about resolving their business and individual life cycle problems.

Every stage of individual, family, and business development comes with certain capacities for change, which the FWTP adviser can use in creating role clarity and development plans. For example, Stage Three families often lack time and money. They have limited resources to take on new roles, and are often relieved when a plan removes a role they find burdensome. Stage Three families, however, are often especially committed to FWTP, and especially role clarity and development plans, because they fear the impact on their young children of a lack of plan. Using this capacity for change may be helpful in Bart Jr.'s situation.

Role clarity and development plans work best when they recognize the complementary and sometimes conflicting needs, capacities, and constraints of each overlapping life stage. Moving from one stage to another is not an event; it is a transition that may take years or decades.

Adapting governance systems and role development plans to account for these needs, capacities, and constraints is critical.

The Impact of Family Wealth Behavior Patterns on Role Clarity and Development

A few lucky families seem to adjust roles effortlessly, but most families have to work hard to define existing roles, and especially hard to change them. The reason this work can be so difficult is that family patterns of wealth behavior affect both existing roles and future ones. A family may be able to ignore certain patterns when deciding on a wealth transition structure, and even on a governance system, but once roles are on the table, recognizing and discussing these wealth patterns become inescapable. Inability or unwillingness to discuss these patterns sometimes even compels some families to terminate the FWTP process before they create a complete plan. For others, these issues seriously interfere with the implementation of the wealth transition plan.

Rigid families have no trouble defining existing roles, but find that changing them is difficult. Chaotic families have the opposite problem. Because their roles change so often and lack a discernable pattern, finding a stable footing on which to develop roles is challenging. The special challenge for enmeshed families is untangling their existing roles and developing separate and distinct roles for the future. These families often have overlapping and intensely connected roles. Developing a governance system that separates the management and oversight roles will be hard for them, and avoiding role confusion and misbehavior will pose an ongoing challenge. Finally, the disengaged family may find it easiest both to define roles and to stick to them. But these families have trouble developing the collaborative skills that allow roles to work together to build family wealth continuity.

The advisory team plays an important role in assisting families in discussing these issues in productive, nonthreatening ways, and creating accountability for implementation of new roles. As summarized in *Figure 10.1*, every family wealth behavior pattern has important ramifications for the process of achieving role clarity and developing new roles, but a few take on special importance in the process. Ultimately, the way a family views its wealth may be measured by the degree of congruity between how the family identifies and incorporates individual values and the vision of the future that drives their wealth transition plan.

FIGURE 10.1 Key Challenges in Role Clarity and Development Plans Arising from Patterns of Wealth Behavior

Key Challenges in Role Clarity and Development	Key Strategies for Change	Key Challenges in Role Clarity and Development
Indiscriminate Communication via Fantasies: • Describing existing roles and functions honestly	*Authenticity:* • Checks and balances on information • Communication pathways • Methods of decision making using that information	• *Blocked Communication via Cold Hard Facts:* Imagining new possibilities and allowing experimentation with new roles
Inaccurate Communication Due to Entitlement Assumptions: • Honesty about "special" status and performance	*Empowerment:* • Creating opportunity and accountability for performance in new roles	*Inadequate Communication Leading to Shame:* • Unworthiness • Inability to participate
Incohesiveness Due to Rigidity: • Inflexibility of current roles	*Structure:* • Small steps to big changes • Oversight for implementation and practice	*Incohesiveness Due to Chaos:* • Lack of boundaries in current roles • Implementation, follow-through, and consistency with new roles
Lack of Adaptability/Over Structured Control: • Replacing benefits of control • Awareness of how control is exercised • Faith in others	*Engagement:* • Defining old and new functions and boundaries for roles and preparing members to fill them	*Excessive Adaptability/ Abdication of Responsibility:* • Fear of making mistakes because of lack of experience and knowledge • Fear of damaging relationships
Enmeshed Conformity: • Fear of allowing freedom: what would happen?	*Individuation:* • Working with strengths to find the right pathways for members	*Disengaged Rebellion:* • Unwillingness to take on any role for fear of being sucked in
Rigid View of Intrinsic Value of Wealth: • Self-worth tied to wealth • Inflexibility in disposition of wealth	*Congruence:* • Articulating values • Taking long-term view of focusing wealth on achieving values	*Chaotic View of Instrumental Value of Wealth:* • Failure to see legacy issues • Participation in defining proper uses of wealth

The Theme of Control and Abdication

—THE WILLIAMS FAMILY—
Helen Williams, age forty-eight

I decided to tell John I wanted a trial separation because every time I look at him I get so angry that I can't see straight. I was all ready to do it, when I realized that I was completely unprepared to handle it. Taking care of all these kids, especially Lisa, and the finances, and everything myself. It's the little things, like taking the twins to soccer practice or what would happen if the circuit breaker blows, that would be too much to handle if I had to do them. It was too scary altogether. I guess the good news is that it made me realize that moving out to Long Island is a stupid idea, because it would make things even more complicated. I hate to admit it, but I'm afraid I can't stand on my own two feet. That was a wake-up call for me. I'm forty-eight years old, and I should be able to handle all of this.

Families and family members arrange themselves along a continuum of control versus abdication that can range from requiring absolute control to completely giving up one's authority. Feedback loops within the family ensure that if one family member claims the control end of the continuum, others gravitate toward abdication. That's what's happened in the past between John and Helen: John's control encouraged Helen's abdication. As Helen looks forward in life, she sees no other way of operating. To her, a separation from John would mean that *she* would have to control everything, allowing John to abdicate his responsibilities. At this juncture, she can't see a middle ground of joint responsibility for their life, even if they separated. Two steps help in situations like John and Helen's: defining existing roles and developing new roles.

Defining Existing Roles

Families influenced by control and abdication issues are easy to spot when they are honest about what they actually do on a day-to-day basis. Some families combine their struggle with control/abdication issues with a penchant for fantasy over facts.[3] In those situations, it can be difficult to see how they use existing roles to implement their choices. These families tend to create roles for family members that carry apparent authority but no real power. Few families want to admit that a family member has abdicated authority. They involve the person in what appears to be decision making, but in fact that person is going along with others without any real understanding of the stakes of the decision or how to make it. Creating these roles helps a family maintain a fantasy of involvement and consensus.

Developing New Roles

The goal of a family trying to move from the extremes of control and abdication is to define roles that allow for engagement by family members in decisions in which they have a stake. Engagement is involvement, not abdication. It is participation, not control. It requires preparation for responsible participation.

To achieve engagement, those on the control end of the spectrum must be motivated to bring their experience and influence to bear, which requires them to see how both they have exercised control and the specific benefits of change. Their need for a meaningful role, whether within a business or outside it, must be met, and they will need time to adjust. In the end, however, letting go of control is a matter of faith in the FWTP process. This requires serious attention to role development components that will prepare others to step up to the desired roles and become responsible stewards of wealth.

Ironically, those who have practiced abdication face even greater challenges than their controlling counterparts do. They may not see the benefits of engagement, especially if the control/abdication pattern has allowed them to lead a carefree life or pursue their own interests. Those who have not been involved will need education as to what a role entails. They probably fear making mistakes, and they know that those previously in control will be scrutinizing their every move.

The Theme of Trust and Fear

—THE HERNÁNDEZ FAMILY—
Luisa Hernández, age thirty-three

I called up my brother Bart and gave him a piece of my mind about how he's treating José in the construction business. I know Papá made it for both of them, not just Bart. I told him that freezing José out wasn't what this family was all about. I just couldn't stand it anymore, hearing José and my father talk about it—not to each other, of course, or to Bart, just to me. Bart tried to tell me that José has no interest in the business, and wouldn't do what it takes to make it run, and that he gave him plenty of chances. He was pretty specific and now I don't know what to think. Sure, my brothers have their faults, but neither one of them is a liar. I know that much for sure. So what's going on? My boyfriend, Angus, says to leave it alone, it's not my problem, let them work it out, but I just can't.

Families that struggle with trust/fear issues face special role clarity and development challenges. Defining the sources of fear and the areas of trust is the first step. Luisa is confident that neither brother is lying. So they must be seeing the same events from vastly different perspectives, which is often a sign of fear and trust issues.

During transition planning, transferors often have unarticulated fears about what role changes might mean, such as:

❑ The fear that they will no longer be valued within the family without serving in these roles.

❑ The fear of having nothing to do if their roles are taken away. Driven entrepreneurs, in particular, may not have made time for hobbies, charitable organizational involvement, or other ways to pass the time outside of work. Leisure activities may not provide the same degree of emotional satisfaction as running a business. If they are in a life cycle stage of searching for meaning, this will be a special issue, because leisure activities may not suffice.

❑ The fear of loss because their business cannot be nurtured properly by anyone else. Typical founders believe that no one could possibly understand the needs of the business as well as they do. This problem is exacerbated by a belief in the intrinsic (as opposed to instrumental) value of the wealth represented by the business.

❑ The fear that they will not have enough money on which to live. The senior generation may have no retirement plan. The founders may have plowed every nickel back into the business. The founders may expect to receive a salary or distributions throughout their remaining life, and staying in control helps make sure this expectation is met.

❑ The fear of risking other assets if the business is not well run. Business owners often provide personal guarantees for various

obligations, so they risk losing assets if the next generation doesn't
manage the business or property well.

❏ The fear of change. As people age, they often get more risk averse
and any change in role, particularly changes that are undefined or
unfamiliar, seems risky.

Transferees face different kinds of fears. They may fear that they
will never be able to put their personal stamp on the business, or that
the transferors will never truly let them participate in governance.
They may fear that their siblings will not act fairly in allocating the
benefits and burdens of the business within the family wealth system.
They may fear erosion of family relationships when they have to make
hard choices. They may fear that they will fail, thereby destroying their
family legacy.

Trust cannot automatically replace fear just because the FWTP advisers think that it should. Instead, governance systems and role clarity
and development plans produce a series of interactions that, over time,
build trust to replace fear. Governance systems are the intellectual exercise that creates feedback loops explicitly designed to build trust. Role
clarity and development plans tell people what they should do, how they
should act, and whom they should talk to in order to put that governance system into place. Over time, if people fulfill their roles, a series
of positive interactions will build trust as people learn to count on each
other to build wealth collaboratively.

Role Accountability

For almost every family in business together, measuring performance in
a role is difficult. Conducting employee reviews for nonfamily members
is hard enough; evaluating one's brother, child, or mother may seem
impossible. The role is likely amorphous enough so that measurement
is difficult, and the relationship is not just about business. Many families
forgo any kind of evaluation, opting instead for a nonconfrontational
Thanksgiving dinner together.

This lack of accountability can easily accentuate the destabilizing
effect of certain trigger events. Perhaps an owner is sued for sexual
harassment, or the person who has been overperforming to make up
for others' underperformance has a heart attack or finally just quits.

This problem will be particularly acute for families who want to face their entitlement/shame issues and move toward empowerment. A culture of entitlement, whether it is entitlement to employment, income, prestige, influence, or any other benefit of family wealth, aggravates problems of nonaccountability.

An important part of any governance system is its accountability features.[4] Various processes of communication, decision making, and transformation serve to increase the accountability of management to the family. This same concept of accountability should be built into any role filled by family members within the company, whether it is a management or oversight role. The time to do this, of course, is as part of the FWTP process during role development because issues of accountability often dominate the conversation. If they adopt it as a package during the planning process, and consistently implement it thereafter, the participants are more likely to accept the process of creating accountability for each role. Families may increase accountability by adopting tools such as:

- ❑ Employment contracts with performance expectations.
- ❑ Annual performance reviews.
- ❑ Using outsiders to evaluate management's performance.
- ❑ Engaging compensation consultants to evaluate the link between performance and pay.
- ❑ Board self-assessments.
- ❑ Outside evaluations of board functioning.
- ❑ Realistic job descriptions.

General Competencies to Foster Stewardship—Lifelong Learning Plans

The previous sections have discussed role clarity and development as it relates to a family business. But family wealth can take any number of forms, and most families are interested in developing roles that will result in responsible stewardship of wealth of all kinds. Any family can identify the kinds of competencies needed to manage wealth responsibly. Depending on the kind of wealth, and how it is deployed within the family system, a family will require different skill sets and kinds of expertise. A wealth-mapping process offers families and their advisers tools for assessing the current state of financial, human, and social capital within a family's wealth system. That information can be extrapolated to develop a plan for role clarity and development. The competencies needed by any particular family will change over time. Thus, a good role development plan will include goals, timelines, and a system for monitoring progress.

CHAPTER NOTES

1. See Chapter 6.

2. See Chapter 9.

3. See Chapter 6.

4. See Chapter 9.

CHAPTER 11

TRANSITIONS OF WEALTH IN THE WILLIAMS FAMILY

THE PRESSURES IN the Williams family's wealth system have been building for some time. John recently had heart surgery, and seems distracted and unhappy. He is increasingly uncomfortable keeping his secrets. John's sister Sara feels estranged from Helen, and is pressuring her brother to come clean. Both John and Helen's fathers have died, leaving their mothers widows. Helen has become increasingly frustrated with John's lifestyle and its effect on his health. His heart surgery in the past year woke her to her vulnerability to his sudden death. It also woke John up to the enormous consequences of keeping this secret from Helen for so long. Now, Helen has discovered his secret and begun to see its implications. She has learned that her father knew about this situation long before she did, and did not tell her. Helen is also seeing a different side of her mother, who is taking an active role as trust beneficiary and wants to simplify her lifestyle by selling the family home. She hardly knows how to broach the Cindy–Brad subject with her mother, much less with John. So her strategy with John was to leave the bill from the accountant who uncovered the purchase of the co-op on John's desk with instructions to "pay this soon!" Helen and John are hurtling toward a crisis in their family subsystem, and the ripple effect throughout their family wealth system is already beginning to show.

Success

The Williams family brings into sharp focus the need for defining *success* in family wealth transition planning (FWTP) terms. Any adviser to the Williams family will start by focusing on healthy family relationships,

253

stewardship of wealth in all its forms, and a family legacy. Yet this is a family in crisis. Sometimes, a full discussion of family wealth continuity must await a decision on what the contours of the family will be. But some issues cannot wait much longer. The family must address the possibility of untimely death so that the children's needs (especially Lisa's) are met. For the family wealth transition planning adviser team, *success* might be an interim plan now, and a larger plan later, when the family law issues have been resolved. Or it might require just putting everything on hold, with a confirmed date to revisit the plan.

Ethics

Chapter 2 discussed some of the difficulties of assisting Helen or John with FWTP during this crisis. The couple will, in due course, have a swarm of team members: individual counselors, couples therapist, accountant, trustees, and other advisers. The FWTP adviser (and others) will have to think carefully about leadership of the team as well as roles for the advisory team members. This is a situation in which Helen's adviser is not likely to take a leadership role. The team leader will have the job of keeping all of the team members in the loop, deciding on the format of meetings, and managing the inevitable starts and stops of a family in crisis. All of the advisers involved will have the difficult job of evaluating the wisdom of participating in the proposed format, given the likelihood of divorce litigation in the near future. Regardless of format, if an adviser assisting either John or Helen wants to meet with the other spouse, they must only do so with presence of or consent from that spouse's adviser(s). If a party's therapist is involved, still other kinds of consents will be necessary.

If Helen and John Williams are able to rebuild their marriage sufficiently so that FWTP can proceed, the adviser must have access to multiple perspectives. Early in the process, the adviser must resolve the question of format. Will the adviser arrange individual interviews, or will group meetings best serve the process? Group meetings often produce the most helpful information when it comes to testing assumptions and discovering similarities and differences in beliefs and meanings. Moreover, meeting with Helen and John jointly supports them in their goal of putting the marriage back together. Yet emotions are likely to run high at group meetings, particularly early in the process, as the family adjusts to John's news. A combination of group and individual meetings might work best, but in this potentially inflammatory setting, clearly delineating the process and identifying the relevant confidentiality issues is critical.

Process

The Williams family offers an opportunity to illustrate in a linear fashion the methodology described in this book. The FWTP adviser can take this approach by analyzing the family wealth system: mapping the Williams family's sources of wealth, their overlapping cycles of change, their patterns of wealth behavior, and the external forces at work upon them. Mapping these within the Williams family wealth system as a whole will help identify the family's needs, capacities, and constraints as well as the linkages and sensitivities that the adviser must attend to during planning.

What will immediately strike any adviser about the Williams family wealth system is that it comprises a relatively small number of people. Helen and John are central figures, as are their four children, including Rebecca, whom John adopted when he married Helen. John has only one sister, and Helen is an only child. Both Helen's and John's fathers have recently died, leaving their mothers widows, one of whom lives far away. Cindy and Brad's places within the system aren't yet clear. The limited universe of people appears to simplify the planning process by reducing the number of potential stakeholders with differing interests. But it also raises a red flag for the FWTP adviser. These few people may be on role overload, and there does not appear to be a group of people available to relieve stress, or take on the new roles that will arise as the family wealth system evolves.

The Williams family wealth system is made up of a family subsystem, a business subsystem, and an investment/office subsystem. While the family may have charitable interests, these have yet to be developed. *Figure 11.1* illustrates this family wealth system.

The Williams situation also illustrates a fundamental premise of the FWTP process: turbulence in the family subsystem sends particularly potent waves throughout the other subsystems. Change within any subsystem has the potential to create positive or negative consequences throughout the system, but changes in the family subsystem have a disproportionately large impact.

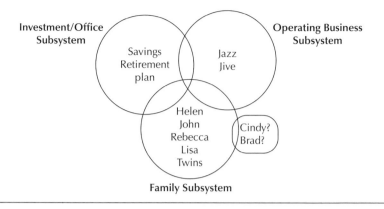

Investment/Office Subsystem

Operating Business Subsystem

Savings Retirement plan

Jazz Jive

Helen John Rebecca Lisa Twins

Cindy? Brad?

Family Subsystem

FIGURE **11.1**   Williams Family Wealth System

Sources of Wealth

While both Helen and John are stakeholders within each subsystem, they each have strictly defined responsibilities for the wealth in these subsystems. Helen is primarily responsible for the human and social capital within the family subsystem. She cares for the children, makes social arrangements, and carries on religious traditions; essentially, she handles the family. John participates when he can. His responsibilities include managing the finances in both the operating business subsystem and the investment subsystem. He has been solely responsible for the development and management of all forms of capital within these other systems.

The vulnerability of human capital in the Williams family wealth system is conspicuous. When their fathers died, both Helen and John lost important capabilities within the system. While John does have friends he can call upon in business, and can also rely on Cindy for business matters, there appears to be a lack of other people on whom the Williams can rely to expand the capacities of their relatively small family. Both John and Helen are on role overload, for very different reasons. John had heart surgery last year, and even now seems unwilling to attend to his health properly. Helen's propensity to depression seems to cause people to walk on eggshells around her and excuse her from full adult participation in financial life. Although Rebecca is successfully launching into a musician's education, the three young children in the Williams home rely heavily on their parents. One of these, Lisa, has special needs.

If anything happens to John, Helen may have to return to the workforce after many years of working in the home. She knows nothing of the family's finances or their investments. If something happened to both Helen and John, John's sister, Sara, would be the children's guardian. But how well could she really cope with her career, her own children, and her nieces and nephews? Helen's father knew John's secret, as does Sara, so these relationships have been adversely affected. Is Sara still willing to be a guardian, knowing what she now knows? Even if she is, the schism in the relationship between Helen and Sara is causing their relatively small store of social capital to shrink even more. Helen may be able to rebuild her relationship with her sister-in-law, but her father is dead, and she cannot confront him about John's secret and his role in keeping it. This erosion of trust may never heal.

The financial wealth in the Williams family requires special analysis. Helen's assumptions about the core family's healthy financial situation were incorrect, and there is some continuing ambiguity about the status of the retirement plan, which in turn raises questions about every other asset in the family's investment subsystem. There needs to be an honest appraisal of what the couple used to own and what they own now, so that they can manage the differences between the two.

There are ongoing ambiguities that no one is talking about: for example, just how much have Helen's parents been helping them, with education expenses or otherwise, and is that likely to continue given the changes in the family wealth system? How much does Jazz Jive really contribute to the family finances?

Finally, Helen's father's death has fundamentally changed the family's investment subsystem. The sudden influx of wealth into Helen's life via her father's trust may change the balance of financial power in their lives.

It is easy to see John's health problems affecting the family subsystem. Other issues are hidden; however, paying attention to what is happening in other subsystems may reveal them. John's other family is a stressor on the family subsystem that echoes throughout the system, whether or not the secret is revealed. It has already affected the investment/office system; this occurred when John withdrew large sums to buy an apartment for Cindy. It affected how Jacob passed financial wealth to Helen. It has also affected the business subsystem, because child support has been built into Cindy's salary. John may not be able to evaluate her performance objectively, given their history and their ongoing connection through Brad.

Overlapping Cycles of Change

Helen and John's crisis has brought to light many of the needs and constraints of the family that arise from their overlapping life cycles. Helen is struggling with Stage Two individual life cycle issues as she tries to overcome dependency constraints and become more autonomous. John seems to ignore his Stage Six intimacy and isolation issues. He has no one who really knows him; each person in his life has had the opportunity to experience only a slice of him.

Helen has her hands full with her Stages Three and Four family: three children at home, one in college, and a newly widowed mother. John is on role overload partly because he has not just one but two Stage Three families, with no way in sight to resolve the situation. No matter how little he may be involved in Brad's life, he still sees Cindy every day, and his responsibilities weigh on him. He also feels the stress of caring for his own mother. She lives in the Midwest and visiting her is a major undertaking, given his other responsibilities.

Moreover, like any entrepreneur, John feels the stress of building a business. Jazz Jive has survived its entrepreneurial growth period, but is not yet a cash cow. It has particular needs for investment of financial and human capital, and relies heavily on John's special charm to continue to build its brand. But how much longer can John be charming?

Patterns of Wealth Behavior

—HELEN WILLIAMS, *age forty-eight*—

I've been off everyone's radar screen—not just yours—for the last six months, sorry. I really appreciated your referrals to a couples therapist and individual counselors. I see mine, he sees his, and we see ours—we're supporting all those expensive Upper East Side apartments in Manhattan, I think! It's really hard. He moved out for a while, but now he's back, and the kids are so happy with that. I think everything is going to be okay, but things are going to have to change—a lot.

I had a hard time confronting John. Even that little trick I told you about—leaving the accountant's bill on John's desk—was because

I couldn't confront him. Eventually, though, things came to a head. He came into the kitchen one night with that bill and asked, "What's this all about?" I just snapped. I asked him what crazy idea did he have that I would put up with him having two families and stealing our family's money to buy a condo for that Cindy Jones and did he think I wouldn't find out? And what was he thinking having another child when he didn't even have time for the ones he already had? The worst was about him having an affair just after Lisa was born, when we were all reeling from the news and I was deep into a postpartum depression. It went on all night, and he just sat at the kitchen table with his head in his hands. We spent a full four months on these same issues, in the therapist's office every week, until I could say the name "Brad" without crying. Of course, now I watch John like a hawk. It's exhausting.

I guess I've learned a few things too. I used to hand over all the financial decisions to John, I didn't even think about it. I just figured he would do everything like my father did; he just took care of everything. I didn't set foot in John's bars or restaurant unless I had to, and it was so easy to avoid it because the kids always needed something, we'd have to get a sitter, and so forth. That's how my mother was with my father's business—he made the money somehow, and she painted and played with me. That wasn't what I wanted my life to look like, and that's not how it was when we first got married, but with the kids and Lisa and everything, I think it was just easier to do things like my parents. Anyway, if I had been down there at Jazz Jive more, I would have known about Cindy. Everybody there sure did. Not that John's actions are my fault, not at all, but I do think the way I acted helped him keep secrets and get in deeper and deeper. I always kidded him about being AWOL [absent without official leave] from the family with his business and all, but I think I was absent too. I also found out that everyone thinks they have to protect me from the cold, cruel world, as if I'm some kind of fragile doll. They think they can't tell me the truth because I'll . . . what? Crack up? I've told my whole family, "Hey, people—those days of treating me like a child are over. Give me the bad news first. I can take it."

The danger in the Williams situation is that the current crisis—the revelation of the secret of Cindy and Brad—can overshadow the underlying issues that would be there regardless of John's mistakes. An adviser to the Williams family is likely to begin by creating an overall typology of the family along the adaptability, cohesion, and communication continuums (see *Figure 11.2*). By doing this, the advisor can delve into the wealth themes at work within the family.

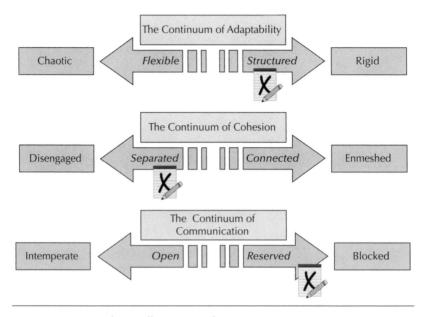

FIGURE **11.2**   The Williams Family

Although there are a number of behavior patterns at work in the Williams family, these three are most critical to understanding the family's needs, capacities, and constraints in planning:

❏ Control and abdication
❏ Coping with conflict
❏ Trust and fear

The Theme of Control and Abdication

John and Helen have a classic control/abdication pattern.[1] They had originally taken a joint decision-making pathway, and their collusion in abandoning a pattern of joint decision making to build capital within the family led to many of the problems they are currently experiencing. After John's surgery, Helen realized that her family would slip into chaos if John suddenly died or became incapacitated. This motivated her toward change. Of course, it wasn't just Helen who abdicated responsibility. John had his own method of abdicating his responsibilities, by being too busy at work, by becoming involved with Cindy, and by having a second, secret family with which he is not, or cannot be, involved on a familial level. All of these represent an abdication of responsibility in critical areas of the family wealth system.

Exploration of how John and Helen ended up in this control/abdication pattern is helpful to the FWTP adviser team. Perhaps their approach is an artifact of their lives, particularly because they have the pressures of a new business and three small children in the home, one with a disability. Certainly, the model Helen knew best came from her own family, where her father "took care" of everything. John may have come from similar stock.

The control/abdication pattern brings with it certain specific needs, capacities, and constraints that help the adviser create suitable processes and suggest an agenda.[2] The succession of trigger events she has endured has motivated Helen to change. The violation of others' duties to her may have freed her of any sense of obligation to continue in the same pathways as before. Yet she is inexperienced in the stewardship of financial wealth. She may fear the unknown and she has little free time to learn, so she needs a mentor, but one who will treat her like an adult. John, too, is constrained by not knowing how to change. He may fear that sharing information will lead to questions he cannot or doesn't want to answer. He may not believe Helen will step up to the responsibilities of being part of an entrepreneurial family. She has never before shown an interest in the business, and educating her will take time. Indeed, time may be the fundamental constraint on family wealth continuity for the Williams family. Helen and John need time to negotiate and adjust to new roles, but doing that in the face of crisis is nearly impossible. To succeed, they will need the support of their FWTP adviser team and a schedule that accommodates the uncertainty of crisis.

The Theme of Coping with Conflict

The second theme at work in the Williams family relates to how its members communicate, and especially how they cope with conflict.[3] It is immediately apparent that the Williams family is "reserved" in the communication arena, and even blocked in certain areas. Jacob couldn't communicate with his daughter about his discovery of John's infidelity or with his wife about the changes in his estate plan. John doesn't communicate with Helen about the most important facts of their lives. Sara presses her brother to come clean about his secret, but doesn't communicate directly with Helen, even though she knows it may ruin their sisterly relationship. Helen, too, struggles with how to confront John, choosing an indirect pathway rather than a direct one. The overlap of John's second family and the Jazz Jive bars also interfered with his ability to share the ups and downs of the business with Helen. Moreover, Helen seems baffled by her mother's evolution: Miriam seems to understand the investments in her trust, even though Jacob took care of this before, and Miriam doesn't want to live in Long Island, preferring the Manhattan lifestyle.

The Williams communication style has supported the family's inability to cope with conflict. Yet once John's secret was revealed, this family had to do just that. They obviously had help, through therapists and other advisers. Helen is seeing how her family feared being open with her, and how that supported her pattern of abdication. Moreover, Helen's predictable reaction has been to move to the other end of the communication continuum by demanding an excessive amount of openness from John. John has acquiesced, at least for now. Helen is clearly struggling to find an accountability structure that will support her own autonomy and protect her from further breaches of trust.

The Williams family is receiving appropriate professional help in learning to cope with conflict. An adviser must take this into consideration when designing the transition process, and if FWTP is to go forward, this family will need assistance in finding a safe forum for discussion. They will need to move away from long-standing patterns of conflict avoidance and toward effective structures for participation in decision making.

The Theme of Trust and Fear

Helen's trust in John has been destroyed. Previously, Helen and John consistently believed in one kind of trust: they trusted one another's abilities within their respective spheres. But Helen's confidence in John's integrity and benevolence (the principle that he is looking out for her best interests) must be restored. These issues affect the governance systems that the family will put in place in each of their subsystems. At the same time, for some reason John did not trust that he could be honest with Helen. He feared the consequences of sharing his big secret, even though he knew that every passing day magnified those consequences.

Helen's family also struggled with trust and fear. Those around Helen feared that she would slide into clinical depression again, as she has done on at least two occasions. Helen's father, sister-in-law, and maybe even mother lied to her about the framework of her world in a misguided attempt to protect her. The lies arose from a lack of trust in Helen and themselves. If a FWTP adviser asked Helen's family members if they trusted her, they would certainly answer "yes." They did trust her integrity and her benevolence, which are the things that really count. Otherwise, Sara would not have loved her "like a sister." They also trusted her ability to be a good mother in a very stressful situation. What they didn't trust was her ability to care for her own mental health, and they did not trust their own ability to intervene appropriately in her depressive cycles. It became easier to protect her than to struggle with questions of autonomy, responsibility, trust, and fear, which would arise from telling the truth.

External Forces

The crisis that the Williams family faces is internal, and in fact arises in the core of the family wealth system: the family subsystem. It is tempting, therefore, for the family to ignore the external forces at work on the system. But one of the facts of life of business families is that they are particularly vulnerable to external forces. Ignorance of these forces is perilous.

In the Williams case, there are several outside forces that must be considered immediately. The first involves the health of Jazz Jive—the micro- and macro economy in which it operates. At this stage of the business life cycle, John cannot take his eye off the business for too long; he needs to be constantly on the alert for adjustments in reaction to economic conditions. The possibility that he will sell the business to outsiders means that he must take certain steps to prepare the business for this eventuality. The second force arises from his actions with regard to Cindy and Brad. The IRS may be demanding penalties and interest for an early withdrawal from a retirement account. Child support laws do not make it optional for John to support Brad. The potential loss of Cindy means a different set of managers for the business.

Finally, the new influx of investment assets into the system creates new challenges for Helen and John. Now they must attend to a different set of economic conditions that affect their family wealth. Their income tax situation will change when trust distributions are made to Helen, and their estate may be so different as to require completely new transfer tax planning.

Core FWTP Challenges

An analysis of the family wealth system of the Williams family reveals certain core challenges that the adviser must address in selecting components of the wealth transition plan. Like every family, the Williams are facing a blend of core challenges. Their fundamental challenge will be to resolve the trust and fear issues that have haunted their marriage. This appears to be occurring, to some extent, through couples therapy and individual counseling. The Williams must also face the implications of the retirement plan withdrawals, and address the future of John's business. Most importantly, their family subsystem has experienced a major shock: the introduction of another child under unusual circumstances. This involves all three components of the FWTP process: wealth transition structures, governance systems, and role clarity and development.

One way to help client families create a plan is to organize these core challenges into the three categories of plan components. *Figure 11.3* summarizes the Williams family's core challenges.

Role Clarity and Development

In the Williams situation, the shock to the family subsystem created a core challenge that FWTP must address before any other issue: who is *family*? Prior to this event, Helen thought she understood who the members of her family were. She had parents, children, and in-laws, including John's sister, Sara, and her husband. While Sara's recent withdrawal from the Williams family had puzzled and saddened her, Helen still thought of Sara as family. Now, two new people are potentially within the family subsystem: Cindy and Brad. For John, these two are family in a legal sense, whether he wishes it or not.

The more clarity Helen and John have about including Cindy and Brad in the family, or excluding them, the easier it will be to create governance systems and wealth transition structures to fit the family's

FIGURE 11.3 Core Challenges for the Williams Family in FWTP

	Role Clarity and Development	Governance Systems	Wealth Transition Structures
Core Challenges	• Who is "family"? —What is Brad's role? —What is Cindy's role? —Brad's? —Grandparents'? • What is John's role in the care of family members? • What is Helen's role in family decision making?	• Divorce scenario • How will Helen and John share responsibility for family financial decision making?	• "Just-in-case" plan vs. long-term transition plan • Child support for Brad (and for other children if marriage fails) • Custody/visitation • Future of business • Helen's rights and risks (penalties?) in retirement plan • Lisa's special needs trust or similar vehicle

needs. These systems and structures must be flexible enough to accommodate changes in the way Cindy and Brad fit into the Williams family.

The Williams face other role clarity and development challenges as well. Primary among them are the new roles John and Helen will play in family decision making. If John and Helen remain married, they must find a way for Helen to participate and engage in the family wealth decision-making process. She may need to cede some control over family matters to make room in her life for education about family finances, and to develop her role as a partner in this process. The good news is that she seems motivated to do so. Even prior to the revelation of his secret, John's surgery had made Helen aware of her family's vulnerability. She was actively lobbying to sell the business and move the family to Long Island. She can channel this newfound motivation into education and development of her new role. Moreover, she has found an accountant in whom she has confidence, and this person may play a key part in Helen's role clarity and development.

It is not just Helen who faces role development challenges. John has some of his own. He had been in sole control of financial matters, and was the only family member calling the shots in the business. He now must learn to let go of the control role and move to a more collaborative decision-making model. This may be difficult for him, but just as he felt relief in finally revealing his secret, he now may be relieved to have a partner in decision making. Both he and Helen will have to grapple with the implications of Jacob's trust for Helen and her children. It is probable that this gift has fundamentally shifted the balance of financial power in the family, so if John and Helen stay together, they must learn how to maneuver with this new component of their investment subsystem.

Helen and John have a good example in Miriam. She seems to have embraced new roles, such as that of an informed beneficiary. She is trying to help Helen complete Stage Two of her individual life cycle, at Jacob's posthumous request. She even seems to have accepted that Brad is an important part of the family.

Governance Systems

—JOHN WILLIAMS, *age fifty-one*—

Getting it all out on the table by telling Helen was a relief. I told her everything. She knew most of it already, of course. I must have been crazy or something not to have just told her when Cindy got pregnant. I told myself that I couldn't hurt her when she was so down about Lisa, but the truth is that I was just scared. Helen was—is—so angry with me, and I wonder if she's ever going to get over it. She calls me all the time when I'm at work, and always opens all the mail before I get to it. She's paranoid, and for no reason. I broke it off with Cindy years ago; our only bonds are work and Brad. Helen and I go to counseling together every week, and I go to my own counselor, too, and we're working on what I need to do to build trust with Helen, and what to do about Cindy. Helen is adamant: Cindy cannot continue working in the business. She still won't come down to the Jazz Jive; she says she doesn't want to see Cindy. I rely on Cindy a lot and I can't just fire her. Helen knows nothing about the business. And we have to figure out what to do about Brad. Is he part of my family, or not?

Helen does not have a pattern of family governance from which she could adopt a joint decision-making system. Whether or not John has a model that worked for his family isn't clear. This couple, like most, is going to have to invent a decision-making system for their family and investment subsystems that provides a substitute for trust until trust can be rebuilt. It is likely that until then Helen will insist on joint decision making instead of delegating any authority to John. Ultimately, they may choose to share decisions differently, delegating some to John and some to Helen, with agreed-upon rules of oversight and accountability that draw upon the components of accountability.

Rebuilding trust will also require immediate, candid, and straightforward attention to the financial arrangements between John and Cindy. Helen needs to understand these fully, from the co-op to the child support built into Cindy's salary.

Helen is still not involved with, and doesn't understand the workings of, the family business. John is still in control, but Helen is adamant that a major change must occur. The result is an impasse. If they are to keep the business, they will need a governance system to ensure that Helen has some degree of oversight. She needs to understand the business more fully and assume a role consistent with her interests as a stakeholder. If the business is organized as a corporation, she should be a shareholder and sit on the board. If it is organized as a limited liability company, she should be a member, under an operating agreement that gives members significant oversight powers in terms of transparency, substitute decision making, and transformation. Either structure will require her to participate in a meaningful way, requiring yet more education, time, and energy on her part.

John may well bristle at all this. He may not want Helen involved at all. But by involving his business and its manager in his breach of trust, he highlighted the need for an oversight structure. More fundamentally, it may be time for transformation of the business by sale or closure.

Wealth Transition Structures

Whether or not John and Helen's marriage survives, the Williams family needs the basic tools of the estate planning trade: wills or revocable trusts that create testamentary trusts for the children, powers of attorney, and directives for health care. In particular, John and Helen need to make arrangements for Lisa's care, probably through use of a special needs trust. They have to discuss guardianship of their children with Sara and Phillip in light of both couples' changed relationship. John and Helen may struggle with one another and with their respective advisers over the implications of John's having breached the prenuptial agreement by withdrawing retirement plan money for

Cindy's apartment. The divergence of interests on these topics means that Helen and John require a team of advisers, and need to be represented by different firms.

Brad's Status

Now that Brad is a reality for everyone in the Williams family, the family needs specific legal arrangements for his support. They also need to involve him in John Williams' life and, by extension, into the lives of the entire Williams family. Building child support into Cindy's salary is no longer necessary; whether it is desirable is a matter for the family law and business attorneys. Visitation arrangements will have to be made. These legal arrangements are the tip of the iceberg, however, when compared to the emotional arrangements that must take form within the Williams family subsystem. Whether Brad is welcome or not, and whether the family is truly open to its new members or not, will have an enormous impact on family wealth continuity.

The Business

For the Jazz Jive bars and restaurant, John faces only three options: close the business, keep the business, or sell it. Helping John and Helen evaluate these options requires an understanding of the business and the stage of its life cycle. This makes closing the business an unattractive option, and probably not one that John could tolerate, because Jazz Jive may be poised to move to a somewhat easier stage of operation. Its current stage, however, makes it particularly vulnerable in a sale. Its success still depends on John's presence, charm, and guiding hands, and perhaps Cindy's as well. The business is difficult to value, because the goodwill hasn't yet translated into steady and significant cash flow. The longer John's family continues in turmoil, or the longer John fidgets over the decision to sell, the more likely it is that the value of the business will drop precipitously.

Keep the Business?

If Jazz Jive is on the brink of becoming an enterprise that will generate significant cash flow, the Williams family may wish to keep it in order to realize its true potential. This choice, however, would require its members to resolve the fundamental life cycle problem that propelled Helen into an adviser's office in the first place: preparing for the untimely death of the owner/operator. If the Williamses are to keep the business, John must, at a minimum, be able to establish a lifestyle that supports his health rather than undermining it. The family must also develop a plan for sudden death. Given Cindy's role in the management of the business, John and Helen may find that their plan for sudden death is quite similar to Cindy's desire to buy the business.

Sale to Cindy or to Outsiders?

If John and Helen are going to sell Jazz Jive, the absence of any Williams family member ready and able to take over the business gives them only two options for sale: sell to a stranger or sell to Cindy. Helen would probably find the idea of selling to Cindy unpalatable, at least initially, but whether she knows it or not, it may be the option most consistent with Helen's needs, for a number of reasons:

❏ Cindy is the person most likely to believe in the future of the business, and be willing to pay the best price for its goodwill, even though the business is not yet a cash cow.

❏ Cindy would be less likely to stay if the business were sold to an outsider, which may make it more difficult to sell.

❏ Cindy is the only one able to take over the business and make a success of it without John, or with him staying on board for a relatively short transition period. Other buyers would likely require one or two years of postsale assistance, and perhaps more if Jazz Jive becomes part of a chain. These approaches are inconsistent with Helen's view of what John's health issues require.

❏ Cindy might be the only buyer willing to buy stock rather than assets. Typical buyers of high-risk enterprises such as Jazz Jive insist on purchasing assets, because a stock purchase brings with it all the outstanding liabilities, contingent or not, of the company. This generally leads to higher taxes for the seller. Cindy knows about the potential liabilities of the business, and may be willing to buy stock so that John and Helen could enjoy the attractive 15 percent federal capital gains treatment on their gain. They may also be able, depending on the structure of the business, to claim an exclusion of a portion of the gain under Internal Revenue Code Sec. 1202.

If John and Helen are to make the best possible decision about the business, they must be careful to put aside the emotionally laden issues of mutual trust and evaluate their options. They need to rely on their FWTP adviser to help them make this decision wisely.

Ten Months Later . . .

—HELEN WILLIAMS, *age forty-eight*—

For us, this whole family wealth continuity thing was a mixed bag. Some things we did really right. Other things, well, we just couldn't get there from here. John and I didn't get a divorce, but it was really rocky there for a while. But with all our kids, and especially Lisa, we just had to stay together. Now we live out here on Long Island in my parents' house. Mother sold it to my trust when she wanted to move to Manhattan. I had hoped she'd live with us, but she's turned into quite the socialite. She even raises money for research into Down syndrome.

John ended up selling the business to Cindy, with some complicated plan for stock in trust for Brad. I understood it at the time—I made sure of that—but I couldn't describe it now, except to say that I thought it was fair. John has spent a lot of time and energy trying to regain my trust. He's an open book, I can ask him anything and I get the truth. I make sure I know what's going on financially with our family. We sit down once a month and go over everything. I'm teaching the kids how to do that too; I don't want any of them to end up in the dark like I was. Since John's not working, he's spending a lot more time with the kids, and I've been able to get back into teaching and even perform some. We've taken up ballroom dancing, of all things. It's good to be back like old times with Sara and Phillip. But John and I still go around about the Brad and Cindy thing. I finally said "enough already." I am so done with seeing counselors. John sees Brad regularly and sometimes he takes the kids. Even my own mother goes sometimes. But I never do.

Helen considers her and John's success in creating family wealth continuity "a mixed bag." Certainly, she has come a long way in developing her role as a steward of family financial wealth, and she is teaching her children to do the same. She has learned to deal effectively with advisers, although she had to learn through trial by fire. She and John are reinvesting in their marriage and family, and John has worked hard to make up for the repeated withdrawals of human capital from the family that his dishonesty engendered. The family is even participating in philanthropic activities, through Miriam's raising funds for research into Down syndrome. Helen will need to continue to develop her role as a manager of wealth, as she will doubtless inherit assets from her mother and will need to learn how to manage investment wealth. Her own trust may eventually terminate, leaving her in charge of its funds. Helen's development as a good steward of financial capital is likely to be a lifelong process of learning.

John and Helen have also come a long way in creating healthy family relationships. No longer in a marriage with a big secret, they have become open books to one another. Their children seem to be doing well. Helen and John are trying to have fun together. Only one difficult area remains: Brad and Cindy. Although John and the children seem to be creating healthy relationships by connecting with Brad, Helen cannot bring herself to do so. Only time will tell whether she will eventually be able to do so, or whether it really matters.

Missing from Helen's story is any hint that she is helping to create a family legacy. Is the family home a part of their legacy? Do the strong ties among the Williams children, and especially their care for Lisa, constitute their legacy? Will Miriam's charity work be part of that legacy? Helen and John's experience is too recent, and has left them feeling too raw even to consider these larger issues. In due course, they and the extended family may wish to reflect on what their family legacy will be.

CHAPTER NOTES

1. See Chapter 6

2. See Chapter 6, Figure 6.5.

3. See Chapter 6.

CHAPTER 12

TRANSITIONS OF WEALTH IN THE HERNÁNDEZ FAMILY

THE HERNÁNDEZ FAMILY has traditionally relied on deep reserves of family social capital to carry them through difficult times. This family has also created a significant amount of financial capital in just two generations. The clothing business was a success, and yielded a good nest egg for Clara and her family. It is not clear how much of that sale was attributed to Elena, or how much Bart Sr. inherited from her. But because Bart Sr.'s primary source of wealth and activity, his real estate, is neither liquid nor self-supporting, Bart Sr.'s continuing involvement in the business is necessary. This may or may not be consistent with his stage in life and the life stage of his core family unit, which is itself in flux. In any event, he appears to have no retirement savings, except for Elena's share of the proceeds of the sale of the clothing business, and he relies on the hardware store for at least part of his support. The future of that store is in question: Bart Sr. is semiretired, José is unhappy with his role there, and Bart Jr. thinks he wants to buy it to keep it in the family. The family previously had turned down offers to sell, and now the big-box stores are horning in on the market. At the same time, the other businesses created by Bart Jr. and Luisa are in their growth stages, requiring their day-to-day commitment and resources. Although this appears to be consistent with their goals and individual and family life cycle needs, at least at this time, the drain on their family lives and family financial capital may continue to be significant.

José and Bart Jr. seem equally stuck, each in his own way: Bart Jr. has too much responsibility and José has too little. Bart Jr. spends too much time working, and is losing touch with his core family members, Susan and María. José lacks a clear path in life to which he can feel committed. Their father, Bart Sr., has survived the death of the two most important women in his life and now seems ready to establish a new relationship with Samantha. Yet he worries about the impact of this on his children, and the financial entanglements he has with each of them doesn't make sorting out their relationships any easier. His sister Clara seems set for life after the sale of the clothing business, but can any Hernández of that generation actually retire? Things are coming to a head between the Hernández sons, yet their conflict may lead the family to a better understanding of its core family wealth transition planning (FWTP) challenges.

Success, Process, and Ethics Questions

—BART HERNÁNDEZ JR., *age forty*—

Susan's always after me to be more of a role model to José, saying that he needs a big brother. She doesn't understand how we can't get along, but to make her happy we invite him over sometimes. That's what happened last Friday. My daughter María adores him, and they played until it was time for her to go to bed. After, we were just sitting around watching TV and having a beer. All I said was something like, "Bro, you can't live at home forever, you know." I didn't mean anything by it. But all hell broke loose. He was like a crazy man, shouting that I had no right to talk, that I didn't know anything. Before I knew it we were going at it, fists and all. He hit his head on the coffee table. Susan screamed at us to stop. We both happened to look up at the same time and saw María cowering in the hallway, clutching her blanket. I think that's what stopped us. I had to take José to the emergency room to get stitches. He was very quiet. Me too. I didn't know what to say. I took him home, and I know that Papá's going to have a few choice words for me. What's wrong with us, that we could end up this way?

The cracks in the Hernández family are fast becoming chasms. As the individuals, families, and businesses in their wealth system make their way through their life cycles, family members are struggling with the unarticulated values and expectations that both support and constrain the family. The challenge facing the FWTP adviser is that the Hernández family is unaware of its own wealth themes, and has little history of talking about them, resolving family members' ambivalence about them, or changing them. Getting the Hernández family members in the same room to discuss these issues with generosity and grace, either together or sequentially, requires both imagination and cultural sensitivity. It also requires careful consideration of how both José and Bart Jr. will be involved in the process, if they can be. The conflict between José and Bart Jr. must be addressed if José is to embark upon his individual path, and if these brothers are to share wealth successfully in the next generation. Although, as we shall see, they make a significant breakthrough on their own, one round of reconciliation does not erase years of mistrust and miscommunication.

Success

An inherently generous father, Bart Hernández Sr. has made capital (in all forms) available to his family members on an ad hoc basis as he saw needs and opportunities arise. These have ranged from confronting his own father about allowing his sister Clara to return home, to purchasing the hardware store, to financing Luisa's independent medical practice. Even Bart Sr. recognizes that the explosion in complexity of the Hernández family wealth system requires some method for making capital available to members. After all, he wants to be fair to his children. Thus, success in FWTP for the Hernández family will mean putting in place a full array of wealth transition structures, governance systems, and role development plans. Together, these elements adapt the family wealth system to achieve family wealth continuity by nurturing healthy family relationships, encouraging family members to become responsible stewards of wealth in all its forms, and creating a family legacy. These goals will be the guideposts for choices to be made, largely by Bart Sr., but also by others within the system, particularly as they face the changes in Bart Sr.'s and José's lives.

Process

As a preliminary matter, an adviser to the Hernández family must consider the makeup of the FWTP team. Members must be aware of both the cultural and generational differences in the Hernández family. Many of the stories that reveal family wealth themes rely on culturally specific ideas. Speaking Spanish will help. Providing advisers from matching generations may help the Hernández family in sorting out its issues.

José, in particular, may trust and respond better to a younger adviser than to an adviser from his father's generation.

The process described for the Williams family closely followed the linear methodology outlined in this book. Because the Hernández family's extreme enmeshment is immediately obvious, the FWTP adviser can choose a different methodology to explore the family wealth system: stakeholder analysis. Stakeholder analysis is especially useful in identifying interdependencies and sensitivities within the family wealth system, and offers clues as to important family wealth patterns. The visual result, a chart showing how people within the system are connected, is often helpful to client families who have never before focused on the roles their members play within their family wealth system.

As issues arise during the process, the FWTP adviser can supplement stakeholder analysis with an exploration of particular aspects of the family wealth system. To help both Bart Jr. and Bart Sr. understand how José may have unarticulated needs that Bart Sr. has already satisfied in his own life, for example, an adviser might focus on the multiple overlapping life cycles in which Bart Sr. participates.[1] An analysis of the sources of wealth within the Hernández family system and the external forces at work on those sources may also be helpful. The following sections, however, focus on stakeholder analysis as a means to sorting out much of the complexity of the family wealth system.

Ethics

Chapter 2 discussed some of the ethical challenges of assisting the Hernández family. While Bart Sr. is the likely central figure in any representation, any significant change for him will require complementary changes for every other family member. In this setting, as with the Williams family, obvious conflicts between family members require that the adviser carefully structure the process to protect confidences while involving family members appropriately in the process.

The FWTP adviser, however, is not without family resources. Bart Sr. is motivated to get his family back on track. He and the adviser can probably call upon the influence and practicality of the new family matriarch, Clara, as well as Luisa's emotional intelligence. Working together, these three family members may be able to break through whatever it is that's going on with the brothers.

Stakeholder Analysis of the Hernández Family Wealth System

Figures 12.1 and *12.2* present a stakeholder analysis of the Hernández operating business subsystem. We have illustrated only the operating business subsystem, because of its importance in this entrepreneurial family, but one can extend this analysis easily to any other subsystem, such as the investment system in which Bart Sr.'s real estate would be located. Figure 12.1 shows eight stakeholder groups of family members

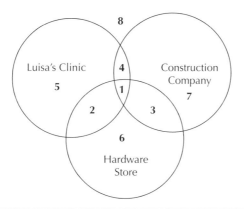

FIGURE **12.1** Family Stakeholder Groups in the Hernández Operating Business Subsystem

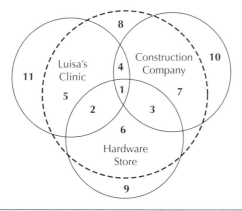

FIGURE **12.2** Hernández Business Stakeholder Groups Including Nonfamily Members

who are involved in the three current family businesses. Figure 12.1 does not include the children's clothing business that was sold, because there is no longer any family ownership.

Figure 12.2 adds nonfamily stakeholder groups. This figure shows that the three Hernández businesses extend beyond family members. Three nonfamily stakeholder groups exist, one for each of the businesses.

One of the biggest challenges for the FWTP adviser who uses stakeholder analysis is defining membership within each stakeholder group, because what is obvious may not always be accurate. There are many possible ways in which to define the stakeholders. In Figure 12.2, the dotted circle represents the family boundary. Each business extends beyond the family group to encompass other stakeholders. Family members are inside the dotted circle according to their involvement in some identifiable capacity within the businesses. Some of these roles have legal and financial implications, which the FWTP process ultimately must either respect or change. Nonfamily members are outside the dotted line. *Figure 12.3* summarizes the membership of both stakeholder groups.

FIGURE 12.3   Summary of Stakeholder Group Membership

1 Involved in all businesses	Bart Sr.
2 Involved in clinic and hardware store	Bart Sr. Luisa
3 Involved in hardware store and construction business	Bart Sr. Bart Jr. José
4 Involved in construction company and medical clinic	Bart Sr.
5 Involved in medical clinic	Luisa Bart Sr.
6 Involved in hardware store	Bart Sr. José Perhaps soon Bart Jr.?
7 Involved in construction business	Bart Sr. Bart Jr. José
8 Family not involved in any formal role in business	Clara Bart Sr.'s other sisters and their spouses, children, etc.
9 Nonfamily involved in hardware store	Customers, employees, etc.
10 Nonfamily involved in construction business	Customers, employees, etc.
11 Nonfamily involved in medical clinic	Patients, employees, etc.

Using Stakeholder Groups to Explore the Family Wealth System

Stakeholder groups are an effective way to focus on the sources of family wealth as well as the connections among them. It is likely that members of the same stakeholder group will have aligned interests, so conflict between them points to important discontinuities within the system. When an individual is a member of multiple groups, important questions about roles and priorities emerge. Finally, membership in multiple groups suggests connections that any FWTP process must understand and protect or replace.

Bart Sr.

The most obvious conclusion of stakeholder analysis for this family business is that Bart Sr. plays a significant role in all the family's businesses. This creates one of the system's most critical sensitivities. If Bart Sr. suddenly died, or needed or wanted to retire, all the businesses would be vulnerable. There are no formal loan agreements that specify the terms and rate of interest for the loans to Luisa's clinic or the construction company. Bart Jr. and Luisa both see the loans as a liability that must be repaid. They may even see their father as their silent partner, or as the family bank. He may or may not share their views. If the loans are not repaid before Bart Sr. dies, there are no agreements for what happens next. If Bart Sr. remarries, his second wife could demand repayment of the loans. She might see herself as having a right to be involved in each of those businesses as more than a lender. She might see herself as José's boss if Bart Sr. dies without specifying whom he chooses as his heirs to the store. She could even insist that her children receive jobs in the store, and leave the store to them rather than to Bart Sr.'s children.

Bart's central role provides ample opportunities for exploring the family wealth system's evolution. Key questions include:

❏ How did Bart Sr. come to play such an important role in all family business ventures?
❏ Why did Bart Sr. and Elena keep the hardware store after they had received attractive offers to sell it? What role does the hardware store play today in the family wealth system?

❑ How did Bart Sr. decide to finance his sons' construction business? What was the discussion and decision process? What were the expectations of his sons and why? Why did he insist that José be included?

❑ What are his plans for the future? What are his fears or concerns?

❑ What is his wish for these businesses?

❑ Is his financial future secure? What are his financial fears or concerns? What are the fears or concerns of family members?

Luisa

Stakeholder analysis reveals that Luisa's role is just the opposite of Bart Jr's. In contrast to her father and brothers, Luisa seems isolated from the family's businesses. She appears in only a couple of the stakeholder groups and has no financial involvement with either the hardware store or the construction business. This raises several opportunities to test assumptions, including:

❑ If Bart Sr. truly believes that all of his children should have a place at the table, what does that mean for Luisa? Would she be welcome as a silent partner, or in some other role? Should she take on a role in these businesses? Or has her move to Los Angeles left her out?

❑ Bart Jr. and José currently participate in the wealth created by the construction business and hardware store, both of which owe their existence, in varying degrees, to Bart Sr. Both brothers have expectations about inheriting from Bart Sr. Does Bart Sr. view this as equitable? Did he help Luisa with the costs of her education? When he dies, how will he create an equitable sharing of wealth among his children, given Luisa's profession and locale?

❑ If the medical practice is the sole source of Luisa's financial wealth, what has she done to protect that source from internal or external events, such as disability or health care reform, that could prevent her from practicing?

❑ Luisa's father encouraged her to "get out there and be somebody." He insisted, when her mother died, that she stay in Los Angeles and not move back home. Yet the two brothers remain in Fresno, one apparently content, the other chafing under his father's oversight. The stories of José as a slacker continue to spread in a family that practices what it preaches: the value of hard work. Why didn't José break free from the family, as Luisa did? Why didn't his father encourage him to find his own path, as he apparently encouraged Luisa to do?

The Brothers

Stakeholder analysis offers important clues about the relationship of the two Hernández sons. Each stakeholder group that contains one also contains the other. Neither has a stakeholder group in which he stands independently of his brother. That may be an important source of conflict, as the establishment of autonomy and independent identity is a critical part of the individuation process. Bart Jr. hinted at this earlier when he wanted to start the construction business on his own, but was afraid to take on his father. Although Bart Sr. currently exerts his influence to keep things under control, if Bart Jr. and José don't find a way to work through their conflicts more effectively, the business and all of its stakeholders will suffer the consequences, because Bart Sr. cannot play this role forever.

Moreover, there appear to be no explicit agreements, formal or informal contracts, or agreed-upon rules of the road that define the roles of the two brothers in their businesses. Yet their interests are potentially adverse. In the construction business and the hardware business, each has taken advantage of his position to direct benefits away from the other: Bart Jr. is stripping earnings through salary, and José is thwarting his brother by changing prices on materials.

Outsiders

Figure 12.2 focuses the family and the FWTP adviser on stakeholder groups that a family in conflict often neglects. It is easy for a family in conflict to focus its attentions inwardly and begin to ignore external stakeholders. Stakeholder Group Eight comprises members of the Hernández family that do not play formal roles in the businesses. This group is vulnerable to conflict within Bart's core family, before or after his death. Consideration of Stakeholder Groups Nine and Ten, comprising nonfamily stakeholders in the Fresno businesses, reminds the family that without the support of these stakeholders, their conflict over the businesses may become moot. In some cases, the family and its advisers can call upon resources within these groups, such as key employees or companies in related industries, when creating options for the FWTP process.

Stakeholder Analysis as a Key to Family Wealth Themes

—BART HERNÁNDEZ SR., *age sixty-two*—

When José came home from Bart's with those stitches and told me a bold-faced lie, that he'd run into some guys and got into a fight, I knew I had to put a stop to all this nonsense. I made them both meet me at the hardware store the next day. I told them that our family didn't come to this country and work as hard as it did to have them shame us by acting like idiots. I told José that both he and his brother need to learn to get along like family, or else he's going to have to move out and get a real job. I told Bart Jr. the same thing: that I held him responsible, and that he can forget getting any more help from me until he figures out how to be a real brother to José. Their reaction was not quite what I expected. Both those boys looked at each other and started laughing, as if I was saying the funniest things they'd ever heard. I was pretty steamed, but what happened was this: I guess that fight was just what they both needed, because they finally talked it all out about the construction company and hardware store and what they both wanted to do. It seems Bart Jr. wants to buy the hardware store because he thinks I need or want it to stay in the family as some sort of heritage or something, and he thought José was running it into the ground. José doesn't want to run it anyway. I guess I knew that all along but didn't want to say it. But what really hurt is that he's only been hanging around here because of me, thinking I needed his help after Elena and Mamá died. I didn't. José wants to go back East to art school in Rhode Island. He has a girlfriend who is already there. That's news to me. He and Bart Jr. have been working out how this all can happen as if it's a done deal. My sons seem to be making decisions about the family and me without even asking my opinion. I have to say I'm floored. I don't want to make José run the store if he really doesn't want to, but it's a good job until he finds some other career. No way is he going to some art school. Nobody can make a living as an artist. We'd be supporting him forever. And with some girl we've never even met? His mother would turn in her grave. That boy can just forget it.

Stakeholder analysis is an important tool for obtaining insights into family typology and related family wealth behavior themes. *Figure 12.4* illustrates the Hernández family typology. The overlap among the stakeholder categories clearly shows an enmeshed family. This family is also flexible, without becoming chaotic. It has been able to marshal its financial, human, and social capital in the right combinations to successfully

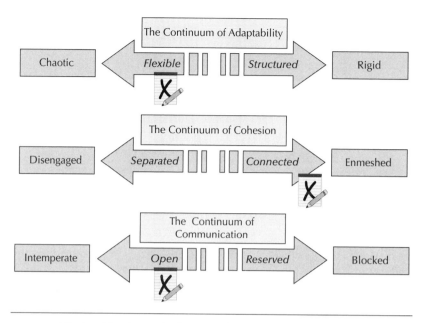

FIGURE **12.4**   The Hernández Family Typology

create and sell businesses over the generations. Traditionally, communication has been open in this family, but the conflict between Bart Jr. and José, and all that led up to it, is threatening that traditional openness. As always, these typologies alert the FWTP adviser to potential themes at work in the family wealth system.

Understanding the roles each stakeholder plays also helps an adviser see how those roles contribute to a family's historical conflicts and play out in repetitive patterns of behavior. José is stuck: he receives the benefits of a job he doesn't want, and he knows that his family does not respect him. If Bart Sr. can fully explore the roles both his sons play in the family's businesses, he may also come to see that working in the hardware store doesn't meet José's (or the store's) needs. He may be able to let go of his assumption that they both have to work in the businesses in order to be owners, thus freeing up the options available to the family for its future. Bart Sr.'s central role in the family operating businesses creates certain predictable feedback loops. He struggles with the conflicts arising from his muddled roles of older brother, dutiful son, hands-on manager, and business owner, while neglecting his roles as husband and father. He may see his older son taking a similar path toward too much responsibility. The challenge for the FWTP adviser is to determine which themes are most important in the family wealth system of this particular family, and how these play out in needs, capacities, and constraints in FWTP.

Control and Abdication

Although the Hernández family appears to be at the "flexible" end of the adaptability continuum, a FWTP adviser should be alert to the possibility that Bart's participation in all his children's endeavors could give him an inordinate degree of control, should he choose to exercise it (as he tried to do in the preceding case study). Most clients would be reluctant to acknowledge this potential for control. Bart Sr., in particular, may be reluctant to examine this issue, because he may be personally invested in the ideal of the benevolent patriarch. Another clue that control/abdication themes are at work in the Hernández family is that José appears to be abdicating responsibility for his own life, and has allowed his family to define his pathway, such as it is.

Yet Bart Sr.'s situation illustrates that an individual can temper control so that it does not derail family wealth continuity. If control is truly an issue with Bart Sr., he has been able to rise above it in significant ways. Years ago, he defied his father to make sure his sister Clara could return home after her early wild days. He supported Luisa in being one of the first Hernández family members to move away from Fresno, and staying the course when her mother and grandmother died, even when she felt it was her responsibility to return home. His loan to her to start a medical practice didn't seem to come with strings. He also seems to have been supportive of Bart Jr. in his construction business, without interfering, except for that first fateful decision requiring José's involvement. Perhaps most telling is that his sons feel free to laugh at his trying to use his financial power to make them settle their differences, which are theirs, not his, to resolve. Bart Sr. has a choice: be angry at this apparent disrespect, or view it as an invitation to cede control of their own well-being to his adult children at last. He may choose to give them the gift of trust that each Hernández child is fully capable of learning how to communicate more effectively and to value each other as siblings and as business partners.

Entitlement and Shame

The theme of entitlement and shame appears to be alive and well in the Hernández family. As we discussed in Chapter 6, the family perceives José as having an inappropriate sense of entitlement, and he does not help matters. However, it is not just José in whom this theme plays out. Bart Sr. has made it clear that any Hernández is entitled to a place at the family business table, and has facilitated that by buying José's place in the construction business and hiring José as the manager of the hardware store. He did not insist upon protocols, structures, or processes in the management of the hardware store that would have either helped José do a better job or alerted Bart Sr. to problems. José has no formal job description, no formal performance reviews, and no formal training program for how to be an owner/manager should he be Bart Sr.'s successor. Bart Sr. has been wearing his "father hat," not his "owner hat," in relationship to José's involvement in the hardware business. He has wanted to make a place for everyone in the family within this family business stakeholder system, so he has kept José in this stakeholder group without defining performance outcomes.

José's story is different from that of many who have an entitlement mentality. He put his life on hold because he felt that his father needed support, and that there were no other family members who could genuinely provide it. He didn't share this perspective with anyone, or share his sacrifice (if that is what it was), or even share what he saw his father going through. He probably kept silent out of respect for his father. Bart Sr. believed he coped well with the deaths of the two most important women in his life. Other family members probably felt the same way, because Bart Sr., given his gender, place in the family, and age, was unlikely to share his true experience with others, even close family members. José saw something that others did not; after all, he was living with his father at the time. He was the one to see his father roaming the house at night, unable to sleep and perpetually irritable. Once José put his life on hold, and lost his girlfriend to the path he really wanted, he simply got stuck. This is not unusual, but getting him back on track will probably require a different path than any other Hernández family member has traveled.

Conformity and Rebellion

The theme most likely at work in the Hernández family is that of conformity and rebellion. Now that José's situation is sorted out, it seems that he, like forebears such as his deceased uncle Ramón and his aunt Clara, is rebelling against the family's expectations of conformity. Clara ran away rather than face failing her family in its expectations of her. José, too, thought he would have to run away because he saw no way to have a place in the family as something other than a hard-working businessman. Bart Jr. wanted to rebel against his father's insistence on including José in the construction business, but couldn't do it, and ultimately conformed. Bart Jr.'s recent idea of purchasing the hardware store, when between the construction business and studying to be an engineer he hardly has time to see his own family, suggests that he may have overly conformed to family expectations. This overconformity may have resulted from early childhood, when Bart Jr. had very different experiences in the family hardware business than did his much younger siblings.

Although Bart Sr. likely believes that he supports his children's individuation, he seems to have a deep-seated need to have them, or at least his sons, follow in the family footsteps. Bart Sr. was willing to purchase a place in the family businesses for José, but, by doing so, he has removed José's opportunities to both follow his own path and fully participate as a valued member of the family. Bart Sr. did support Luisa in her choice of a different path in life, and part of exploring this theme is why that was acceptable for Luisa, but is not for José. Undoubtedly, Bart Sr. does not see the situation like this, and teasing out the expectation of conformity will be difficult for him. It's important to understand what value conformity provides to members of the Hernández wealth system, and what purposes it serves. By doing so, the family will be able to define meaningful roles for each family member, especially as Bart Sr.'s role changes.

The Hernández family illustrates the importance of addressing a family's expectations of conformity in light of the inevitable movement toward increasing complexity in families through generations. Bart's three children are on very different paths, and their courses are likely to continue to diverge as all three adult children establish families of their own. Bart Sr. has the opportunity to help change family patterns so that nonconformity does not require as complete a break with the family as it has in past generations. He has successfully practiced doing this with Luisa, and now José, admittedly a harder case, needs that same support. Along the way, both Bart Sr. and Bart Jr. may find themselves escaping from overcommitment and may have a new freedom to choose where they put their energies. But for this to succeed, Bart Sr. will need the FWTP adviser to attend to processes and structures that support his needs for family connection and commitment to a common purpose. While these family members love one another, some of their mutual trust has been eroded by the ongoing, unresolved conflicts now surfacing. They are having to rebuild trust as their roles and opportunities change.

Core FWTP Challenges for the Hernández Family

The information gleaned from stakeholder analysis of the Hernández family reveals certain core challenges that the FWTP adviser must address in selecting the components of the family's plan. Bart Sr. has always been open to change, and sees how his own life is changing after Elena's death. He is also beginning to realize the depth of his sons' conflict. The adviser must spend some time with Bart Sr. helping him understand how his family's degree of enmeshment, without clarity on roles or responsibilities, has led to conflict. The adviser must be cautious, however, because this enmeshment has arisen naturally from Bart Sr.'s living out his core values: generosity, hard work, and a commitment to family. Bart Sr. must be confident that he will not have to abandon these values in this process of creating a plan, and that the plan will support those values as part of the family legacy.

Figure 12.5 summarizes the Hernández family's particular challenges of role clarity, governance, and wealth transition structures.

FIGURE **12.5**   Core Challenges for the Hernández Family in FWTP

	Role Clarity and Development	Governance Systems	Wealth Transition Structures
Core Challenges	• Clarifying Bart's roles in wealth subsystems: How does he want to participate, and why? How can he disentangle from them, if he is willing? • Clarifying others' roles in each business • Preparing others to assume Bart's roles, as appropriate • Finding ways for José to get back on a track that will move him forward and that the family can support	• Decision making in hardware store • Decision making in construction business: management vs. oversight • Decision making with respect to real estate	• Letting go of endeavors that don't work anymore for family wealth continuity • Formalizing loans, and distinguishing them from gifts • Creating "fairness" among children, e.g., determining Luisa's share of wealth in businesses in which she does not participate • Real estate ownership structures to reduce estate taxes and transfer ownership • Prenuptial agreement for Bart Sr. and Samantha? • A family foundation?

Governance Systems

—José Hernández, *age twenty-seven*—

Susan really got to me the next day when she called me up and told me that María was scared of both of us and we should be ashamed of ourselves. So I went back over to their house and we made up some story to explain my face, that I was just dressed up for Halloween or something, and we made sure Maria was okay. Then Bart Sr. and I finally talked it out. I told him how I hated him for leaving me out of the construction business when I was supposedly an equal partner. I just knew he would deny it, or try to blame it on me that I wasn't any help, but he didn't. He told me that Dad made him include me, not that he was blaming Dad. Bart Sr. said he didn't have the guts to stand up to Dad then, to say he needed to do this by himself, and to turn down Dad's money rather than including me. Bart actually said he was sorry. (Which made me feel like a complete jerk, because I'd been jacking him around on prices at the hardware store.) Bart Sr. would make room if that's what I wanted, but I don't. Not anymore. I want to go to Rhode Island. So Bart Sr. said in that case we'd figure out a way that the business could provide some money for me so that I wouldn't have to rely on Dad. He said he thought we should both ask Tía Clara to go over the books with us and help us figure out what's happened and what would be fair for the future. Tía Clara's tough. She doesn't let anybody pull any crap on anybody else. She'll be able to keep us both in line.

In creating a FWTP process for Bart Sr., it may seem odd to begin with a governance system for his sons. Yet they are the ones that seem ready to address a fundamental issue: building some sort of governance system that will allow them to share the benefits of that business equitably, despite having very different relationships to it. Not only will resolving the sons' conflict ease Bart's mind, but it will also provide a model for what needs to happen in many other areas of Bart's world: clarifying relationships, creating governance systems, and implementing wealth transition structures that support family wealth continuity. Seeing how Bart Jr. and José rebuild their relationship will be instructive for all of the members of the family.

The Hernández brothers have embarked upon a somewhat rebellious process. Without including their father, they have begun the process of sorting out how they can share the wealth generated by the construction business, within which they will have very different roles. Bart Jr. will be the manager, while José will be a passive investor. Yet the brothers want to direct an equitable share of the benefits of the business to José. How do they want to share governance of the business? Relying on an outsider arbiter such as Aunt Clara is a good start, but this is likely to be just an interim step toward a more formal and sustainable governance system. Given what has happened between the sons over the years, it is likely that they will choose a system that has advanced accountability structures embedded within it. These accountability structures will help the brothers rebuild the trust that has been eroded between them.

Of course, selection of an appropriate governance system is intimately tied to both role development and wealth transition structures. The structure of the company and the legal structures needed to implement the transition plan will determine certain roles. These roles may be unfamiliar to the family, and may require thorough role definition and development.

It is not only the brothers who must wrestle with governance systems. If Bart Sr. chooses to step away from his central roles within each subsystem of the family wealth system, he will leave a governance vacuum. In the past, Bart Sr. probably made most of the business decisions himself. He may have consulted with family members, but these consultation processes were likely informal and ad hoc. They probably varied from business to business, but whatever the business, it is certain that the legal structure of governance did not match the reality. A successful role transition for Bart Sr. and his children, including Luisa, will require that the family explicitly choose a governance system for their businesses, particularly the hardware store and real estate ventures, and that they practice using this system prior to Bart Sr.'s departure. This will give them the opportunity to create a smooth transition without huge negative reverberations within the family wealth system.

Making all this even more problematic is the possibility of Bart Sr.'s marriage to Samantha, a woman with two children. Bart Sr. must also address governance within the context of sharing wealth with her, if that is their decision about roles.

Role Clarity and Development

—CLARA HERNÁNDEZ PAZ, *age fifty-one*—

The boys have worked it out so that some of the construction company money will go to José, enough to live on, and he's got a partial scholarship. He can get a job, too. He'll be just fine. But I know that's not what's bothering my brother. He just can't bear to let José go. With Luisa, it was different. She was smart—he ended up thinking it was his idea that she go to Los Angeles and become a doctor. And of course, she's not all the way across the country. We can still see her anytime, really. José is more like me—if his father doesn't agree, he'll just leave anyway and be gone from our lives forever. So, I sat my brother down and told him straight up: he must let José go. I reminded him of when I ran away, that we didn't want that for José. We have to make it okay for these kids to leave and okay for them to come home—just as he did for me. Now he's got Samantha and her kids to love (he rolled his eyes, but I know how he feels about her). I told him I have a new project, too: I'm using some of the sales proceeds from our business to start a foundation that will help other women start their own businesses. I told him that because he was so helpful to us, if he wants to he could be involved, too. We'd like that.

Clara is right. The Hernández family is in transition, whether or not Bart Sr. likes or accepts it. The core challenge for the FWTP adviser assisting Bart Sr. is to help him accept these events as a normal and expected part of his individual, family, and business life cycles. These trigger events offer an opportunity for Bart Sr. to examine how he wants his own life to be in the coming years. Helping Bart Sr. evaluate his desires and needs for financial and social capital will be critical in helping him define a new role. Moreover, just as the Hernández family wealth system is vulnerable because of Bart Sr.'s role in every subsystem, these connections bind him in ways that he may or may not want to continue, particularly if he establishes a new family. He may choose to reexamine his own expectations of conformity as he enters his sixties.

As Bart Sr. seeks to define his own role, he and José may or may not come to an understanding of José's path in life. Bart Sr. must weigh his strong support of family against his need for his sons to conform to a certain way of life. Helping Bart Sr. understand the role of individuation as a natural part of the life cycle, and how "hard work" can manifest itself in any number of occupations, may help him accept a different role for José. If José is able to pursue his art degree in Rhode Island, the family faces the hard question of what to do with the hardware store. If it is to stay in the family, how will the family fill the manager's role? The family must also address José's continuing role, if any, in the construction business. Whatever that role may be, it will be an unfamiliar one to José and the rest of the family. Defining and developing the roles within the construction business will be a challenge for the brothers, as well as their father.

Bart Sr.'s possible future with Samantha complicates the process of role definition. Will he take on the role of provider for Samantha and her children? What are her views on his role? If Bart Sr. expects his children to support his marriage, he needs to define his relative commitments to them and to his new family. He must be clear about his role and the plan for wealth transition. This must come from Bart Sr., and not from Samantha or from Bart's children.

Finally, Bart Jr. has his own role development challenges. If Bart Sr. chooses to step out of a central role in all the family wealth subsystems, Bart Jr. is the natural choice to succeed him in managing the family real estate. Yet Bart Jr. is fully occupied with the construction business and studying to be an engineer, and wants to spend more time with his core family. His plan of adding the hardware store to his responsibilities seems unreasonable, at least at this juncture. Helping Bart Jr. explore the reasons for his interest in this business venture will help him evaluate whether this is a role he really wants to assume.

Wealth Transition Structures

—SAMANTHA PARSONS, *age thirty-eight*—

I've tried not to involve myself in the Hernández family problems that have been going on. I just try to be supportive of Bart, and not stick my nose where it's not wanted. One thing I know for sure. With Luisa in Los Angeles and now José going—maybe—to Rhode Island, Bart is feeling a little lost. He's wondering what he will do with his life. Bart Jr. is really self-sufficient and his business is going great. Luisa's all set in her new practice. José's finally launched—we hope. Bart Sr. does have his real estate to manage, but he has to decide about what to do with the hardware store. Clara tells him in no uncertain terms that it's time to sell the thing, but Bart Sr. needs to come to that conclusion himself, in his own time. There are just too many memories there for him to walk away from it just like that, I think. I know Bart Jr. said he'd like to buy it, but I can't imagine him taking on one more thing. His wife Susan is already laying down the law to him about being home more.

Bart Sr. and I have talked about marriage. He's very traditional, and it's a stretch for him to think about "just dating" a woman with two kids. The idea of living together would shock him to the core. Bart Sr. needs to work out his problems with his children before he mentions marriage to his family. I want Bart Jr., Luisa, and José to know that their inheritances are secure, that I'm not looking to their father to support my children—or me. My real estate business is doing just fine.

Bart Sr. needs all the usual estate planning documents, and perhaps one more: a prenuptial agreement with Samantha. But before all this can be put in place, Bart Sr. must clarify his role within his new family, and define the balance between that role and his roles in his existing family, particularly with respect to financial wealth.

The two brothers must, with a FWTP adviser's help, create a shareholders' agreement tailored to their specific circumstances. They will need all the usual provisions, such as what happens upon death, but in their case they will also need to include agreements as to what decisions are reserved to the shareholders, as opposed to the board of directors. (Examples might include managers' salaries or distributions.) They will also need exit provisions that do not overly favor the brother with greater resources, and do not encourage competitiveness. Given their history of distrust, dispute resolution procedures that offer progressive interventions are appropriate.

It is in their shareholder agreement that the brothers may choose to address the issue of making a place at the table for either of them, or for anyone with Hernández DNA. The challenge is to balance this desire against the needs of a profitable business in which employment and other roles go to those with the abilities to carry them out. They should consider including in their shareholders' agreement separate decision-making processes for the hiring, evaluation, and termination of employment of family members.

This might extend to any other role that directs wealth generated by the business to family members. At first, the boys' Aunt Clara might serve in this role, but ultimately they will need a process that doesn't depend on just one person. The idea is to slow down, and have independent review of, the process of hiring and firing family members, establishing expectations, and evaluating family members who work in the business. This will prevent managers from freezing out family members or imposing unrealistic demands on them. Setting standards and performing a genuine evaluation of family members employed by a family business helps ensure that the business doesn't become a dumping ground for family members with an overly developed sense of entitlement.

Real Estate

Bart's real estate, which is made up of single-family homes and apartments that he uses as rental property, cries out for a limited liability company (LLC) or family limited partnership (FLP) as a legal transition structure. The adviser must pay careful attention to the governance documents for this entity. All three of Bart's children are likely to inherit interests in the real estate entity, and because their situations are so different, they will likely have different preferences regarding income, growth in value, cash, and continuing investment. Bart Jr. is the likely choice for manager, and Luisa, a busy doctor in Los Angeles, is unlikely to object to his serving in this role. But José's path is still unclear, and given the brothers' past difficulties, defining the governance systems within these entities will be crucial to ensuring a smooth transition whenever it comes. How will the managers decide about distributions, additional investments, and similar business matters? What will be the communication pathways among the owners, and between the manager(s) and the owners? How will they balance oversight and discretion? The creation of the LLC operating agreement or FLP partnership agreement raises all the same questions that the Hernández brothers must face in creating their shareholders' agreement, with a few additional wrinkles. Will the real estate venture, like the construction business, also make a place for any Hernández who cares to participate? Rentals offer fewer opportunities for active employment, so this value may not translate well. Will Samantha, who is in the real estate business, be involved, and if so, how?

Ten Months Later

—BART HERNÁNDEZ SR., *age sixty-two*—

I couldn't tell José that I agreed with his plan to study art, because I didn't. I thought—and still do—that a man needs a trade that will support a wife and children. We didn't part on the best of terms, but since then we've talked a lot on the phone and I've visited him out there. It looks like that school helps its students get really good jobs in New York and places like that. So I guess I was wrong. That thing with his girlfriend didn't last, but he's still glad he went. Bart Jr. had to adjust to taking less salary from the construction business, so he could split the profits with his brother. Clara is the arbiter between the boys, and they've had a few arguments, but everything's worked out. Clara is working nonstop on her foundation. Her son Ramón helps her some, when he can. I decided not to get involved. I have my hands full with the rentals and I'm getting ready to get married.

Everybody said I should sell the hardware store, but I didn't. I had some good offers, but I felt the future of that business is with the big-box stores. So I closed up shop. I had a plan. I leased the property to the boys' company. Bart Jr. redeveloped it into offices and upscale retail. Samantha knows how to get the right tenants, so it's been a great move financially.

I've put all my rentals, and the land where the hardware store used to be, into LLCs. They produce a decent income, which is good since I don't have any retirement plan to speak of. I've given interests to all three kids, but I've kept the majority interest and will be the manager until I die or give it up. Let's face it; it will be when I die. Then Bart Jr. will take over, along with either Luisa or José. Samantha and I have a prenuptial agreement that says the LLCs stay in the family. I believe that I have a responsibility to Samantha. If I die, as long as she's living she will have an income from a share of the LLCs. My kids didn't care too much for that—Samantha's younger than Bart—but that's just too bad for them. Samantha says she'll just give that share to my kids—she doesn't need it—but I want her to have it just in case. She and I have plans to travel some. Her younger son is entering the U.S. Naval Academy in the fall, so she and I will drive with him out there and see José at the same time.

The Hernández FWTP process illustrates a good balance of the three components of family wealth continuity. The strife that was endemic in the family at the outset of the process has worked itself out. While the brothers still have arguments, as most brothers do, they have a structure in which they can work them out. Bart has soothed his children's anxieties about his new family by having a prenuptial agreement and creating the LLCs. Along the way, Bart Sr. is expanding the family, and embarking upon the adventure of a new Stage Four family. Perhaps facing the family's conformity issues made this step easier for him.

The Hernández family also has taken steps to become better stewards of its wealth. While Bart Sr. continues to play a central role in the family businesses, the creation of governance structures in the construction company and the LLCs protects the family from many of the negative impacts of his sudden exit from the system. Clara has expanded the realm of family capital by creating a philanthropic foundation, which will cause the family to begin to look outward in a new way.

Legacy

What is the Hernández family legacy? One thing is clear: the hardware store is *not* the family legacy. It occupied a special place in the memories of family members, and was a safety net for family members still searching for a place in the world. It was probably difficult for Bart Sr. to close it. But Bart Sr. made the right choice. Rather than keeping the store well beyond its usefulness to the family, he chose to close the store and transform it into a different kind of wealth.

If it is not the store, then, what is the legacy? For the Hernández family, it is probably their continuing strong family ties. They have strengthened these ties, which were probably never in danger of being shredded, but did become a bit frayed. Along the way, Bart Sr. and his family have learned a lot about themselves. Learning about and working through their tendency to require family members to conform to certain kinds of expectations makes it easier for the next generation—María and her cousins-to-be—to find their own paths in the world. José and Luisa and their cousin Ramón will all serve as models for how to leave the family, yet stay connected to it.

CHAPTER NOTE

1. See Chapter 5.

CHAPTER 13

TRANSITIONS OF WEALTH IN THE MARSHALL FAMILY

THE MARSHALLS' BIG CRISIS occurred when a tragic crash took the lives of three people (two of them Marshalls), severely injured others, and caused ripple effects throughout the family wealth system. Yet things are still not well in this family. Johnny Ray plans to disinherit Arnie, to the dismay of his brother, Robert, and sister, Ruth. Arnie and Johnny Ray bicker constantly, and Arnie's imminent departure from the ranch and business threatens to wreak havoc in the family and the family business. Ruth Ann and her family are returning to the ranch, determined to fix these problems with a radical solution very different from any the Marshalls have yet seen. Yet West Texas might not be as welcoming as they hope to a same-sex couple. Robert's place in the scheme of things is not clear. He seems firmly ensconced in the life of a professor, so how much time or energy can he devote to family in Texas? His own marriage is on shaky ground and his son is in and out of drug rehabilitation clinics. The one bright spot in his life is his math whiz of a daughter, Corrine, who is in college. Finally, Eddie's role within the family wealth system is even harder to fathom. Is he disabled? Is he just a difficult sibling with a lot of pent-up anger? Will he able to adapt to the changes that will inevitably occur?

Success

If family wealth continuity means making the right kinds of capital available to the right people, in the right way, at the right time, the Marshalls are headed for a disaster unless they act quickly and with resolve. The

Marshall family is approaching the loss of its patriarch and matriarch with no transitional structures in place. Not only is the family likely to face estate taxes without a source of liquidity with which to pay them, but there is no plan for how to pass control of their far-flung businesses to the next generation. On top of it all, the effects of the car crash seem to have brought the family to a standstill. For the Marshalls, any modicum of success requires *movement:* progress toward any of the three goals of family wealth continuity.

Ethics

Chapter 2 discussed some of the ethical issues raised by the Marshall family's need for help with family wealth transition planning (FWTP). Any family wealth transition planning adviser to whom the Marshalls turn for help immediately faces an ethical dilemma: identifying the client. When we first met the family, the siblings Ruth Ann, Robert, Arnie, and Eddie were meeting with the long-time lawyer to the Marshalls and their businesses. All of these members are shareholders in the family business, but the principal shareholders, Johnny Ray and Jenny Lynne, were not in attendance. The FWTP adviser has information about a new will made by Johnny Ray, which disinherits Arnie, and knows of Robert's negative views on this arrangement. How the other siblings would react to the new will is not clear, as the meeting terminated when Eddie stormed out. All of this creates a fundamental dilemma for the lawyer: who is the client?

The fundamental problem is that Johnny Ray and Jenny Lynne are not involved in planning. While it might be possible to structure an engagement in which Marshall Enterprises is the client, or a coalition of siblings are clients, this will be awkward, impractical, and likely unethical without at least some cooperation from the senior Marshalls. And without this cooperation, any plan will include a precipitous transition of wealth at Johnny Ray's death, which may not be optimal for family wealth continuity.

The FWTP adviser's job in such a situation is to think creatively about removing the barriers that prevent the senior Marshalls from being involved in the process. It may be as simple as asking Johnny Ray the right way, or invoking Jenny Lynne's influence within the family. Yet the major barrier to effective FWTP appears to be the Marshall family's unresolved grief about the car crash, which is playing out in different ways for different members of the family. Finding ways to prevent them from circling the wagons or endlessly repeating their current stories about the event will be critical. Ruth and Robert seem ready to help the family move beyond these events, and the adviser can call upon them to persuade the family to cooperate. Ruth's idea of using a family charity as a catalyst to heal her family can also be explored as part of the grief healing process. In assembling the team, the FWTP adviser may wish to enlist the assistance of a grief counselor, to work with the family if the members will allow it, or to work "in the background" with the FWTP adviser if the family cannot accept that it is truly grieving after these many years.

Process

Compared with the FWTP needs of the other families discussed in this book, the Marshalls' FWTP engagement is likely to be the most complex. This chaotic, enmeshed family does not lend itself to a linear process of analysis similar to that used in Chapter 11 with the Williams family. Stakeholder analysis, the process employed with the Hernández family in Chapter 12, would likely reveal that Johnny Ray is at the center of the Marshall universe. And that might be exactly as Johnny Ray likes it, leading to the conclusion that "we are just fine, thank you very much." A perceptive FWTP adviser will choose a process that will highlight how vulnerable the Marshall family wealth system is to future trigger events. This is a message that is not likely to sit well with Johnny Ray, or even with other family members, who are still reeling from the events of five years ago. The FWTP process should help family members recognize the extraordinary degree of interdependence among the components of the Marshall family wealth system and begin to find ways to adapt the system to dampen the negative effects of this interdependency.

The process will be a guided journey through each of the subsystems of the Marshall family wealth system. The FWTP adviser guides the client family through a discussion of each subsystem, examining the

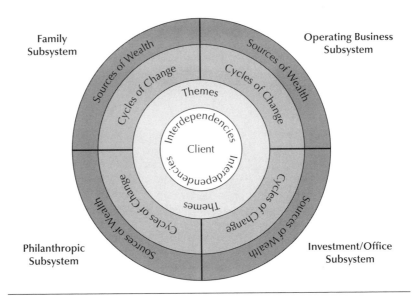

FIGURE 13.1 A Guided Tour Through a Client's Wealth System

sources of wealth within that subsystem, the cycles of change affecting the individuals, families, and businesses participating in that subsystem, and the family wealth themes that affect that subsystem. The final step is to identify the interdependencies among subsystems, so as to find ways to adapt them through components of the plan (*Figure 13.1*).

The Marshall Family Subsytem

—JOHNNY RAY MARSHALL, *age eighty-five*—

It was damn lucky that my grandson cut school that day. He snuck in our back door; he figured Jenny Lynne wouldn't call his parents, it being the last few days before Arnie and his family moved away. So it was Billy Rob who found Jenny Lynne lying on the floor in the kitchen. That boy kept his head and called 911 and then his mother. Made sure Jenny Lynne was breathing, covered her with a blanket, and stayed right with her, telling her everything was going to be okay. Me, I was down on Knickerbocker Road. I knew something was wrong when I heard the rescue go by and then saw Arnie in his truck, drivin' like a house afire. We followed the rescue right to the emergency room in San Angelo.

I got to see Jenny Lynne before they took her to get the operation. She was lying there half-dead-like and it about scared me to death. But being half dead didn't stop that woman. No, I think she saw it as a golden opportunity to assign me one of her famous "Undertakings." My personal experience is that an Undertaking is just a big ol' whopper of a job, one that's going to take a long time, and be a real pain in the butt, and build your character whether it needs building or not. Jenny Lynne's only given me a few Undertakings during our marriage, thank the Lord. Anyhow, I couldn't make out her exact words, but I surely got the gist of this particular one: "If you want to see me come out of that operating room, you'll start right now and reconcile yourself with your son...." I knew for a fact she could just up and die if she wanted to. That's what her own mama did; she just decided one day to give it up. So I did as she asked.

Jenny Lynne mended up pretty well. She'd had a little stroke, not too bad, but that's probably what caused her to fall and break her hip. The docs didn't want to let her go from the hospital, but she was stubborn and said she wanted to go home. So Betty Ann is tending to her. Arnie and them have their plans on hold.

The Marshall ranch is a busy place. The senior Marshalls live there, as do Arnie and his family, at least for now. They live together and work together. Over the years, each sibling has built a house on the property. Although Ruth and Robert do not live there, they feel free to visit whenever they like, along with their families. But Marshall Enterprises owns the land on which the houses are built. Jenny Lynne has effectively run the personal side of things on the ranch for years. This family is deeply enmeshed. As a result, it was doubly wounded in the crash, not only from the death of family members, but also from the severance of ties with Robert Lee (Bobbie Lee), his wife, Florence, and their children as Robert Lee (Bobbie Lee) and Florence seek to deal with their marital problems and their son's addiction.

The members of this family are ignoring the cycles of change that must occur as Johnny Ray and Jenny Lynne, now in their mid-eighties, continue to age. Perhaps they fear that their family cannot survive another abrupt decline in its storehouse of human capital. The death of two cousins and the injuries to the third certainly interrupted the progress of the Marshall families through their natural cycles of development. Arnie's and Robert's families both suddenly had to adjust to radically different family constellations, with immeasurable effects on the surviving cousins, Corrine and Billy Rob.

Of all the sources of Marshall wealth, it is their family social capital that is the most uniquely "Marshall." Family relationships are important and enduring in the Marshall clan. In the past, at least, the family has been open to newcomers, although Ruthie's relationship with Pam may test the limits of that openness. Most important, however, the schism between Arnie and his father threatens the family's strong ties. It may be the first real schism within the family, and its importance is a clue to a fundamental communication theme at work throughout the Marshall wealth system: the family's inability to cope with conflict. Sixteen-year-old Billy Ray suggests that in the past, his grandfather faced issues head on, such as when he and Ruth had it out in the barn over her relationship with Pam. Whether this is an accurate perception, no one knows. But now, at least, Arnie and Johnny Ray are not able to air their problems openly. Father and son cannot communicate about a critical issue: their guilt, shame, and blame surrounding the crash. It is easier for Johnny Ray to blame the tragedy on Arnie, the father of the drunk driver, than to see it as part of a longstanding family pattern of behavior. Johnny Ray probably relies on the *if only* approach: if only Arnie had been a better father, if only he had not been such a hard drinker, if only he had disciplined his son earlier, or better, none of this would have happened. However much his father blames him, Arnie blames himself twice as much, and now has returned to his old habit of drinking secretly. Johnny Ray doesn't want to remember how he used his influence to sweep multiple drinking and driving incidents under the rug. Neither he nor Arnie wants to remember how they laughed and said "boys will be boys" to excuse this behavior instead of creating consequences, or how they left the boys unsupervised, knowing what was really going on. No one in the family wants to remember how they ignored all the signs of alcoholism in a teenager and would not listen to repeated warnings from pastors and teachers. Nor does anyone want to acknowledge that bootlegging was a source of Marshall wealth just two generations ago. This Marshall clan has probably been living in a fantasy world for years about its connection with alcohol. Now the family has a choice: to name this problem and deal with it or to continue living in fantasy.

There *is* hope for this family. But the Marshalls' inability to deal with conflict in the family subsystem is not restricted to its relationship with alcohol. It is evident in the family's refusal to say what is really going on with Eddie, for to do that would spark one of Eddie's famous outbursts and perhaps focus the family on its perceived failures. So everyone just works around the problem instead of braving the conflict that dealing with it would require.

The Marshall Investment/Office System

—ROBERT L. (BOBBIE LEE) MARSHALL, *age forty-seven*—

I guess we all grew to rely on Marshall Enterprises for those regular dividends. I know I did, and when they stopped coming it was a problem for us, especially since we were paying for Larry's rehab and getting ready for Corrine's college. When my parents decided to make payments to the victims of the crash with money from the business, I knew that wasn't appropriate. Dad and Mama didn't listen to the lawyers' advice, they just did what they thought was right. I didn't feel I could insist because it would seem like I was only interested in keeping the money coming to me. I can't believe the accountants let them get away with that plan, but probably they thought it was a one-time thing and what's done is done. Anyway, the dividends dried up and all of us had to tighten our belts.

Remarkably, no one in the Marshall family has mentioned having significant savings, retirement funds, life insurance, or even health insurance. The one investment asset, which no one ever talks about, is the oil leases on the ranch property. These apparently generate significant cash flow, but are essentially passive in nature.

The business, not individuals, made payments to the victims of the crash. The pending lawsuits raise questions: against whom are they filed, and what are the possible sources of wealth to satisfy them, if it becomes necessary? The only possible conclusion is that Marshall Enterprises is the source of investment wealth for the senior Marshalls, and their unwillingness to acknowledge their place in the life cycle or to plan is likely intimately tied to this issue. Letting go of the company raises the fear of not having enough and having to trust their children to provide for them. This suggests a theme of fear and trust at work in the investment subsystem, even though it is devoid of specific investment components other than the family business.

The Marshall Operating Business System

—JOHNNY RAY MARSHALL, *age eighty-five*—

All that time Jenny Lynne was up at Shannon Hospital, I couldn't just hang around doing nothin'. So I decided to spend some hands-on time at the truck yard instead of being a phone call owner. That Steve, he's one top hand, it's hard to believe he's only forty-eight. He knows every driver by name and driving record. Heck, he even knows their wives' and kids' names. It was good to see Eddie work and see how Steve gets the best out of him—something I could never do. I thought we were just trying to keep Eddie in a job. But he's pulling his own weight and getting along just fine. It was Steve who made this thing work and he sure doesn't need me hanging around. So I told Steve privately that I'd like him to think about buying the whole outfit; I'd give him a good price and good terms. His jaw dropped to the floor. He said he was sure honored but he knew he couldn't afford it. I haven't told Arnie or the other kids. They'll squeal at the price I'm determined to give Steve, but a business should belong to its operator, not some absentee owner, that's what I've always said.

The Marshalls' operating business subsystem is dominated by Marshall Enterprises, Inc., the home of the family's ranching, trucking, and drilling businesses. These businesses are probably in a mature stage of their life cycles, but it is interesting that all are in high-risk industries. By some accident of history, along with a failure to plan, all three businesses are within one corporate structure, further adding to the risk. Probing the family's beliefs about Marshall Enterprises will reveal important aspects of the sources of wealth within the operating business subsystem as well as family wealth themes.

The Marshalls have invested much of their financial and human capital in the business. Johnny Ray, even at eighty-five, goes to the office every day. He participates in all the businesses and even talks on the phone frequently with Steve, the key trucking company employee.

The Marshall operating business subsystem is chaotic. There is no apparent plan for continued financial investment in the businesses, and the roles of the family members in the businesses are blurry, to say the least. It isn't clear whether Johnny Ray is truly in charge, or the family is just pretending he is. Arnie works in the drilling and ranching businesses, but who defines what he is supposed to do and how that relates to others' roles? In all likelihood, nobody knows what roles anyone is really playing. Eddie's role at the trucking company seemed particularly ambiguous, at least until Johnny Ray started to pay closer attention. Even then, no one in the family seems willing to talk openly about Eddie's capacities and constraints.

The FWTP adviser must distinguish between the control/abdication theme and the trust/fear theme in order to decide on appropriate components for the Marshalls' plan. It is tempting to view Johnny Ray as being caught up in issues of control, but the fact that his children have successfully individuated suggests otherwise. It is more likely that the theme of trust and fear is at work in this subsystem, just as it appears to be in the investment subsystem.

Exploring this theme may be new territory for the Marshalls. Prior to the 2004 crash, their strong web of human and social capital allowed them to assume that those bonds also created a high level of trust within the family. Now that those bonds have been threatened, they must address their fear and trust issues explicitly. Now in their eighties, the parents' continuing exercise of control within the family and its businesses, whether real or imaginary, signals some level of fear: fear of change, loss of autonomy, or, perhaps, identity. They may also fear that their children will not be good stewards of wealth, financial or otherwise. Important components of their transition plan will have to assuage those fears, not just with words, but also with a plan for role development and governance systems designed to build trust.

The theme of fear and trust isn't the exclusive domain of Jenny Lynne and Johnny Ray, however. The Marshall children also have trust issues to address. The paradox of the successful family is at work in the Marshall family. Arnie, Ruth, and Robert Lee (and to an unknown extent, Eddie) have individuated, and have pursued their own, very different paths. They have little experience (pro or con) with each other as adults who share decision making or responsibility. Although Arnie has been intimately involved in the ranch activities, his critical role has been hidden from his siblings' view. The speed at which change is coming toward them means that these siblings will have to share wealth before they can build a history of belief in each other's competency, openness, and integrity. Some structures will be necessary in the interim to substitute for trust, and these may have a longer-term impact on Eddie than on the other Marshall siblings.

The Marshall Philanthropic System

The Marshall philanthropic subsystem is in a nascent state. The Marshalls have made donations to their church during their lifetimes, and each sibling probably engages in personal charitable activity. Ruth works for a charity. Jenny Lynne and her friends at church do what they can for the victims of the crash.

Yet all of this is about to change, if Ruth is successful with her plan to move home, create a family foundation, and get family members involved in helping her run it. This plan, apparently hatched unilaterally by Ruth and Pam, will reveal two wealth themes for the Marshalls. One is familiar to them: control. Ruth is obviously a strong personality and expects that the family will jump on her bandwagon because she believes she has the answer to their problems. She may well have an answer that will help heal them, but the family may chafe under her apparent need to control the outcome. Moreover, signing on to Ruth's plan will require the Marshalls to examine a theme that has probably been tucked away in the attic for generations: what is wealth *for*? The Marshalls have two assets that perfectly illustrate the intrinsic and instrumental value of wealth, respectively: the ranch and the trucking business. The ranch, which has been in the family for generations, represents their connection to the past, a gathering place for family, and a legacy for the future. The trucking business creates a job for Eddie, period. If Ruth wants to use any of the family wealth to heal the Marshalls and the community, she will need to be able to reconcile their ideas about the value of that wealth with their concept of a family legacy as well as their practical needs for funds.

Interdependencies in the Marshall Family Wealth System: Core FWTP Challenges

The FWTP process reveals a number of interdependencies among the subsystems of the family wealth system. These interdependencies suggest core challenges for the Marshall family wealth transition plan (summarized in *Figure 13.2*) that the adviser will want to meet through specific components of the wealth transition plan.

For the Marshall family, perhaps the most far-reaching of the interdependencies is the aging of the Marshall clan. The matriarch

FIGURE **13.2**   Core Challenges for the Marshall Family in FWTP

	Role Clarity and Development	Governance Systems	Wealth Transition Structures
Core Challenges	• Natural processes of aging: what will change for the Marshall family members? • What are Arnie's roles in each business: ranching, drilling, trucking? What are his expectations? • What are Eddie's needs, capacities, and constraints? • Do siblings understand each business sufficiently to participate effectively? • What is Billy Rob's plan for the future?	• How can FWTP components be implemented with lawsuits pending? • Who decides on the settlement of and strategy for lawsuits? • For businesses that siblings will share, how will they share decision making? • How to share personal enjoyment of and responsibility for the ranch?	• Johnny Ray's new will that disinherits Arnie: Discuss? Keep? Modify? • How to separate businesses in Marshall Enterprises? • How to separate personal and business assets? • What wealth will the siblings share after the death of parents? • Trucking business: keep or sell? How to ensure Eddie's participation? • Ruth's charitable foundation: Possible? Advisable? Structure?

and patriarch are in their eighties, and their children are approaching retirement age. Yet throughout the subsystems of the family wealth system, there appears to be an assumption that a youthful clan is ready to take on the Marshall personal and business activities. Caring for Johnny Ray and Jenny Lynne on the ranch appears to be the unstated duty of Betty Ann, and there is no acknowledgment that outside resources might be necessary, which precludes a discussion of the cost of these resources. The fantasy that the Marshall universe will spin in perpetuity permeates all of these subsystems, and leaves each one vulnerable to the death or disability of Johnny Ray or Jenny Lynne, the departure of Arnie and his family, and the diverse expectations and needs of Ruth, Robert Lee, and Eddie, who have all established lives well away from the ranch.

The endemic chaos of the Marshalls' businesses ripples throughout the family wealth system, creating added vulnerability. The Marshalls lack any sort of clarity about roles and responsibilities for their various businesses, which precludes the evaluation of the performance of family members employed in them, or even of the performance of the businesses themselves. Because all family members depend on the businesses for cash, yet only a few are closely involved in them, misunderstandings and distrust can grow out of proportion to actual events. Left unchecked, this could undermine the Marshalls' most precious form of wealth, which is their social capital.

Finally, at this time the Marshall family wealth system is particularly vulnerable to outside forces. The Marshall businesses are all in high-risk industries, and are sensitive to macroeconomic changes in demand, interest rates, and commodity prices. Liquidity is tight. Lawsuits are pending, and they significantly reduce the flexibility of FWTP for the Marshalls, as Marshall defendants may be precluded from rearranging the ownership of assets within the family, even for legitimate reasons. The adviser will need input from the lawyers handling the lawsuits to understand the likely outcome of those lawsuits, how previous payments affect them, the sources of payments, and the constraints on transferring assets pending resolution. Again, the concentration of the businesses in one corporation ensures that these lawsuits affect the entire wealth system, as none of the Marshall wealth appears to be safe from these suits.

Wealth Transition Structures

—STEVE REYNOLDS, *age forty-eight*—

I was floored when Johnny Ray said he'd like to sell the business to me. I run the place, sure, but I always knew I was running it for the Marshalls. The family's been good to me over the years. I make good money and it's a good fit for me. I actually don't mind Eddie's crazy habits; they work well here in this business. As long as I manage the people and he manages the rolling stock, we're just fine. I worry, though, that the other Marshall kids are going to have a big problem with this. I don't want to cause a big family fight, but I would like to see if this would work.

Johnny Ray and at least three of his four children seem to be coming to the same conclusion from different perspectives: they do not want to play the role of owner/operators in the trucking business in the long term. Johnny Ray is further along in this process than any of his children know, but before any transition structure can be devised, the family must resolve important governance issues: whether the business is for sale, to whom, at what price, and, most importantly, who makes those decisions? Selling the business to Steve is a trigger event that can serve as an important catalyst for putting in place the other legal transition structures the Marshalls will need. Selling the trucking business independently of the drilling business is not as easy as it sounds to Johnny Ray but will be the perfect opportunity for imagining the disposition of all the family business assets in the wills or revocable living trusts for Jenny Lynne and Johnny Ray.

A Spinoff

The structure of Marshall Enterprises, Inc. lends itself to a traditional spinoff transaction. A spinoff offers both operational and planning advantages. Each of these high-risk businesses would be isolated within its own corporate structure, a move that the family lawyers probably have long advocated. The governance structures for each business could be very different, even if all stay within the family. Separating these businesses will eventually have to occur in order to prepare these businesses for transition either within or without the family. Completing the spinoff during Johnny Ray's lifetime is likely to be smoother than waiting until his death, and his desire to sell the trucking business to Steve can act as an impetus for the overall plan.

The Trucking Business: Sale to Steve

The likely legal transition structure will be the sale of the business, and fortunately, there is an attractive buyer on the horizon: a key employee. Although Steve doubts he will be able to afford to purchase the business, if the business is economically viable there are a number of options available to make this transaction succeed. An installment sale is almost certainly in the picture.

There are other, more imaginative ways to make the business affordable for Steve if the spinoff is accomplished. An ESOP might be suitable, depending on the profits of the business, its periodic needs for capital, and the desire for employee ownership. Putting the arrangements for Eddie into the mix also opens up some opportunities, but only if the family has first clarified Eddie's roles and capabilities.

The Ranching and Drilling Businesses: Shared Corporate Ownership

The family's discussion of role clarity and governance systems in the ranching and drilling businesses will set the stage for the design of legal transition structures. The wise FWTP adviser will have listened to the discussion about prospective roles and responsibilities, and weighed them within the context of family wealth themes.

A high level of trust requires less complexity in the legal transition structures. Traditional transfers of stock of a single class, with basic shareholder agreements in place, will generally suffice. Even families with high degrees of trust, however, can benefit from including these just-in-case structures in their transition agreements:

❏ Sensible buy–sell agreements that do not encourage brinksman-ship or create imbalances because of differences in wealth among owners
❏ Buyback provisions for divorce or other trigger events, to ensure that the family businesses stay within the family
❏ An understanding of how much authority will be retained by share-holders, as opposed to the board of directors

In the Marshall situation, it appears that the family is kidding it-self that shared ownership in the next generation will be easy. The FWTP team will be called upon to design legal transition structures that will mitigate the impact of this fantasy. These structures will tip the balance of discretion and accountability, producing either more discretion for the manager, or more accountability for the nonmanager owners. While they may seem cumbersome to family members at the outset, these structures can do much to preserve family wealth conti-nuity by providing both a substitute for trust and a way to build trust organically by establishing reasonable expectations and a mechanism for meeting them.

Funding the Charitable Gift

If the family adopts Ruth's approach to healing the family through the creation of a family charity, it will have to work through myriad questions about the nature of the charity. What is its mission? Will it be an operating charity, offering programs and services for teens, for example? Or will it simply make grants? Will the Marshall family control it? Will others be involved? This charity will represent a new legacy for the Marshall family, and the family as a whole must define the contours of that legacy before any legal transition structures can be created.

Answering these questions will guide the FWTP team in recommending a suitable funding source for the charitable gift. This gift must be coordinated with the transition plan and ideally will also generate an estate or income tax deduction. But funding the charitable gift will be one of the most challenging aspects of a wealth transition plan because the Marshalls appear to lack significant liquid assets such as retirement plans, life insurance, or savings. Their wealth is tied up in family businesses and family real estate, so any charitable gift must come from these sources.

Role Clarity and Development

—ARNIE MARSHALL, *age fifty-nine*—

I was weighing in my mind whether vending machine coffee was better than no coffee at all when Dad came out from seeing Mama. He looked like hell. He stomped right over to me, got right in my face, and I thought, "Okay, here it comes—finally we are going to have it out, right here in the waiting room." The family went all silent like they do whenever he and I start circling each other like mad dogs. "Son," he said (he hadn't called me that in a long time), "I have undertaken to put things right between us. I don't pretend I know how to do that, but it will be my own responsibility. I humbly need to ask you and your family to put your moving plans on hold until your mother is better, so you can see in due course that I am serious. For right now, I want to offer you my hand." He held his hand out to shake, and I took it. You could've heard a pin drop in that waiting room, and just then Ruthie and Pam showed up and Ruthie said, "Hey, where's Mama? Is she going to be okay?" And then everyone was jabbering all at once while Dad and I just stood there on each side of that vending machine. He said to me, "The first thing you and I need to do is round up some real coffee, that's for sure. They say it's going to be a long wait for your Mama to come out of surgery."

Johnny Ray has taken important first steps toward change in the Marshall family. He accepted responsibility for healing the relationship between himself and his son. But even more importantly, he has acknowledged that he doesn't know how to change the situation. He begins symbolically with offering a handshake, calling Arnie "son," and proposing a joint mission, a role he and Arnie have shared thousands upon thousands of times. Johnny Ray's openness to the ambiguity of the situation (a new role for him) creates opportunities for them, and the others, to clarify, redefine, and develop their roles within the family wealth system.

Johnny Ray and Arnie's pathway toward reconciliation will be difficult. Johnny Ray will forget his Undertaking from time to time, and Arnie may understandably harbor resentments toward his father for the way he has treated him. A skilled adviser will recognize that this family probably requires the intervention of another team member before the FWTP process can truly begin: a family therapist skilled in grief counseling. The family has not reconciled itself to the loss of so many family members, and the reverberations of this loss continue to rock the family wealth system as a whole. Until the family comes to grips with its grief, it will not be possible to consider role clarity or role development issues. Resolution, of course, will mean different things for different family members. For Johnny Ray, it may mean moving away from blaming Arnie and seeing him in a new light: as a responsible adult. For Billy Rob, it may open up a wider world than his current fears will allow, as he can live on the ranch but attend a local community college. For Arnie and Betty Ann, it may mean letting go of the guilt engendered by their inability to rein in their son when he was headed for disaster. For Robert and Florence, it may mean either a divorce or a strengthening of their marriage. For the entire family, however, it will mean facing its collective fantasies about alcohol and the family's connections to it.

The trigger event of Jenny Lynne's stroke and broken hip may also serve as a wake-up call to clarify her role in the ranch operations and her husband's role in the family businesses. Are they really in control? Now that Jenny Lynne will be recovering for some time, someone else will need to step up to the plate. Some family members say that Johnny Ray makes all the big decisions in the family business, but others suggest that Arnie really controls the drilling business, and the key employee, Steve, really runs the trucking company. What, exactly, is Johnny Ray's role? Is the family colluding in an illusion of his control over the business decisions? If so, for what purpose? Defining Johnny Ray's and Jenny Lynne's current roles opens up the discussion of how to fill these roles now and in the future. It will also raise the question of Johnny Ray's and Jenny Lynne's identities if others begin to fill those roles.

The key question for the Marshalls will be whether to continue ownership of the ranch, the trucking business, and the drilling business. Because these businesses are tied up in Marshall Enterprises, separating them, if necessary, will require some complex legal transition structures. But whether the family even needs those structures depends on whether they *want* to assume any of the roles involved in owning these assets. Family members have different depths of knowledge about the various businesses and what it takes to run them. The operations are far flung. All are high-risk enterprises. The family must analyze whether it wishes to keep these businesses within the family, and if so, who will own and operate them.

As part of this process, the Marshalls will have to come to grips with the appropriate role for Eddie in the family businesses. The Marshalls would clearly like to view him as merely eccentric. Although Eddie appears to be functioning in his job at the trucking business, where he works in a very specific area (logistics), he seems to have problems interacting with family. He has displayed a propensity for disruption, and various family members have described characteristics consistent with Asperger Syndrome or mild autism. As part of the FWTP process, the family must honestly evaluate Eddie's desire and capacity for participation in the family business. To do so they may need the help of a specialist in adult developmental disorders. Whether Eddie would participate in such an evaluation remains to be seen, but Ruthie—the one family member to whom Eddie listens—may be able to help in that process. Once Eddie's capabilities are clear, the family can begin to fashion a role development plan for him within the trucking business and the wealth transition as a whole.

All of these are difficult questions, but they are in fact quite tame compared to the issues surrounding the ownership of the ranch. The ranch isn't just a business; it's the family legacy. The ranch and ranching business were handed down through generations that worked the land, but today only a few Marshalls are involved in the ranching business or live on the ranch. Defining the future roles in the Marshall family vis-à-vis this asset will be a critical part of creating governance systems and legal transition structures for them.

Governance Systems

—RUTH ANN MARSHALL, *age fifty-three*—

After Mama came home from the hospital in late November, the whole family came down to Texas for an early Christmas. A couple of days after we all got there, Robert cornered Arnie and me and said, "Let's go down to the Peerless, where we can actually talk without everybody hearing every word we say." He wanted us to finish what we started last year with the lawyers down in Dallas. Robert and I were on the same page, that something had to be done or we were going to end up paying a heck of a lot of estate taxes, and for nothing, because the businesses would be in shambles anyway unless we had some sort of plan in place. Robert's point was that maybe Dad would be more open to a real discussion now that we've had this scare with Mama, if we could approach him just the right way. Me, I think we can save a lot of estate tax, and heal our family, which is really what's important, by creating some sort of family charity. We should find ways to make sure a crash like we had—with teenagers drinking and driving—never happens to any other family. Who better than us to do this? Our family's bootlegging past has come back to haunt us, so let's stop acting like we are so ashamed about that and do something positive for a change. Robert and Arnie were intrigued with that, I could tell. But Arnie nailed the problem on the head: we have to have our act together before we can even bring anything up with Dad. Arnie's still plenty raw, of course, given all that's happened with Dad, but you can tell he's looking for a way to stay on the ranch, not move his whole family down to Galveston. He feels he could easily run the ranch and the drilling business. And even though the trucking company is a cipher to all of us, we all know we can't just put Eddie out on the street. Either we figure out something, or Bobbie Lee and I become long-haul truck drivers, I guess. Arnie says it's up to us to show Dad how all four of us can work together to make these businesses last. Only then will Dad feel like he can begin to make a plan. Arnie said he didn't want us to take it personally, but he might as well be honest: he doesn't mind sharing the fruits of these businesses, but if he's running them, he doesn't want any interference from the rest of us. He didn't get specific, but I know just what he means. He doesn't want Bobbie Lee lording over him with his PhD, telling him he should do this or that, or me barreling into the office making promises to everybody about Marshall Enterprises sponsoring this or supporting that. All this made me really uncomfortable, because as far as I know, Daddy still hasn't changed that will that disinherits Arnie.

Unlike families with significant investment wealth, such as the Williams family, the Marshall siblings will inherit wealth intimately tied to three operating businesses. They must, at least for a time, share that wealth in order to preserve it. Yet their family has grown ever more complex as its wealth has grown. The four siblings lead very different lives; only two are involved in a family business, and even their roles are quite different. Two siblings have teenagers, and one has a very young daughter. One sibling has never married or had children. One is charitably minded, while others are not, at least for now. The ranch is an operating business, but also a homestead and a vacation destination for family members. Finally, the 2004 crash has had very different effects on all the siblings. This complex family must find a way to govern itself, hopefully before Johnny Ray's death, so its members will be good stewards of their wealth. Arnie is right: if Johnny Ray can learn to trust his children's ability to work together as stewards of wealth, he is much more likely to participate in making a plan. If they can practice sharing wealth before their parents' death, they will build trust among themselves that will ensure a relatively smooth transition after their parents' deaths.

What is the current Marshall family governance system? Testing assumptions about who is in control may reveal a traditional system in which Johnny Ray is in control. Or, it may reveal a family illusion of control, in which only Johnny Ray is in the dark about his lack of control. In either event, the formal organization of the family corporation doesn't match the governance system currently in place. Nor will the current governance system adequately serve the needs of the family as wealth is transferred to the next generation. The core challenge for the Marshalls is to create a governance system that will serve their needs for the drilling and trucking businesses, the ranching business, and the ranch itself.

Complexity leads most systems toward some sort of centralized management. In a family business, this evolves toward a system in which a manager manages the business on behalf of other family stakeholders, who in turn exercise appropriate oversight of the manager. The Marshall Enterprises structure, while currently only a governance shell, has the potential to house a powerful governance structure, if the Marshalls can participate in a meaningful conversation about governance.

Structuring that conversation is tricky, of course. While involvement of all the family members is optimal, this is unlikely to happen in the Marshall situation; it is Arnie, Ruthie and Robert who are motivated to have preliminary conversations and to prepare for future conversations with Johnny Ray and Jenny Lynne. If initiated with the explicit proviso that these are exploratory discussions, their conversations can be framed in terms of the siblings' possible future roles. They might want to put the trucking company aside for the moment, and focus on the three areas in which they seem to have some inkling of a plan: the drilling company, the ranch, and the family charity.

Sorting Out Personal Assets and Business Operations

The muddling of personal and business assets and liabilities within the Marshall family wealth system will require some clarification as part of the FWTP process. The Marshall homes are located on the ranch, which is owned by the corporation. The corporation paid money to some of the victims of the 2004 crash. Various members of the Marshall family rely on the businesses for income, and probably for other benefits. Sorting out which assets and liabilities are personal and which are business related will be an important precursor to the design of governance systems as well as legal transition structures, because both of these components may be different for personal assets than for business assets.

Ranch and Drilling Businesses

If Arnie were the manager of the ranch and drilling businesses, what would be the roles of the other siblings? The goal is to devise a system in which Arnie has sufficient discretion to manage the businesses, but the other siblings feel comfortable with their level of oversight of his management and believe that their financial interests are protected. A good system will build trust among the siblings. To that end, they must consider issues such as areas of management authority, joint decision-making definitions between ownership and management, and establishing communication processes and protocols that will help define family, management, and ownership boundaries.

A skilled adviser will listen to conversations about these topics with an eye to predicting whether the family will be able to find a workable balance between discretion and accountability. The FWTP adviser's job will be to combine governance systems and legal transition structures to help achieve this balance, taking into account the particular capacity of the family members for trust and collaboration.

Family Charity

Ruth is committed to exploring the use of a family charity to move her family toward healing. The contours of such a charitable effort are vague at this point, and she has a great deal of work to do before the governance systems of such an organization can be designed. If her family works with a grief counselor, this idea may be shaped within that process. In any event, her goal is to persuade them that a commitment to charity can help the entire family come to grips with the accident and its causes and effects. She is not advocating just any act of charity, of course, but instead a long-term, coordinated approach to solving the problem that has haunted her family. She must draw upon her family's capacities, including its deeply held belief in the value of social capital and even its penchant for fantasy, to focus them on the future rather than the past, on responsibility instead of blame. Her primary governance challenge at this stage is to prove to her family that they can come together in this joint effort.

Trusts for Family Members?

Ultimately, Johnny Ray and Jenny Lynne must make the hard choice: is Eddie capable of effective participation as an owner of a family business, or must they put a governance structure into place for him? If they decide that Eddie (or any other member of the family, for that matter) is not capable of effectively participating in the governance systems of the family businesses, they may choose to explore the use of a trust as a governance structure for him. Rather than allowing Eddie to disrupt the governance system, a trustee will hold his shares in the family businesses and manage them for him, and will make distributions to Eddie according to the terms of the trust agreement. However, unlike some beneficiaries, Eddie is highly functioning: he supports himself and lives independently. He is likely to resist the imposition of a trust structure on him if all other members of his family are given shares outright. In designing this particular trust, the FWTP adviser should create consultation and communication processes between beneficiary and trustee that will support Eddie's autonomy and participation in the family, while not unduly interfering with the trustee's ability to participate effectively as the owner of the shares.

Ten Months Later

—ROBERT L. (BOBBIE LEE) MARSHALL, *age forty-seven*—

You know that Dad died about a year ago? He fell off a horse and hit his head, and though they got him to the hospital, he never regained consciousness. At least he was doing what he liked best—we should all be so lucky. Dad did end up changing his will, using that Odessa lawyer. He and Arnie reconciled, and so he got rid of that whiskey-to-Arnie nonsense, but he couldn't bring himself to do any complicated estate planning. He just left everything to Mom. She's doing great, and has agreed to do some things to reduce estate taxes. What we're going to do is similar to the plan we talked about: separate the businesses into three different corporations. But then we are going to donate most of the ranch to Ruth's charity, where most of it will stay. It will be connected with Shannon Hospital's mental health program for teenagers, and they're planning a kind of outdoors treatment program for kids with alcoholism or drug addiction. Some of the ranch will be sold to support the charity. But we'll still have the part of the ranch where our houses are, so all the grandkids—and their kids—can always come home. I don't mean to say we did this all out of charity, you know. It also helped us settle those lawsuits. But we're all behind it.

Arnie and Betty Ann are still on the ranch and Arnie's running things there, and at the drilling business too. It's going all right, given the times. Arnie finally gave up all his drinking, period. Billy Rob is headed off to college next year at Texas Tech and has turned into a fine young man. Unfortunately, my own family isn't so happy. Florence and I divorced, and my son Larry is in really bad shape, addicted to heroin and HIV positive. He's agreed to give treatment one more try, at the Shannon program. God willing, it will take this time; maybe the ghost of his grandfather will help him. Corrine, though, she's just great. Her aunt Ruth invited her and Billy Rob to be on the board of the charity, and since Corrine is such a whiz with numbers, she's already brought a lot to the project.

We're still talking about what to do with the trucking business. We want Steve to have it, but we want to protect Eddie and make sure he keeps his job as long as he can. It's not that we don't trust Steve, but anything can happen. So the tentative plan is to do a recapitalization, sell voting stock to Steve, and give some of the nonvoting stock to Eddie along with a long-term employment contract. Some of the proceeds would also go into trust for Eddie so if things don't work out there he'd have a little something. It's not a perfect plan, and we're still negotiating the price. Some days I don't know why we bother, though, because Eddie has been one big pain in the butt since Dad died. Arnie, Ruth, and I are at our wits' end. Mom doesn't want to treat him any differently from us in her will, but we keep telling her he's really getting worse. He won't even listen to Ruthie any more. If we are going to share the family business after Mom dies, we need some way to manage him.

The FWTP engagement has produced remarkable results in terms of family wealth continuity for the Marshall family. The Marshalls have restored many of the relationships that were in danger of fracturing when the process began. The family has carefully considered its legacy, and how its multigenerational business—the ranch—can be shaped into a new kind of legacy that heals the family. Younger family members can be encouraged to take a leadership role under the tutelage of their Aunt Ruth. And all Marshalls, of whatever age, have a place to come home to, even if it is a smaller version of the ranch that once straddled two counties.

Robert's story illustrates how the themes a family faces in the FWTP process may continue to haunt it during implementation and thereafter. The process is not a cure for these issues.

The plans Robert describes appear to be reasonable in light of the family's needs and capacities, and manifest the essence of good stewardship. Missing from Robert's picture is the actual impact of these plans on the financial wealth of the family. Eddie is taken care of, in a sense, but will the family's remaining financial wealth support it in years to come? How will that reduced wealth be divided among the siblings? How will they share the proceeds of the sale of the trucking business? Can the family really afford to give a large portion of the ranch to charity? At this stage, the Marshall FWTP process is skeletal, but it represents real movement toward healthy relationships, good stewardship, and a robust family legacy.

CHAPTER 14

THE FAMILY WEALTH
TRANSITION PLANNING
ADVISER'S PRACTICE

RESEARCHERS DELUGE FAMILY wealth transition planning advisers with estimates of the trillions of dollars of wealth destined to change hands in the coming decade. These estimates range from $10 to $40 trillion, depending on a researcher's assumptions regarding age and wealth. Many of these estates will generate significant estate taxes, unless careful planning is completed prior to death for the owners of this wealth. But regardless of the outcome of Congressional estate tax wrangling, family wealth transition planning (FWTP) advisers will have their hands full designing transition strategies to accompany this demographic sea change.

As previous chapters have illustrated, however, when a family business is at stake, transferring the wealth from one generation to the next poses special challenges for families and their advisers. More and more advisers will face this challenge over the coming years. It is impossible to know with certainty the number of family businesses in the United States, or even have a realistic assessment of their size or impact on the economy. Yet researchers suggest that 70 to 90 percent of the businesses in the United States are family owned, and the value of capital in family or closely held businesses was about $2.4 trillion as far back as 1990. Today, closely held businesses generate between 30 and 60 percent of the nation's GNP and contribute just over half of the total payroll in the United States. Conservative estimates place the number of family firms, independent of sole proprietorships, at about 1.7 million entities. Including sole proprietorships in the count increases it to a whopping 12.9 million businesses. With a significant percentage of the capital associated with these firms being controlled by the founders, who established the firms after the 1940s and 1950s, the coming transition of wealth in the form of family businesses is staggering.

In the past, advisers have worked primarily with one or perhaps two generations in FWTP. Given increasing life expectancy, in the future attorneys might easily be working with three or four generations, greatly complicating the development of family wealth transition plans. It is clear that there are acute generational differences in work ethic, hopes and expectations about life and lifestyle, and even language for discussing these issues among senior-generation Veterans, Boomers, X-ers, and Nexters.[1] When these individuals are involved in a family business, the differences loom still larger.

Advisers serving the wealth transition market, whether they work as solo practitioners or within practice groups in firms, can take steps to position themselves to serve this business family market. Serving business families better helps ensure a firm's own long-term sustainability. When a business family trusts its advisers to help family members in the second, third, and even fourth generations to find a meaningful place within the family wealth system, the firm will earn the loyalty of the family throughout its generations. When a business family recognizes that a firm's role is not only to assist with structures and transactions that are a part of FWTP, but also to assist the clients to negotiate a smooth transition through their natural individual, family, and business life cycles, they will more frequently turn to their adviser for help. Business families gravitate toward firms that genuinely believe in family wealth continuity as the goal of planning. The challenge for any adviser's practice is to find its authentic path within this market and communicate its values through action.

Many firms worry about losing clients during the transition of a family business from one generation to another. As children take the reins from their parents, the younger generation may wish to change firms, engaging an adviser whom they have chosen rather than one selected by their parents many years ago. A successful FWTP engagement for a business family strengthens the relationship between the family and the firm and helps allay transferees' fear that only the transferors' needs will be met. The younger generation also will begin to understand the firm's depth of understanding about the business and how difficult it would be to educate another firm. After a successful FWTP engagement, the family as a whole will likely have greater confidence in the firm's ability to meet its needs. Moreover, the firm will be better equipped to do so, having gained a deep understanding of the choices the family made in constructing its transition plan. Staying involved, as appropriate, in the implementation phase of developing roles and monitoring governance further strengthens this relationship.

How advisers did and did not help the three families whose stories were traced in this book illustrates practical lessons for advisers and firms serving this market. The following sections explore these lessons and more.

The Adviser for the Williams Family

The adviser helping Helen Williams faced what is the most difficult problem of all for many in the profession: how to say *no*, or at least *not yet*, to a request for assistance. Helen's world started to fall apart just as she showed up for her initial FWTP consultation. The events that transpired in the Williams family wealth system created thorny ethical challenges for the adviser, and raised insurmountable barriers to creating an effective FWTP process at that time. Helen was probably a needy client during this time, repeatedly asking for help from the adviser to whom she first turned. The adviser's wise counsel was to wait: survive the current crisis, find some family stability by making the right decisions within the right time frame, and only then focus on the transition process.

Yet Helen's FWTP adviser was also able to help her by quickly activating a robust referral network of other professionals. Helen needed an accountant with whom she could communicate, and with whom she would not feel even more foolish. She needed a divorce lawyer. She needed a family therapist and an individual therapist. She needed help communicating with her father's lawyers. And she needed these resources right away. There was no time to waste.

Only after the crisis passed, and the family entered a stage of some stability, could Helen and John return to their adviser for FWTP help. This required the adviser to understand the ethical duties owing to Helen and John and the children, including Brad. Because Helen and John's interests with respect to Brad were potentially adverse, the adviser had to spend time sorting out the likely conflicts and obtaining Helen and John's informed consent for the adviser to assist John with the business sale, the creation of the trust for Brad, and the traditional estate planning documents.

The Williams situation offers the following lessons for FWTP advisers seeking to help a family in crisis:

❏ The adviser must decide on a role, clarify it, and stick with it. This is difficult when the client is a member of any blended family, but is particularly hard when that family is in conflict.

❏ An adviser must have a healthy referral network of other professionals. The FWTP adviser's professional network should include not only lawyers, accountants, and therapists, such as the ones that Helen needed, but also financial advisers, bankers, business consultants, physicians, those who can act as trusted advisers, mediators, and even drug and alcohol dependency programs. The adviser must be familiar with how to access these resources. The adviser must also have a sense of the helping style of these professionals in order to match the needs of diverse clients with appropriate professionals.

❏ An adviser must know how to act as a good member of a team. The Williams family's FWTP adviser did not act as a team leader, because the focus of Helen and John's core work was their continuing marital relationship. They stayed in counseling, and they faced financial issues in rebuilding the funds taken by John from the retirement account. Adding value as a member of this team required finesse. Many advisers find being a member of a team more challenging than being team leader, yet any FWTP adviser must be ready to act in either role. The section of this chapter entitled "The FWTP Adviser Team" discusses the issues of constructing a team and team leadership.

The Adviser for the Marshall Family

The adviser helping the Marshall family had a full plate of challenges. The family's many business and personal issues, along with its large population and propensity for fantasy, created numerous process challenges. The pending lawsuits required coordination with other advisers and limited the options available as components of the plan. The Marshalls tended to engage multiple law firms from time to time, without bothering to inform the advisers of this fact. The family had to address its ongoing business issues even as the landscape was changing as a result of planning and internal family changes.

Before FWTP could commence, the Marshall FWTP adviser had to decide, in consultation with the family, on the right process and the right role for helping the family. The longtime advisers to the family had to take a hard look at whether the adviser should engage an outside party to manage this process.

A firm positioning itself to serve a family like the Marshalls in transition planning might reflect on the following lessons that the Marshalls illustrate:

❏ The firm must develop a deep understanding of the ethical rules as they apply to complicated families and to legal structures within family wealth systems. Developing a library of information on these matters, including sample letters to advise clients of potential conflicts and obtain consents, is helpful. A formalized in-house program of ethical review can help FWTP advisers avoid pitfalls.

❏ A firm with multiple advisers must develop a strong in-house referral and information-sharing culture. The FWTP adviser must be able to communicate effectively with the family's other advisers to ensure that their efforts are coordinated. The adviser must be able to draw upon the long and complex legal history of a family like the Marshalls to help construct a plan. Developing a database of information about a family and its businesses will assist in this process, and will also help sort out ethical issues. Viewing a business family as "belonging" to a transactional lawyer, for example, makes it difficult for a firm to help clients in planning. The plan must be part of the natural transition of the family, and an expected part of serving the business interests of the family.

❏ Given most families' desire to maintain privacy, and the adviser's obligation to do so, it is often challenging to provide examples of how other families address these issues. A firm seeking to help business families should seek to develop a library of information about family systems, family businesses, and wealth transition options. Ready access to these resources strengthens the adviser's role as team leader or member. It makes it easy to provide clients with copies of books or audiovisual materials, or bring in speakers for private client meetings. Some advisers' practices collect case studies and subscribe to a clipping service that collects stories about family wealth transition.[2] Information about families and their needs must be part of an advising firm's inter–practice group discussions. This helps advisers inform families about their options, and also helps them avoid the pitfalls of getting too close to the family to meet its needs objectively. The FWTP adviser assisting the Marshalls, for example, undoubtedly faced the challenge of not buying into the family's fantasies and stories that avoided the family's long history with alcohol. Too much conversation with the very reasonable Robert and Ruth, for example, might have influenced the adviser to share their view of Eddie without testing the assumptions and beliefs that created this view. Institutionalized discussion within a firm can support an adviser by untangling the adviser's own biases from the themes of the family.

The Adviser for the Hernández Family

The FWTP adviser helping Bart had the distinct advantage of a single, identifiable client for whom even traditional estate planning could make a great deal of difference. Yet special constraints were at work in this family. The family was enmeshed, and unused to acknowledging conflict or settling differences openly. Bart's central role made change difficult. The Hernández family offers significant lessons for a firm creating a FWTP practice.

The cultural origins of a family are critical. Thus, the adviser assisting the Hernández family was required to have some understanding of the culture of this family. While families of wealth across cultures face the same complexities, these complexities will play out differently in various cultures. For the Hernández family, the fact that their FWTP adviser spoke Spanish and sought to understand the ethos of immigrant families built trust with the family as it began to reveal its challenges. An adviser practice that seeks to serve business families must be willing to invest in learning about different cultures, such as the Latino culture of this Fresno family, the different religious backgrounds of the Williams family, or the deep Texas ties Marshall family.

Representing Multiple Generations

A practice seeking to serve multigenerational families must provide multigenerational advisers to help them. Younger members of a firm are often better able to connect and communicate with younger members of the family. Building positive experiences for younger advisers and younger clients binds the family to the firm and shows the family that the firm values every member of the family. Senior advisers must take special care to treat next-generation family members with the same respect they show the parents. To do this requires the adviser to be aware of how easy it is to take a protective attitude toward parents during the natural transition to wealth of the next generation, and know how to avoid this trap. Along the way, the firm can provide a model for what the family really wants: a smooth transition of wealth to the next generation. The clients should leave the office saying, "If they can do it, so can we." A later section of this chapter discusses specific opportunities and pitfalls in representing multiple generations of the same family.

Inherent in the goal of providing multigenerational lawyers is an intra-firm wealth continuity plan. While the goals of a firm in creating a sustainable, long-term practice may not be quite the same as the goals of family wealth continuity, they are similar. Advisers want to be good stewards of the wealth generated by serving clients: they want to earn a good living and have someone on whom they can rely to take over their practice when they are ready to retire. They want to have good relationships with their clients, partners, associates, and staff. And many advisers are in practice to build something larger than themselves and create a thriving, interesting practice that will survive them and make a contribution to community. To do this, the adviser's practice itself will need a plan for wealth transition to the next generation.

An adviser practice starting to formalize its FWTP strategy must recognize that planning for existing clients rarely has a formal starting place. Multiple members of a family may seek advice well before the FWTP process becomes part of the family's formal or informal agenda. When the advice involves family dealings with outsiders, such as the daughter dealing with problems with her condominium association or the son fighting a DUI, for example, this doesn't usually raise ethical issues. However, when multiple generations seek an adviser's guidance on wills, trusts, shareholder agreements, or any other set of legal rights

and duties within the family, potential conflicts of interest and confidentiality issues arise, and all of the rules discussed in Chapter 2 potentially
apply.

The FWTP Adviser Team

It is the rare adviser that can meet all the needs of a business family.
Usually, it is necessary to call upon other advisers for their specialized
expertise. Experienced estate advisers are familiar with working with
other professionals on complicated estate plans. These skills will help
build an efficient adviser team.

Many of the obstacles to involving team members from within a firm
are familiar to advisers, and not unique to FWTP. These involve timely
prediction of the need for assistance, communication between practice
groups and among advisers, organizing priorities, and ensuring quality
control. What is unique about FWTP for business families, however,
is the complexity of their family wealth systems. Getting a colleague
up to speed on that complexity is time-consuming and expensive for
the client, who may balk at the expense of educating a colleague about
the details of the family wealth system. A firm that can find ways, using
technology or other innovative methods, to communicate the essential
information efficiently will be better able to include other advisers, and
other team members, in the process.

The Role of Team Leader

The FWTP approach for transition engagements assumes that there will
be an experienced team leader who will be involved with family members throughout the process. The adviser team leader's job is to manage
needs, capacities, and constraints, and specifically to:

- ❑ Develop and articulate the desired outcomes for the adviser team.
- ❑ Choose the right team members, in consultation with the client.
- ❑ Prepare the selected team members for participation in the team.
- ❑ Manage the constraints within which the team must work, such
  as time, money, or less tangible constraints, such as an impatient
  patriarch.

❑ Coordinate communications within the team and family.
❑ Assess the progress of the adviser team.
❑ Ensure that the output of the adviser team meets the needs of the family.

The team leader is not the boss of the group. It is the client that determines the appropriate outcomes. The team leader thinks about the most effective process, reminds the group of its desired outcomes, and keeps it on task, asking a little more here, a little less there, and moving the group toward adaptations of the family wealth system that will generate family wealth continuity. Each adviser team member brings new capacities to the team, but also presents special challenges, as well. For example, sometimes all team members are "Type A" individuals who are used to being the adviser team leader. Managing the adviser team dynamics is often as challenging as managing the family dynamics.

The team leader within a FWTP engagement has two difficult process tasks. The first is handling fees and billing. The second is moving the group toward resolution. For many families, and for some teams, it is tempting to avoid resolution and to keep all options open. (After all, no one has died yet.) By making choices, the group closes the door on certain options. While no decision is final in the sense that it cannot be changed, the team needs the skills of a good team leader to move the family and team to decisions that create a transition plan.

Throughout this process, second-guessing decisions is the dark side of the team approach. The team leader needs to be ready to meet this challenge by constantly checking assumptions among all participants and maintaining as much transparency as possible.

Team Members in the FWTP Practice Group

Experienced estate advisers are familiar with working with other professionals such as certified public accountants, bankers, financial advisers, and insurance professionals on complicated engagements: these professionals are equally likely to be involved in the FWTP process described in this book, and, for the most part, their participation does not raise special ethical issues. However, using the approach described in this book, the FWTP adviser may want to expand the team's capacities to include family systems experts, mediators, or even family therapists.

The team composition should reflect the client family's needs and the goals of FWTP. During the assessment phase, the needs and goals of the engagement should be explicitly identified and accepted by key stakeholders. The adviser team needs clear goal definition, action plans, and timelines that specify the responsibilities of each team member. When adviser teams are new, they need to identify their working relationship protocols. Who sets meeting agendas and notifies other team members? Who keeps meeting minutes? How are work-in-progress documents shared? Has the client signed off on sharing all or specific information with key team members?

Increasingly, clients are telling their advisers that they want to have a younger person on the team, even if it means a greater cost. "Great plan," they say. "But who will be here to make sure it's working when you and I are tottering around unable to tie our own shoes?" Many clients appreciate knowing that there is someone in the firm whose life cycle more closely approximates that of the transferee generation and who has been sufficiently involved to understand the needs of the family as expressed in the FWTP process.

Fees and Billing

The FWTP approach described in this book is more expensive than a traditional estate planning engagement, because it is more time-consuming. The lead adviser and the team will spend more time gathering information about the family and its wealth system. They will spend more time discussing the needs of a family and the appropriate components of a plan. The implementation will take the team far beyond the traditional estate planning tasks and into involvement with role development plans and practicing and monitoring governance systems. Not every FWTP engagement will be as extensive as those described in this book. The more complex the family wealth system, however, the more expensive it is likely to be.

Clients look around the room at a team of professionals and see wealth draining away from their family wealth system. An all-day meeting of the team can easily run into the tens of thousands of dollars. While the client may understand that, in the long run, this process is cheaper than a failed family wealth transition plan, these costs loom large. These are real costs that must be borne today, while the potential costs of a failed plan are speculative and may be incurred, if at all, many years in the future.

A critical component of the adviser team leader's job is addressing the issue of fees and obtaining the client's consent to proceed, based on a full understanding of these costs. The adviser team leader must have a basic understanding of what processes the team will use and how team members will be involved in those processes, and must communicate these to the client. Then, before commencing the process, the adviser team leader has four tasks related to billing: calculating and communicating costs, determining participation, setting intrateam communication protocols, and proper accounting.

Calculation and Communication of Costs

First, the adviser team leader must determine how the fees for the engagement will be computed and communicate these fees and costs to the client. It is likely that the team members will bill in a combination of ways. The adviser team leader, for example, may choose to bill time on a daily, weekly, or engagement basis. Some other adviser team members may bill hourly for their time, while still others may bill by project. Some may only require payment if the client ends up using a particular product. The adviser team leader is responsible for communicating these costs to the client. The adviser team leader is also in charge of coordinating engagement letters and billing agreements, except for those of outside counsel, which are usually handled independently.

Participation

Second, the adviser team leader must propose a process that involves the team members in the most cost-effective way. Not every team member must be involved in every part of the process. By allocating these resources wisely, the team leader can contain costs while acquiring the wisdom of team members. The constellation of team members involved will likely change as the FWTP engagement continues, but having a plan at the outset will alleviate client (and team member) anxiety.

Intrateam Communication

Third, the adviser team leader will communicate with team members as to projects and confirm fees at that time. When adviser team members are asked to produce a particular deliverable, the team leader must clearly communicate the outcome, scope, and timing of that project. As part of this process, it is critical to clarify the communication pathways by which a team member's time can be committed. One can imagine the chaos that could occur if, for example, any family or team member could at any time ask the accountant on the team to analyze any portion of the plan.

Proper Accounting

Fourth, the adviser team leader will ensure that bills go out at appropriate intervals and will follow up on unpaid invoices. The usual monthly billing approach may be appropriate in a FWTP engagement, but many engagements lend themselves to billing at other intervals, such as when work on a certain phase is substantially complete. The engagement letter should clarify this. The adviser team leader should have a handle on the financial commitment of each professional in the engagement at any time and be prepared to answer any questions the client has about fees.

Succession Planning Within the Adviser's Practice

Many experienced estate planning advisers notice a similarity between the challenges their clients face in transitioning business wealth to their children and the challenges they themselves face in moving their practices to the next generation of advisers. *Goodwill*, the wealth generated by the adviser's practice, is most valuable when it is shared among advisers and in particular with the next generation of advisers within the firm. Without that generation's buy-in to continue to serve clients, and without clients' willingness to be served by the next generation of advisers, goodwill is worthless. Protecting this capital is critical to succession planning in the firm. But, as with families, this capital has intimate ties to human and financial capital. The capacities of the various advisers in the firm, combined with their broader social network of referral sources, long-standing relationships, and community service, must also be supported during times of transition.

While the adviser's practice system is not usually a family business, the subsystems of a firm resemble in many ways the subsystems of a family wealth system. Moreover, if the advisers in the firm have imported family patterns of behavior into the firm, it can certainly feel like a family business. Advisers are continually moving through their individual and family life cycles while the firm itself is moving through its business life cycle. Senior advisers may be contemplating retirement without the firm having a clear plan about how the capacities developed by those partners through the years can be replaced. Many advisers are as ambivalent about retirement as their clients are about retiring from their businesses.

All of the lessons to be derived by families and their advisers about FWTP potentially apply to the transition of wealth within an adviser's practice. By examining how the multiple overlapping systems connect, how the overlapping life cycles interact with each other, and how external forces come to work on the system, the firm can develop its own succession plan for the retirement of partners and the attraction and development of new talent.

Junior partners and senior associates are unlike their predecessors in many ways. Working through the issues may require a different kind of sharing of wealth, a different type of governance, and advisers stepping up to new roles. But it can be done, and continuity achieved.

CHAPTER NOTES

1. Bonnie Brown Hartley and John Gibson, "Are You Multi-Generationally Literate?" conference proceedings, Family Firm Institute, October 2004.

2. See Joseph Goodman's Family Wealth and Family Business Library and Resource Guide, comprising over 120 books and close to 1,800 articles indexed and summarized in 40 topical categories; "So Many Books, So Little Time . . .," *Family Business* (Summer 2000).

Index

ABOUT THE AUTHORS

Bonnie Brown Hartley, president of Transition Dynamics Inc., works primarily on governance systems and lifelong learning systems for client families. She works with family offices, multigenerational business families, and their businesses on mapping and implementing transition plans. As part of that process, she mentors multigenerational families and their advisers on communication and relationship management.

Hartley has published four Fire Drill books for building strength and flexibility in families: *Sudden Death, Unexpected Wealth, The Dynamics of Aging Families,* and *Health Care Issues of Aging Families* (the latter two with coauthor John Gibson). Hartley speaks internationally to business families and their advisers.

Hartley serves on the Attorneys for Family Enterprise board. She is a past Family Firm Institute (FFI) board member, a founding FFI fellow, and holds FFI's certificates in Family Business Advising and Family Wealth Advising. In 2008 she was honored by FFI for contributions to interdisciplinary adviser teams. She is also a member of a national think tank, Psycho-Social Dynamics of Family Business, and the Collaboration for Family Flourishing.

Gwendolyn Griffith is Of Counsel at the Portland, Oregon law firm of Tonkon Torp LLP, where her business and tax practice includes business formations, reorganizations, and dissolutions, as well as the crafting of complex wealth transition structures and governance systems. She has substantial experience representing nonprofit organizations and multigenerational businesses. Gwen is a graduate of Stanford Law School and Rollins College.

Gwen began her career with Akin Gump Strauss Hauer and Feld in Dallas, Texas. She then taught corporate, partnership, individual, and international tax at various law schools, including Willamette University, Florida State University, and the University of Oregon. Prior to joining Tonkon Torp LLP, Gwen was a shareholder in the Eugene, Oregon law firm of Speer Hoyt PC. She is the author of several books on taxation and is a frequent speaker on tax and business-related topics.

Gwen is a member of the Oregon and California bar associations. She is on the executive committee of the Oregon State Bar Taxation Section and is also on the advisory board of *The Tax Adviser,* the monthly publication of the American Institute of Certified Public Accountants. She is also a trained mediator and arbitrator.

ABOUT BLOOMBERG

Bloomberg L.P., founded in 1981, is a global information services, news, and media company. Headquartered in New York, Bloomberg has sales and news operations worldwide.

Serving customers on six continents, Bloomberg, through its wholly-owned subsidiary Bloomberg Finance L.P., holds a unique position within the financial services industry by providing an unparalleled range of features in a single package known as the Bloomberg Professional® service. By addressing the demand for investment performance and efficiency through an exceptional combination of information, analytic, electronic trading, and straight-through-processing tools, Bloomberg has built a worldwide customer base of corporations, issuers, financial intermediaries, and institutional investors.

Bloomberg News, founded in 1990, provides stories and columns on business, general news, politics, and sports to leading newspapers and magazines throughout the world. Bloomberg Television, a 24-hour business and financial news network, is produced and distributed globally in seven languages. Bloomberg Radio is an international radio network anchored by flagship station Bloomberg 1130 (WBBR-AM) in New York.

In addition to the Bloomberg Press line of books, Bloomberg publishes *Bloomberg Markets* magazine.

To learn more about Bloomberg, call a sales representative at:

London:	+44-20-7330-7500
New York:	+1-212-318-2000
Tokyo:	+81-3-3201-8900